60 Classic Essex Matches

60 Classic Essex Matches
First published by m press (media) Ltd in 2010
Designed and printed by m press Ltd, England

ISBN 978-0-9567015-2-7

Further copies are available from:
www.calmproductions.com
orders@calmproductions.com
UK hotline 0845 408 2606

60 Classic Essex Matches

by TONY DEBENHAM, PAUL HISCOCK
& GREG LANSDOWNE

Officially endorsed by Essex Cricket

The Authors

Tony Debenham saw his first Essex match at Ilford against the South African tourists in 1951 and was 'hooked' from that moment. Thirty years as a club cricketer followed, with the occasional visit to an Essex game a seasonal highlight. Retirement from playing (and coincidentally from work) gave an opportunity to be involved with the administration of Essex CCC on a voluntary basis and over the past 20 years he has held a variety of honorary positions at the Club. From a very early age Tony has been collecting 'anything cricket' and now has a large haul of books, postcards, cigarette cards, autographs, photographs and ceramics. Essex items have, of course, always held a special attraction and the photographs in particular have proved useful in the production of this book. It seemed only natural that when Essex CCC sought to establish a cricket museum on the ground at Chelmsford in 2006 that Tony should take a leading role, and he is currently Chairman of its Management Committee.

Paul Hiscock was taken by his father to his first day of county cricket at Ilford as a five-year-old, where he watched the County play Kent, and became addicted to cricket as a result. After many years working in the life assurance industry, he moved into journalism where he covered Essex cricket, home and away, for more than a decade – contributing features and match reports for a number of local daily and weekly newsgroups. He is now a regular contributor to the Essex Cricket website, the County's yearbook, and the Test Match Extra website. He is also the county correspondent for the *Wisden Cricketers' Almanack* and a member of the Cricket Writers' Club. Paul is married with three children and has lived in Essex throughout his life. Apart from his family and cricket, Paul's other passion is following the fortunes of Leyton Orient Football Club.

Greg Lansdowne saw his first Essex game at his local Ilford ground in 1983 and has been following the Club as a supporter, member and, more recently, employee ever since. Greg occupied the role of Communications Manager at Essex between 2003-2008 and continues to work on a freelance capacity as editor of the Yearbook, magazine and various other Club publications. Greg has been working within the sports industry since 1995, initially primarily in football before focusing more on cricket in recent years. Greg has also worked in a freelance capacity for organisations such as the ICC, IPL and Yahoo Cricket – as the Chief Correspondent on the official 2009 World Twenty20 website – as well as launching his own magazine aimed at fans of Asian cricket, *Big Hitter*.

Contents

Foreword

From the time I came into the Essex system, and way before that, through the likes of Tom Pearce (who was still President when I was coming through), Doug Insole (who has been a constant mentor for me) and Keith Fletcher, the ethos of playing to win and risking defeat to do so has always been there at the Club. You can't get points in the dressing room or praying for rain so taking the chance of defeat to set up a win has always been the Essex way. That was particularly evident in the 1970s,

Graham Gooch on his way to a century in the 1979 Benson & Hedges Cup Final against Surrey at Lord's

1980s and 1990s and it was no coincidence that we had a lot of success during that period. Essex had a lot of financial difficulties in the late 1960s and early 1970s so went down to 12 full-time professionals at one point. As a result they were forced to blood youngsters like John Lever, Ray East, Stuart Turner and David Acfield and that side grew together, being added to later on by myself, Neil Smith, Brian Hardie and Kenny McEwan. We blossomed with experience and the development of a harder edge made us a force to be reckoned with. A group of players with considerable ability was held together by a terrific leader in Keith Fletcher and we managed to retain the fun element despite our desire to be successful. Looking at the games chosen for this book, there are a number of three-day matches selected and I think that says a lot about how entertaining that format of the game was, with a lot more tight finishes ensuing on the final afternoon in pursuit of victory with either bat or ball. With the extra day now used in Championship cricket, that has happened less and less although Ryan ten Doeschate's batting fireworks at Derby in 2009 showed that the odd gem can still exist. It is no coincidence, however, that a lot of the more recent games are of the one-day variety. Essex's policy of nurturing attacking players has always been there and we have also brought in some eye-catching limited-overs cricketers from overseas down the years, coming right up to date with Scott Styris, whose incredible effort against Surrey in 2010 receives due recognition in this book. It appeared that the run-rate had got right out of hand in that match before his blitz against Andrew Symonds resulted in another great night at the Ford County Ground. Our supporters now turn up expecting to see that kind of entertainment and we hope that will be carried on over the years ahead to make a second 'Classic Matches' book necessary in the not too distant future.

Graham Gooch OBE

Introduction

As with any book of this nature, it is often not what you put in but what you leave out. There is no doubt that many personal favourites will have been omitted and this is a measure of the level of entertainment Essex County Cricket Club has provided to its supporters over the years. Of course, to reflect the County's history as a whole, it has been necessary to recall some of the lows amongst the highs – the path of true cricket love never ran smooth.

We hope what has been put together is a fair overview of the life and times of Essex since it was founded in 1876. Members and followers have been royally entertained over that period and there is little doubt more of the same will follow in the seasons ahead. If you like what you read, here's to *60 More Classic Essex Matches* in the near future!

Acknowledgements

The authors would like to thank Essex County Cricket Club and its members of staff for granting us access to the archives of the Club. We would also like to thank the following players who provided quotes specifically for the purpose of this book: Robin Hobbs, Graham Gooch, David East, Paul Prichard, John Childs, Peter Such, Mark Ilott, Ashley Cowan, Ronnie Irani, Will Jefferson, James Foster, Alastair Cook and Ravi Bopara. Thanks must also go to the photographers whose pictures have been sourced – most notably Club photographers over the years Clive Tarling, Kieran Galvin (Galvineyes, www.photoboxgallery.com/liveactionsport) and Nick Wood (www.unshaken-photography.co.uk) as well as from the personal collection of Tony Debenham. Thanks to m press for their expert assistance throughout the whole process of putting this book together. Finally, particular thanks must go to all the cricketers who have richly entertained all three authors and thousands of other Essex followers over the Club's proud history so far.

Tour Match

Essex v Australians

3-day match **Venue:** County Ground, Leyton **Result:** Draw

This was the first time that Essex had met the touring side from Down Under and the fixture came at an important time in the history of the County Cricket Club. Seeking every opportunity to extol their virtues as a competitive side ahead of an application to become a first-class county, it was good fortune that allowed the Club to pit their skills against the visitors. On their three previous tours, Australia had been engaged at the County Ground, Leyton although it was to face Cambridge University Past & Present rather than Essex. However, on this occasion, the University was unable to raise a team of sufficient strength and an invitation was extended to the County side to take over the fixture. Essex had achieved some impressive victories during the year. Derbyshire were beaten twice, Hampshire, Leicestershire and Surrey were defeated at Leyton whilst victory was achieved against Yorkshire at Sheffield.

There was still some concern about how they might adapt to meeting such exalted company but those worries proved unnecessary as the performance of Walter Mead against the Australians allayed any fears that Essex might be out of their depth. He took 9-136 and followed-up with 8-69 to allow the County to draw with their illustrious opponents. There is no doubt that

Essex team *circa* **1893**   the outcome of the game convinced administrators that they should be afforded first-class status, which was duly granted the following year. However, because they had not achieved that ranking at the time of this encounter against the tourists, Mead's aggregate of 17 wickets went unrecorded in the record books although he did equal that tally two years later which remains the best match performance by an Essex bowler to this day.

The fixture with Australia was interrupted by rain on the second and third days but there was still enough time for the County to display their ability to compete on level terms with distinguished opponents. Australia batted first and were

---

Slim in stature and with a black moustache, Mead, who was known as 'The Essex Treasure', had an easy action bowling his medium-pace off-breaks and occasional leg-breaks and earned this tribute from renowned all-round sportsman C.B.Fry.
"He is the hardest trier imaginable. One of his best balls is a plain straight one off which you may easily be caught at the wicket. You must also look out for another upon which he puts vigorous leg-break, but which on the contrary, turns slightly from the off."
The *Wisden Book of Cricketers Lives* commented: "In his day, he was one of the most notable of slow-medium bowlers. With an easy delivery and remarkable command of length, he possessed exceptional powers of spin and could make the ball turn on the best of pitches. His best season for Essex was that of 1895 when he took 179 wickets and in three successive innings, he disposed of 24 batsmen for 192 runs."

Toss: Australians won the toss and decided to bat.
Umpires: WB Clarke, RO Clayton.

AUSTRALIANS

JJ Lyons	c Taberer b Mead	7	c and b Mead		29
*AC Bannerman	lbw b Mead	34	c Russell b Mead		29
GHS Trott	c and b Mead	25	c sub b Mead		0
SE Gregory	b Mead	26	c Carpenter b Pickett		5
H Graham	c Taberer b Mead	35	st Russell b Mead		7
W Bruce	c Russell b Mead	56	b Mead		5
H Trumble	b Mead	28	c Mead b Pickett		15
CTB Turner	c Lucas b Mead	27	b Mead		18
WF Giffen	not out	9	b Mead		0
A Coningham	b Pickett	1	not out		19
†AH Jarvis	b Mead	0	b Mead		10
Extras	(1 lb, 1 nb)	2	(4 b)		4
Total	**(all out, 83.4 overs)**	**250**	**(all out, 61 overs)**		**141**

Fall: **1st inns:** 1-17, 2-52, 3-77, 4-104, 5-153, 6-210, 7-223, 8-246, 9-247, 10-250. **2nd inns:** 1-41, 2-41, 3-60, 4-67, 5-73, 6-94, 7-102, 8-102, 9-115, 10-141
Bowling (5 balls per over): **1st inns:** Kortright 17-0-60-0, Mead 41.4-6-136-9, Taberer 4-0-19-0, Pickett 21-7-33-1. **2nd inns:** Kortright 3-0-18-0, Mead 31-11-69-8, Pickett 27-12-50-2.

ESSEX

AS Johnston	b Trumble	7	not out	10
HA Carpenter	c Jarvis b Coningham	42	b Trott	7
HGP Owen	b Coningham	36	not out	2
*AP Lucas	c and b Trumble	15	did not bat	
H Hailey	not out	38	did not bat	
J Burns	b Trumble	7	did not bat	
†TM Russell	c Gregory b Trumble	8	did not bat	
HM Taberer	c Bruce b Trumble	8	did not bat	
CJ Kortright	lbw b Turner	23	did not bat	
W Mead	c Giffen b Trumble	8	did not bat	
H Pickett	st Jarvis b Bruce	25	did not bat	
Extras	(12 b, 4 lb, 4 w)	20	(13 b)	13
Total	**(all out, 119.4 overs)**	**237**	**(1 wicket, 11 overs)**	**32**

Fall: **1st inns:** 1-15, 2-72, 3-101, 4-107, 5-117, 6-127, 7-144, 8-191, 9-200, 10-237 **2nd inns:** 1-8.
Bowling (5 balls per over): **1st inns:** Turner 41-19-81-1, Trumble 58-27-87-6, Trott 6-3-17-0, Coningham 13-6-26-2, Bruce.1.4-0-6-1. **2nd inns:** Turner 5-2-8-0, Trott 5-0-11-1, Bruce 1-1-0-0.

bowled out for 250 with Mead, having taken the new ball, bowling unchanged and by the close of the opening day's play, Essex had reached 72-2. Play was restricted to just the morning session on day two when the hosts lost a further five wickets whilst adding another 111 runs before lunch when rain arrived to wash out hope of further play. Showers also interrupted the final day's exchanges when Essex concluded their innings before lunch having scored 237 with the studious Henry Hailey 38 not out. The tourists were then dismissed for 141 and found Mead equally unplayable as the off-spinner ripped through the order once again, this time taking 8-69 in 31 overs whilst Harry Pickett took the remaining two wickets.

With time only for 11 further overs in the half-hour remaining, Essex had reached 32 for the loss of one wicket when time was called on an inevitable draw. Cricket magazine wrote, "The County eleven deserve to be highly congratulated on their excellent show." A collection taken on the ground raised £12 of which a third was given to Pickett whilst the remainder was given to Mead in appreciation of his fine bowling.

County Championship
Essex v Leicestershire

3-day match

Venue: County Ground, Leyton **Result:** Leicestershire won by 75 runs

In front of an estimated 8,000 Bank Holiday Monday attendance, Henry "Harry" Pickett opened the bowling at the Pavilion End at the start of the day. Within two hours, he had dismissed the Leicestershire side returning the incredible figures of 10-32 which still remains the best individual bowling performance by an Essex player to date. A strong and stocky bowler, who bowled off about eight yards, Pickett had played for the County for 13 years before they achieved first-class status and ranks amongst a number of luminaries such as Walter Mead, Ray Smith and John Lever in his efforts for the club.

The opening day's cricket at the County Ground, on a wicket that initially offered variable bounce with some alarming lift before settling down to evenness, proved absorbing and the difference between the sides on first innings was only 8 runs.

Charles Kortright and Walter Mead were the two main strike bowlers but on this occasion, it was the 33 year-old Pickett who was to enjoy his greatest moment of a long career. Not that he had been in particularly good form coming into the game, having to wait until the third match of the season before claiming his first victim. However, the beginning of June saw the bowler rediscover his form in sensational fashion when he bowled unchanged after taking the new ball and ran through the Leicestershire batsmen. The visitors were shot out for 111 with Pickett, whose previous best figures in first-class cricket were 4-6, almost unplayable.

Harry Pickett: recorded the best bowling figures achieved by an Essex player

Essex, in their inaugural season of County Championship cricket and still seeking their first victory, initially fared badly against Arthur Woodcock and his four bowled victims all had their stumps knocked far out of the ground. The County were in a sorry state of 21-5 at one stage but James Burns fashioned

---

Harry Pickett was a powerfully-built man bowling with impressive speed off about 8 yards using twelve short strides explaining, "A professional who has to bowl day after day at the nets as well as in matches is likely to wear himself out very soon if he takes a long run."

His rout of the Leicestershire side at Leyton received this comment from *The Times* correspondent. "Having found a "spot" on the wicket, he got some work on the ball and the batsmen who attempted to hit him were soon in retreat. Pickett has never done a better piece of bowling and he now takes rank with the men who have distinguished themselves in a similar way. A collection around the ground raised £20."

Meanwhile the magazine *Cricket* wrote: "Though helped by the ground which was very fast and somewhat fiery, Pickett's success was due to grand bowling. He kept a splendid length throughout."

Toss: Not known.
Umpires: W Clements, H Draper

LEICESTERSHIRE

Batsman	1st innings	1st runs		2nd innings	2nd runs
M Chapman	b Pickett	14	(3)	c Mead b Kortright	56
J Holland	c Russell b Pickett	1		b Pickett	4
W Tomlin	b Pickett	9	(4)	b Owen	28
AD Pougher	c Russell b Pickett	10	(6)	c Russell b Kortright	7
CC Stone	b Pickett	0		b Kortright	0
*CE de Trafford	c Kortright b Pickett	29	(1)	b Kortright	44
F Geeson	c Mead b Pickett	4	(8)	b Kortright	9
D Lorrimer	b Pickett	0	(7)	b Kortright	8
A Woodcock	b Pickett	20		c Hailey b Kortright	14
JH King	not out	12		b Kortright	3
†JP Whiteside	b Pickett	7		not out	6
Extras	(5 lb)	5		(11 lb)	11
Total	**(all out, 54 overs)**	**111**		**(all out, 104.3 overs)**	**190**

Fall: 1st inns: 1-2, 2-16, 3-18, 4-35, 5-67, 6-71, 7-71, 8-76, 9-99, 10-111. **2nd inns:** 1-27, 2-62, 3-108, 4-124, 5-124, 6-140, 7-165, 8-169, 9-179, 10-190.
Bowling (5 balls per over): 1st inns: Mead 21-4-50-0, Pickett 27-11-32-10, Kortright 6-2-24-0. **2nd inns:** Mead 41-23-63-0, Pickett 13-3-41-1, Kortright 35.3-10-63-8, Carpenter 7-2-8-0, Owen 8-5-4-1.

ESSEX

Batsman	1st innings	1st runs		2nd innings	2nd runs
*HGP Owen	b Woodcock	1	(2)	c Holland b Geeson	18
HA Carpenter	b Woodcock	2	(1)	c Chapman b Woodcock	17
GF Higgins	c Tomlin b Pougher	3	(4)	c King b Geeson	6
CP McGahey	b Pougher	27	(3)	b Woodcock	54
H Hailey	c Geeson b Pougher	2		b Woodcock	0
AP Lucas	b Woodcock	0	(7)	b Woodcock	3
J Burns	c Whiteside b Pougher	37	(6)	lbw b Woodcock	6
†TM Russell	b Woodcock	0		b Woodcock	0
CJ Kortright	b Woodcock	0	(10)	not out	7
W Mead	not out	25	(9)	c Geeson b Pougher	7
H Pickett	b Pougher	0		c Holland b Woodcock	3
Extras	(6 b)	6		(1 b, 1 lb)	2
Total	**(all out, 46.4 overs)**	**103**		**(all out, 65.1 overs)**	**123**

Fall: 1st inns: 1-3, 2-8, 3-12, 4-20, 5-21, 6-70, 7-71, 8-75, 9-103, 10-103. **2nd inns:** 1-29, 2-56, 3-92, 4-97, 5-98, 6-102, 7-102, 8-113, 9-117, 10-123.
Bowling (5 balls per over): 1st inns: Pougher 23.4-11-29-5, Woodcock 20-3-53-5, Geeson 3-0-15-0.
2nd inns: Pougher 24-10-39-1, Woodcock 24.1-7-62-7, Geeson 13-8-10-2, King 4-1-10-0.

the recovery adding 37 out of 49 for the sixth wicket but despite his efforts, at 75-8, the hosts were still in trouble. Walter Mead took advantage of a missed run-out opportunity to hit a quick 25 whilst Charles McGahey anchored the innings with a vigilant 27 in one and three-quarter hours. Leicestershire enjoyed a lead of 62 runs with nine wickets in hand when play resumed on the second day and they took the total into three figures with the loss of one further wicket. The innings then fell away with the visitors bowled out for 190 as Kortright stepped forward to return his career-best first-class bowling figures of 8-63.

That left the home side requiring 199 for victory on a pitch that was proving increasingly helpful to bowlers. By the close, it was Leicestershire who had gained the upper hand having reduced their opponents to 98-5 despite a half-century from McGahey. It took Leicestershire little time in the morning to complete victory as the remaining five wickets fell for 25 runs with Woodcock taking his match aggregate to 12-115 whilst poor Pickett could only reflect that his record-breaking achievement had all been in vain.

County Championship
Hampshire v Essex

3-day match **Venue:** County Ground, Southampton **Result:** Hampshire won by 171 runs

Having taken 17 wickets in a match one year before the County had been granted first-class status in 1894, the performance of Walter Mead in this game ensured that the player deservedly entered the roll of honour. He returned match figures of 17-119 and remains the only bowler in the Club's history to take that number of victims in one match. He claimed 128 wickets during the season and proved the County's most successful bowler by far.

Walter Mead: set best match figures for the County, a record that still stands

Rain delayed the start of play until 4.30 p.m. on the first day with the bowlers hampered by a wet ball on a damp pitch and the fielders inconvenienced by the wet turf. Vic Barton and Arthur Hill dominated the initial exchanges posting a first wicket partnership that was to prove significant in determining the outcome of the match. By the close of the opening day, the home side had reached 122-4 with Mead serving notice of his effectiveness with three of those wickets, two with successive deliveries. The last six Hampshire wickets more than doubled the score with Barton, who recorded the only half-century in the match, hitting 79 before he was caught in the deep having batted for two and a half hours during which he struck a five and seven boundaries. Mead finished with 8-67 and the sixth of those victims brought his aggregate for the season into three figures.

Essex lost half the side in reaching 50 but a promising stand of 56 in 50 minutes between A.P. 'Bunny' Lucas and Charles Kortright improved the situation with the latter hitting the ball out of the ground on one occasion. Although the visitors managed to avert the follow-on, they were left trailing by 118 runs on first innings and by the time stumps were drawn at the end of day two, the home side were in an imposing position with a lead of 159

The Times correspondent wrote: "One of the best pieces of cricket in the game was recorded by young Walter Mead whose pitch and break were so effective as to yield an aggregate of 17 wickets for 119 runs." Mead enjoyed his best-ever season in 1895 taking 120 wickets for Essex and 179 wickets in all first-class matches. He was named as one of *Wisden's* 'Five Cricketers of the Year' in 1904 when they said of him: "Of the Essex team, Mead has for ten years been the mainstay in bowling, and pages of *Wisden* could easily be filled with a record of his performances. With an easy delivery, which enables him to keep up an end literally for hours without tiring, he combines great accuracy of pitch and, when the ground gives him the least assistance, a splendid off-break. Moreover, he can, on occasion, make the ball do a good deal from the leg side."

Toss: Hampshire won the toss and decided to bat.
Umpires: RO Clayton, J Wickens

HAMPSHIRE

AJL Hill	b Owen	37		lbw b Mead	3
VA Barton	c Carpenter b Mead	79		b Mead	3
EG Wynyard	b Mead	10		lbw b Mead	20
RA Studd	b Mead	0	(6)	b Pickett	8
HF Ward	b Mead	10	(4)	b Mead	10
J Wootton	c Kortright b Mead	9	(9)	b Mead	2
FH Bacon	c Carpenter b Bawtree	28	(5)	b Mead	12
*HWR Bencraft	b Mead	35	(7)	b Mead	0
T Soar	c Arkwright b Mead	30	(8)	not out	37
†MW Deane	not out	0	(11)	b Mead	1
H Baldwin	c Carpenter b Mead	2	(10)	st Russell b Mead	32
Extras	(2 b, 4 lb)	6		(8 b)	8
Total	(all out, 111.2 overs)	246		(all out, 64.1 overs)	136

Fall: 1st inns: 1-76, 2-99, 3-119, 4-119, 5-137, 6-148, 7-193, 8-241, 9-244, 10-246. **2nd inns:** 1-3, 2-10, 3-36, 4-45, 5-58, 6-59, 7-60, 8-66, 9-129, 10-136.
Bowling (5 balls per over): 1st inns: Kortright 15-3-37-0, Mead 47.2-20-67-8, Pickett 18-5-37-0, Arkwright 14-3-52-0, Owen 10-0-28-1, Bawtree 5-1-16-1, Carpenter 2-0-3-0. **2nd inns:** Kortright 6-1-17-0, Mead 30.1-12-52-9, Pickett 25-9-49-1, Owen 3-0-10-0.

ESSEX

*HGP Owen	b Soar	24	b Baldwin	0
HA Carpenter	c Soar b Baldwin	1	b Baldwin	14
JF Bawtree	b Wootton	6	b Baldwin	3
CP McGahey	run out	0	b Wootton	5
AP Lucas	c Wynyard b Soar	37	lbw b Baldwin	0
J Burns	c Wootton b Baldwin	5	b Soar	28
CJ Kortright	b Baldwin	34	not out	20
†TM Russell	c Bencraft b Baldwin	0	b Baldwin	0
W Mead	c Wootton b Baldwin	0	b Baldwin	6
HA Arkwright	b Baldwin	5	b Baldwin	7
H Pickett	not out	5	run out	0
Extras	(10 b, 1 lb)	11		0
Total	(all out, 69.4 overs)	128	(all out, 36.4 overs)	83

Fall: 1st inns: 1-4, 2-11, 3-11, 4-37, 5-50, 6-106, 7-118, 8-118, 9-118, 10-128. **2nd inns:** 1-0, 2-10, 3-17, 4-17, 5-25, 6-64, 7-65, 8-71, 9-79, 10-83.
Bowling (5 balls per over): 1st inns: Baldwin 34.4-18-36-6, Wootton 20-8-40-1, Soar 15-4-41-2. **2nd inns:** Baldwin 18.4-8-42-7, Wootton 7-1-21-1, Soar 11-4-20-1.

runs and seven wickets intact. Matters changed dramatically on the final day as batting became increasingly difficult on a rapidly deteriorating wicket. Having been 45-3 at one stage, Hampshire slumped to 66-8 as Mead continued to flourish with the ball although the home side rallied after wicket-keeper Tom Russell dropped two chances allowing Thomas Soar and Harry Baldwin to put on 63 in 50 minutes before Mead returned to conclude the innings. He had Baldwin superbly stumped and then rearranged the wicket of last man William Deane to finish with figures of 9-52. That left Essex needing 255 for victory but it was a challenge they found well beyond their capabilities. The first five batsmen were back in the pavilion with only 25 runs on the board as Baldwin's right-arm off breaks destroyed the early order and, although James Burns and Kortright added 39 runs in 40 minutes, once they had been parted the end came quickly.

Eight batsmen were clean bowled – seven by Baldwin – and it all made a sorry tale for Essex and for the unfortunate Mead whose team, despite his 17 wickets which included ten clean bowled victims, were comprehensively beaten.

County Championship
Somerset v Essex

3-day match **Venue:** County Ground, Taunton **Result:** Essex won by an innings and 317 runs

Records are made to be broken but one Essex batting record stood for 95 years until the advent of four-day cricket saw the figure surpassed. The statistic in question was the score of 692 made at the County Ground, Taunton where the visitors enjoyed a veritable run-fest. Somerset batted first and Walter Mead and Charles Kortright bore the brunt of the bowling being rewarded with four wickets apiece as the home side lost wickets at regular intervals although they did recover somewhat before posting an under-par 246 having been 93-6 at one

stage. By the close, their opponents were already enjoying a commanding position racing to 224-2 in two and a quarter hours batting. Opening batsman Harry Carpenter discarded his normal staid and solid approach in favour of an aggressive attitude that saw him reach 135 before proceedings ended for the day.

Essex continued to enjoy the batsmen friendly wicket when play resumed although Carpenter only added a further 18 runs before losing his wicket to a fine piece of fielding by Somerset captain Sammy Woods having scored 153 that included a 5 and 26 boundaries. Charles McGahey struck a superbly composed 147 in three and a quarter hours that embraced 23 boundaries whilst A.P. 'Bunny' Lucas, who only scored two centuries in his Essex career, reached an impressive 135 that included a six and 18 fours. He was joined by wicket-keeper Tom Russell in an eighth wicket partnership worth 184 runs before Lucas made his first error of judgement and was caught. Russell was just one run short of a two-hour century when he was caught by a substitute fielder and when the innings closed, Essex had

Charles Kortright: posted the third highest total achieved in county cricket at that time having
his 11 wickets occupied the crease for seven hours and five minutes.
provided a significant
contribution towards
the comprehensive Trailing by 446 runs, Somerset's problems continued when Kortright capped a
victory magnificent day for his team by taking the wicket of Gerald Fowler. Somerset

Prolific wicket-taker Charles Kortright stood six feet tall with a superb physique and, despite a long run-up, he boasted excellent reserves of stamina. In an article written in *Wisden* (1948), he criticised bowlers of that time who bemoaned the 'shirt-front' wickets they were expected to bowl on. "There were many such pitches in my playing days,' he wrote. "The sort on which if we could bounce the ball bail-high we thought ourselves pretty clever. Yet every county fielded two, sometimes three, genuinely fast bowlers, who were not discouraged by the wickets."
Meanwhile in his book, *The Fast Men*, David Frith wrote of the bowler's philosophy. "He believed in bowling as fast as possible, straight at the off stump, and without wasting too many balls in short-pitched deliveries. He scoffed at the moderns who theorised about and believed in swing and cut. To him fast bowling was a simple exercise."

Toss: Not known.
Umpires: G Hay, J Wickens

SOMERSET

LCH Palairet	c Russell b Kortright	33		b Kortright	31
G Fowler	c and b Mead	3		c Russell b Kortright	9
RCN Palairet	b Mead	16		b Kortright	6
RB Porch	not out	85	(6)	c Owen b Kortright	6
JE Trask	c Bawtree b Kortright	7	(5)	not out	26
*SMJ Woods	b Kortright	3		c Bawtree b Mead	17
DL Evans	c Carpenter b Mead	1		c Bawtree b Mead	12
EJ Tyler	b Kortright	45		c Kortright b Mead	8
EW Bartlett	lbw b Owen	4		c McGahey b Kortright	7
†FT Welman	b Mead	43		c Russell b Kortright	1
HT Gamlin	run out	0		c McGahey b Kortright	0
Extras	(1 b, 4 lb, 1 w)	6		(2 b, 3 lb, 1 w)	6
Total	**(all out, 75.3 overs)**	**246**		**(all out, 47.1 overs)**	**129**

Fall: 1st inns: 1-14, 2-40, 3-56, 4-72, 5-90, 6-93, 7-147, 8-156, 9-242, 10-246. **2nd inns:** 1-34, 2-49, 3-55, 4-55, 5-96, 6-98, 7-109, 8-126, 9-129, 10-129 (47.1 ov).
Bowling (5 balls per over): 1st inns: Pickett 13-4-46-0, Mead 33-11-100-4, Kortright 21-3-58-4, Owen 4-1-18-1, Bawtree 3-0-14-0, Carpenter 1.3-1-4-0. **2nd inns:** Pickett 4-0-8-0, Mead 21-8-58-3, Kortright 22.1-7-57-7.

ESSEX

*HGP Owen	c Gamlin b Woods	37
HA Carpenter	run out	153
FL Fane	b Tyler	12
CP McGahey	b Fowler	147
JF Bawtree	c Fowler b Tyler	47
J Burns	c Woods b Tyler	0
AP Lucas	c LCH Palairet b Tyler	135
CJ Kortright	c Woods b RCN Palairet	31
†TM Russell	c sub b Woods	99
W Mead	st LCH Palairet b Tyler	0
H Pickett	not out	1
Extras	(22 b, 7 lb, 1 w)	30
Total	**(all out, 192.3 overs)**	**692**

Fall: 1st inns: 1-80, 2-97, 3-257, 4-358, 5-358, 6-442, 7-499, 8-683, 9-691, 10-692. **2nd inns:** 1-0, 2-10, 3-17, 4-17, 5-25, 6-64, 7-65, 8-71, 9-79, 10-83.
Bowling (5 balls per over): 1st inns: Tyler 60.3-9-215-5, Woods 45-5-171-2, Gamlin 23-6-82-0, LCH Palairet 20-7-50-0, Fowler 25-7-68-1, Porch 4-1-17-0, Evans 3-1-5-0, RCN Palairet 12-1-54-1.

collapsed on the third morning with the outstanding nine wickets tumbling for an additional 91 runs as Kortright and Mead totally dominated events with the ball. Kortright, bowling with pace and enthusiasm, returned 7-57 and match figures of 11-115, whilst Mead offered support with the remaining three wickets. The winning margin was a mammoth innings and 317 runs. After a day's break, the hapless Somerset team found themselves chasing leather once again when Lancashire hit 801 with A.C.MacLaren helping himself to 424, the record individual first-class score in England.

The victory against Somerset left Essex third from the bottom in the 14-team county championship table. They had played nine games and won three and lost five matches which gave them a return of -2 points. In those days, the formula for deciding positions was calculated by deducting losses from wins whilst drawn games were ignored. Surrey were at the top of the table with nine wins and one defeat from 12 matches whilst Kent were the basement county having lost five of their seven matches and still seeking a win.

County Championship

Essex v Yorkshire

3-day match **Venue:** County Ground, Leyton **Result:** Yorkshire won by an innings and 33 runs

This match marked the debut of a player who was to become one of the most famous of Essex cricketers, John William Henry Tyler Douglas, although it proved to be a less than auspicious start for the 18 year-old all-rounder who recorded a "pair" as he twice failed to cope with the pace of George Hirst. Not that Douglas was alone in experiencing difficulty in contending with the visitors formidable bowler. Hirst grabbed six other victims in the first innings and finished with match figures of 12-29 from a total of 18.1 overs.

To dismiss your opponents for 104 but still lose by an innings is an incredible outcome yet that is what happened to the hosts as they endured one of the most humiliating defeats suffered in the entire history of Essex CCC losing

inside a day and one session. Yet the Leyton pitch had attracted comment as "one of the most perfect batting pitches in the country," after groundsman Edward Freeman had apparently cured the wicket of the uncertainties that had bedevilled it in former years.

County Ground,
Leyton *circa* 1901

The first day saw 26 wickets fall, of which 16 belonged to the home side, even though heavy overnight rain delayed the start until 12.45 p.m. Within an hour, Essex had been bowled out for an embarrassing 30 – a score that remains the County's lowest total to this day – with Hirst taking seven wickets of which six were bowled. As wickets tumbled like dominoes, the loss of A.P. 'Bunny' Lucas to an injudicious attempt for a quick single that failed just increased the home side's misery and it was only thanks to some responsible stroke play by Bill Reeves that the total passed twenty. When the visitors batted, they were undermined by Walter Mead and Reeves, both bowling with impressive line and length on a false pitch, that restricted the opposition to a lead of 74.

There were two delays to rain but when Essex batted for the second time, a

Although Johnny Douglas made an ignominious beginning to his Essex career, he was destined to become one of its finest players. He made a total of 459 appearances for the County and captained the side between 1911 and 1928. He also led England in 18 of the 23 Tests he played.
Named as one of the five *Wisden* Cricketers of the Year in 1915, the publication wrote of him: "The position Mr. Douglas now holds in the cricket world has been won by sheer hard work and perseverance. As a batsman, Douglas is essentially a defensive player. Now and then, like all steady bats, he carries caution too far. Watchful to a degree, he is a very hard man to bowl out. As a bowler he has remarkable qualities. Without being abnormally fast, he can keep up a fine pace for hours; his length is very accurate, and just at the end of his flight he has a nasty swerve."

Toss: Essex won the toss and decided to bat
Umpires: RG Barlow, H Wood

ESSEX

HA Carpenter	b Hirst	0	b Hirst	0
FL Fane	b Hirst	1	b Hirst	3
PA Perrin	c Hunter b Hirst	0	c Hawke b Hirst	9
CP McGahey	b Hirst	11	lbw b Rhodes	1
JWHT Douglas	b Hirst	0	b Hirst	0
*AP Lucas	run out	3	c and b Hirst	0
G Tosetti	b Hirst	3	c and b Rhodes	9
W Reeves	c Denton b Rhodes	10	st Hunter b Rhodes	12
†TM Russell	c Taylor b Rhodes	0	retired hurt	1
HI Young	not out	1	not out	0
W Mead	b Hirst	0	st Hunter b Rhodes	2
Extras	(1 b)	1	(2 b, 2 nb)	4
Total	**(all out, 16.1 overs)**	**30**	**(all out, 20 overs)**	**41**

Fall: 1st inns: 1-0, 2-0, 3-1, 4-1, 5-6, 6-17, 7-22, 8-23, 9-30, 10-30. **2nd inns:** 1-1, 2-8, 3-13, 4-15, 5-15, 6-15, 7-32, 8-39, 9-41.
Bowling: 1st inns: Hirst 8.1-3-12-7, Rhodes 8-0-17-2. **2nd inns:** Hirst 10-6-17-5, Rhodes 10-2-20-4.

YORKSHIRE

JT Brown	lbw b Mead	3
J Tunnicliffe	b Mead	10
D Denton	c Mead b Young	5
TL Taylor	b Reeves	44
F Mitchell	b Mead	10
GH Hirst	c Reeves b Mead	0
E Wainwright	c Young b Reeves	4
E Smith	c Fane b Reeves	8
*Lord Hawke	b Mead	7
W Rhodes	not out	9
†D Hunter	lbw b Mead	4
Extras		0
Total	**(all out, 44 overs)**	**104**

Fall: 1st inns: 1-3, 2-12, 3-36, 4-72, 5-72, 6-76, 7-76, 8-91, 9-100, 10-104. **2nd inns:** 1-1, 2-1, 3-71, 4-96, 5-129, 6-129, 7-145, 8-146, 9-146.
Bowling: 1st inns: Young 12-3-28-1, Mead 22-8-40-6, Reeves 10-3-36-3.

further series of batting horrors followed and they reached the end of the day on 15-6 with Hirst taking five more victims. On the day, his impressive controlled line and length bowling had reaped personal figures of 12-23 to leave his side in complete command.

Only half an hour's further action was required to allow Wilfred Rhodes to finish the game for Yorkshire on the second day as their opponents lost their remaining four wickets for a further 26 runs to leave the visitors triumphant by an innings and 33 runs.

Only three Essex players managed to reach double figures in the match whilst nine ducks were recorded over their two innings. There was further dejection for Essex when it was learned that wicket-keeper Tom Russell, who had been hit on the hand and suffered damaged fingers, would be on the sidelines for some time. The victory allowed Yorkshire to move 14 points clear of Middlesex at the head of the County Championship table whilst Essex were left ninth of the 15 counties involved in the competition at that time.

Derbyshire v Essex

3-day match **Venue:** Queen's Park, Chesterfield **Result:** Derbyshire won by 9 wickets

Perhaps of all the counties involved in the first-class game, only Essex could contrive to score almost 600 in their first innings and still manage to lose by 9 wickets – and remember this was in the days of three-day cricket! It was at the fast-scoring Chesterfield venue that Essex achieved this embarrassing feat

after Percy Perrin hit an unbeaten 343, which remains the only triple century recorded by an Essex player in the County Championship. His brilliant innings, full of magnificent drives on both sides of the wicket, included an unprecedented 68 fours. Until 1910 when the law was changed, a six was only recorded when the ball was hit out of the ground and it has been suggested that as many as 14 of the batsman's fours would have been credited as sixes after the amendment was introduced.

Perrin's record breaking innings on a fast wicket and outfield commenced within 10 minutes of the match starting when he went to the crease at the fall of opening bat Herbert Carpenter with only 12 runs on the board. Frederick Fane with 63, Charles McGahey (32) and Frank Gillingham (43) offered good support to the free-scoring Perrin as the innings began to take shape with century stands for the second and fourth wickets. Essex then lost three wickets cheaply before Johnny Douglas contributed 47 out of 130 for the eighth wicket and following his dismissal, Alf Russell accompanied Perrin whilst another 73 were added. When the innings finally closed, Perrin had been batting for 345 minutes.

Percy Perrin:
a triple-century but
still finished on the
losing side

Such was the dominance of the Essex batsman that he scored at nearly 60 runs an hour for six hours despite the presence of four fielders on the boundary for much of the time. Apart from his record number of boundaries, Perrin hit 4 threes, 10 twos and 39 singles. When he reached 197, he passed 1,000 runs for the season and he then went on to beat his previous

---

Percy Perrin, said afterwards, "We wanted to show 'em you see, what we could do in each direction." Some years later, when asked what he recalled of his magnificent innings, he said modestly, "I strolled a few singles, trotted a few twos and just leaned on my bat and watched the rest."

One of the great batsmen of his time, Perrin was named by *Wisden* as one of their Five Cricketers of the Year in 1905 but never played for England and the reason was quite straightforward, his remarkable lack of fielding ability. It was not that he was lacking enthusiasm nor effort for that dimension of the game; simply he was unable to cover ground in an athletic manner. He accepted his shortcomings with humour illustrated by a reply given to a question asking if it was true that he had really stopped a shot from Jack Hobbs that appeared destined for the boundary. He replied, "Oh yes. Mind you they ran eight."

Toss: Essex won the toss and decided to bat
Umpires: S Brown, W Wright

ESSEX

*FL Fane	lbw b Curgenven	63		b Warren	2
HA Carpenter	b Bestwick	5		c Warren b Bestwick	2
PA Perrin	not out	343		c and b Warren	8
CP McGahey	b Bestwick	32		c Cadman b Bestwick	5
FH Gillingham	c and b Warren	43		absent hurt	
EHD Sewell	b Warren	10	(5)	c Cadman b Curgenven	41
W Reeves	b Warren	0	(6)	b Bestwick	0
RP Keigwin	lbw b Ashcroft	14	(7)	c Needham b Warren	0
JWHT Douglas	b Ollivierre	47	(9)	not out	27
†AE Russell	c Humphries b Cadman	23	(8)	b Curgenven	0
CP Buckenham	lbw b Bestwick	3	(10)	b Warren	8
Extras	(2 b, 5 lb, 4 nb, 3 w)	14		(1 lb, 1 nb, 2 w)	4
Total	**(all out, 138.1 overs)**	**597**		**(all out, 39.1 overs)**	**97**

Fall: 1st inns: 1-12, 2-132, 3-179, 4-300, 5-314, 6-314, 7-383, 8-513, 9-586, 10-597. **2nd inns:** 1-4, 2-4, 3-17, 4-21, 5-21, 6-25, 7-33, 8-83, 9-97.
Bowling: 1st inns: Warren 29-3-143-3, Bestwick 42.1-8-160-3, Cadman 22-3-65-1, Storer 7-0-41-0, Curgenven 16-1-67-1, Ashcroft 7-1-38-1, Morton 8-1-39-0, Wright 4-0-15-0, Ollivierre 3-0-15-1.
2nd inns: Bestwick 16-4-34-3, Warren 16.1-5-42-4, Cadman 2-0-10-0, Curgenven 5-2-7-2.

DERBYSHIRE

LG Wright	c Fane b Reeves	68		c Carpenter b Buckenham	1
CA Ollivierre	b Reeves	229		not out	92
W Storer	b Buckenham	44		not out	48
*EM Ashcroft	b Sewell	34		did not bat	
E Needham	b Reeves	47		did not bat	
G Curgenven	b Buckenham	31		did not bat	
A Morton	b Reeves	16		did not bat	
A Warren	b Douglas	18		did not bat	
SWA Cadman	c Douglas b Reeves	34		did not bat	
†J Humphries	not out	2		did not bat	
W Bestwick	lbw b Douglas	0		did not bat	
Extras	(6 b, 18 lb, 1 w)	25		(4 b, 2 lb, 1 nb, 1 w)	8
Total	**(all out, 134.3 overs)**	**548**		**(1 wicket, 30 overs)**	**149**

Fall: 1st inns: 1-191, 2-319, 3-378, 4-401, 5-462, 6-478, 7-499, 8-530, 9-544, 10-548. **2nd inns:** 1-11.
Bowling: 1st inns: Buckenham 43-5-176-2, Keigwin 7-1-36-0, Reeves 51-7-192-5, Douglas 15.3-1-54-2, McGahey 11-2-34-0, Sewell 7-0-31-1. **2nd inns:** Buckenham 13-0-78-1, Reeves 13-1-43-0, Douglas 2-0-14-0, McGahey 2-1-6-0.

best score of 205. Yet he was destined to hold an unwanted record of recording the highest innings ever played by a batsman in a losing team.

Derbyshire's response was sustained by a fine 229 from their West Indian opening batsman Charles Ollivierre who acted as the catalyst for his side's 548 against what was considered a "weak" Essex bowling attack. The home side then rediscovered the incisive cutting edge by whipping out their opponents – on what was by now described as a "crumbling" wicket – for a meagre 97. Only two batsmen reached double figures whilst eight batsmen managed only 25 runs between them including 8 by Perrin this time around although Gillingham was unable to bat because of a thigh injury. There were suggestions that the Essex collapse occurred because the team had celebrated Perrin's earlier record-breaking achievement with too much alcoholic fervour rather than the pitch being the source of their second innings shortcomings. Certainly Derbyshire had no problems in reaching the 147 required for victory cruising to their target with nine wickets to spare as Ollivierre again mastered the visitors' attack.

County Championship

Essex v Yorkshire

3-day match   **Venue:** County Ground, Leyton **Result:** Draw

Johnny Douglas chose this game to record a remarkable bowling feat that included the first hat-trick by an Essex bowler in the Championship during a spell of five wickets in eight deliveries. It could be suggested that the Essex form was enigmatic at the time combining some excellent days with some less than impressive displays and yet they were the only side to beat the

Johnny Douglas: recalled this match as one that had given him the most pleasure in his career

Australians. On this occasion, Yorkshire found them at the peak of their form from the moment the visitors lost the toss and were left to chase leather throughout the first day. Frederick Fane and Herbert Carpenter posted a three-figure opening partnership – the second time in a week they had achieved the feat – although Carpenter was dropped by wicket-keeper Arthur Dolphin when he had scored 10 runs.

Fane took two and three-quarter hours to reach his well-organised hundred with cutting a particularly impressive feature of his game and when he became the second wicket to fall, he had figured in a further century stand. That was achieved with Frank Gillingham who then continued the good work together with Bill Reeves as the pair forced the pace with the latter contributing 71 of the 90 runs that were added in 50 minutes for the fifth wicket. By the close of the first day, Essex were 404 -6 with Charles McGahey unbeaten on 51 and he completed his century the following morning as the hosts added a further 117 runs before being dismissed.

On a wicket playing hard and true, Yorkshire collapsed sensationally and were bowled out in one and three-quarter hours with Douglas proving the instigator of their misery. Joining the attack as first change, he removed five batsmen all clean bowled without conceding a run. With the fifth ball of his second over, he dismissed John Tunnicliffe with a slow yorker and lunch was immediately taken. On the resumption, George Hirst hit across the line and then with the last three balls

Years later, Johnny Douglas remembered the game as one that gave him the greatest pleasure. Summarising the match, The Times correspondent reported: "Essex did their best in the field and with the ball; but this batting of Yorkshire rather exposed the real weakness of the side in the matter of any great bowling talent." The reporter then commented on the unsavoury attitude of a section of the home support. "There was a large crowd gathered to see the finish and it was regrettable to find a slight recurrence of the unsportsmanlike spirit that was noticed in the Lancashire match a few Saturdays before," he stated. "While Yorkshire were fighting so well and courageously an uphill game, a few spectators deficient in manners as well as knowledge of the game, repeatedly jeered at the batsmen. Lord Hawke, who went in, absolutely refused to go on with his innings until the crowd desisted."

Toss: Essex won the toss and decided to bat
Umpires: J Carlin, A Pike

ESSEX

*FL Fane	c Myers b Smith	106
HA Carpenter	run out	69
FH Gillingham	st Dolphin b Smith	82
CP McGahey	b Rhodes	105
SA Trick	c Hirst b Smith	0
W Reeves	c Rhodes b Myers	71
JWHT Douglas	b Myers	2
CE Benham	b Ringrose	42
†AE Russell	b Rhodes	17
CP Buckenham	b Haigh	3
B Tremlin	not out	3
Extras	(11 b, 10 lb)	21
Total	**(all out, 138.4 overs)**	**521**

Fall: 1st inns: 1-116, 2-248, 3-277, 4-279, 5-369, 6-381, 7-467, 8-514, 9-517, 10-521. **2nd inns:** 1-0, 2-93, 3-96, 4-180, 5-182, 6-196, 7-208, 8-226, 9-231, 10-250.
Bowling: 1st inns: Hirst 32-2-111-0, Ringrose 19-1-84-1, Rhodes 29.4-2-107-2, Haigh 23-8-53-1, Myers 15-5-38-2, Smith 20-1-107-3. **2nd inns:** Jessop 13.2-2-41-1, Townsend 13-3-39-2, Grace 20-9-25-0, Roberts 7-1-20-0, Brown 26-8-52-2, Wrathall 9-0-32-1, Wright 15-3-32-4.

YORKSHIRE

(FOLLOWING ON)

J Tunnicliffe	b Douglas	11	c McGahey b Benham	59
JW Rothery	b Buckenham	0	c McGahey b Buckenham	0
D Denton	c Carpenter b Tremlin	40	b Douglas	17
GH Hirst	b Douglas	0	b Reeves	90
W Rhodes	b Douglas	2	b Buckenham	6
S Haigh	b Douglas	0	c Russell b Reeves	12
H Myers	b Douglas	0	lbw b Douglas	9
E Smith	b Buckenham	2	not out	0
*Lord Hawke	b Tremlin	36	not out	9
W Ringrose	b Tremlin	5	did not bat	
†A Dolphin	not out	0	did not bat	
Extras	(1 b, 1 lb)	2	(10 b, 10 lb, 2 nb, 3 w)	25
Total	**(all out, 30.4 overs)**	**98**	**(7 wickets, 150 overs)**	**227**

Fall: 1st inns: 1-1, 2-35, 3-35, 4-39, 5-39, 6-39, 7-42, 8-87, 9-97, 10-98. **2nd inns:** 1-0, 2-22, 3-158, 4-177, 5-193, 6-212, 7-218.
Bowling: 1st inns: Buckenham 12-2-47-2, Tremlin 6.4-3-16-3, Douglas 10-1-31-5, Reeves 2-0-2-0.
2nd inns: Buckenham 32-15-49-2, Tremlin 21-10-24-0, Douglas 26-13-49-2, Reeves 36-24-37-2, McGahey 7-2-8-0, Benham 25-14-29-1, Carpenter 3-1-6-0.

of his third over, Douglas performed the hat-trick. Wilfred Rhodes played on, Schofield Haigh also hit across one and Hubert Myers played over a ball that hit leg stump. Medium-pacer Douglas, maintaining true length but varying his pace, had figures of 3-1-3-5 as Yorkshire capitulated to 39-6.

Essex were then frustrated by two showers and an eighth wicket stand of 45 between Lord Hawke and David Denton but when Hawke was last man out, Yorkshire followed-on and their problems continued. Bad light brought a premature close with the visitors still 408 runs adrift and nine second innings wickets standing. However, they batted resolutely and in six hours of cricket on the final day, only six wickets fell whilst 212 runs were scored with Hirst eschewing any possibility of demise with safety-first technique. He went to the crease at the fall of the second wicket and was only removed four and three-quarter hours later with his side now 212-6. Following his departure, the match-saving task was taken over by Ernest Smith who batted throughout the last hour without making a run to achieve the draw that his side required.

Tour Match

Essex v Australians

3-day match

Venue: County Ground, Leyton **Result:** Essex won by 19 runs

In a low-scoring match completed in two days, only one batsman reached a half-century. An easy victory seemed likely for the tourists when they reduced their hosts to 69-7 but Johnny Douglas batted with his usual dogged resolution to score 28 taking his side to 118 before becoming the last wicket to fall. Essex staged a spirited fightback taking only 22.1 overs to dismiss their opponents. Celebrated batsmen Joe Darling, Clem Hill, Monty Noble and Syd Gregory

Claude Buckenham:
unfortunate not to
have won more than
four Test caps

managed just seven runs between them as the first eight Australian wickets fell for 49 and although Albert 'Tibby' Cotter and Frank Laver added 51 for the ninth wicket, the home side gained a first innings lead of 18 runs. Apart from six overs when Claude Buckenham was given a well-earned rest, he and Bert Tremlin bowled unchanged throughout the match and were subsequently destined to capture all 20 Australian wickets between them.

Wickets continued to tumble on a day when ball totally dominated bat as the hosts closed on 31-3. The pattern of play on day two followed a similar fashion with wickets falling regularly although a couple of decent partnerships between Bill Reeves, Douglas and Buckenham saw the last two wickets add 93 valuable runs setting the tourists 222 for victory. Once again, their batsmen struggled to master the pace of Buckenham and the fast-medium bowling of Tremlin who quickly reduced the opposition to 56-4 and when Noble had his stumps re-arranged by Buckenham, at 126-8 the game seemed over. Albert Hopkins, one of four Aussies who had failed to score in the first innings, drove profitably and together with Charlie McLeod, 31 runs were gathered for the ninth wicket until that partnership was broken with the touring side still 65 runs short of their target. Laver joined Hopkins and with careful batting, added ones and twos plus the occasional boundary to guide the total to 200 and start nervous moments for Essex. However, the game ended with an extraordinary dismissal. Laver, on 18, swung at Buckenham in an attempt to clear the ropes but skied the

In his publication, *Famous Cricketers of Essex*, Dean Hayes described Claude Buckenham thus. "Bowling with great speed and a good high delivery, he would have made a greater name for himself if he'd had stronger support in the field." That assessment was echoed in the obituary in *The Cricketer* magazine on Buckingham's death in 1937. "When Buckingham was in his prime, the weakness of the Essex slip fielding was notorious, and it is significant that when he was chosen for representative matches, he invariably did well," it stated.

For a period of 6 years, he was rated as one of the deadliest pace bowlers in England. In 1909, he was named in the England Test squad to face Australia at The Oval but was omitted on the morning of the match, a decision that the editor of *Wisden* described as "touching the confines of lunacy." Buckenham did play in four Tests against South Africa in 1910-11 capturing 21 wickets.

Toss: Essex won the toss and decided to bat.
Umpires: AJ Atfield, W Attewell

ESSEX

Batsman	1st innings			2nd innings	
*FL Fane	c Cotter b Laver	4		b Noble	16
HA Carpenter	c Laver b McLeod	24		b Cotter	2
CP McGahey	b Laver	0		c Darling b Laver	39
FH Gillingham	c Hill b Laver	9	(6)	c Noble b Laver	21
G Tosetti	c Newland b Laver	14	(7)	b Noble	13
PA Perrin	b Laver	0	(8)	c Duff b Laver	0
W Reeves	c Hopkins b McLeod	11	(9)	c Duff b Laver	37
JWHT Douglas	c McLeod b Duff	28	(10)	c McLeod b Cotter	22
†AE Russell	c Hill b Laver	8	(5)	c Hill b Noble	12
B Tremlin	b Duff	6	(4)	c sub b Noble	0
CP Buckenham	not out	1		not out	20
Extras	(8 b, 4 lb, 1 w)	13		(12 b, 7 lb, 1 nb, 1 w)	21
Total	**(all out, 50.5 overs)**	**118**		**(all out, 74.1 overs)**	**203**

Fall: 1st inns: 1-4, 2-4, 3-20, 4-54, 5-58, 6-60, 7-69, 8-99, 9-116, 10-118. **2nd inns:** 1-2, 2-25, 3-25, 4-55, 5-85, 6-86, 7-110, 8-110, 9-175, 10-203.
Bowling: 1st inns: Cotter 10-3-19-0, Laver 25-8-49-6, McLeod 10-4-20, Duff 5.5-1-17-2. **2nd inns:** Cotter 11.1-3-35-2, Laver 37-11-81-4, Noble 26-8-66-4.

AUSTRALIANS

Batsman	1st innings			2nd innings	
RA Duff	c Reeves b Buckenham	29		b Buckenham	3
*J Darling	c Buckenham b Tremlin	1		b Tremlin	15
C Hill	b Buckenham	5		c Gillingham b Buckenham	15
MA Noble	lbw b Tremlin	1		b Buckenham	42
CE McLeod	c and b Tremlin	12	(10)	c Buckenham b Tremlin	23
SE Gregory	b Buckenham	0	(5)	c Carpenter b Tremlin	0
AJY Hopkins	c Perrin b Buckenham	0	(6)	not out	67
DRA Gehrs	b Buckenham	0	(9)	b Buckenham	2
A Cotter	b Tremlin	38	(7)	b Tremlin	4
FJ Laver	c Perrin b Buckenham	13	(11)	c Fane b Buckenham	18
†PM Newland	not out	0	(8)	b Buckenham	4
Extras	(1 lb)	1		(5 b, 4 lb)	9
Total	**(all out, 22.1 overs)**	**100**		**(all out, 66.2 overs)**	**202**

Fall: 1st inns: 1-12, 2-17, 3-26, 4-42, 5-43, 6-49, 7-49, 8-49, 9-100, 10-100. **2nd inns:** 1-4, 2-28, 3-56, 4-56, 5-98, 6-113, 7-124, 8-126, 9-157, 10-202.
Bowling: 1st inns: Buckenham 11.1-1-45-6, Tremlin 11-1-54-4. **2nd inns:** Buckenham 27.2-4-92-6, Tremlin 33-10-81-4, Reeves 3-0-14-0, Douglas 3-2-6-0.

ball to Essex captain Frederick Fane on the boundary directly behind the wicket where he had posted himself to prevent the possibility of extras being conceded.

The valiant Hopkins was left stranded on 67 not out as Essex claimed victory by 19 runs. Buckenham returned match figures of 12-137 and Tremlin 8-135 and both continued to be effective new ball bowlers ending the season with 90 and 99 wickets respectively. Given that the County had lost six of their first seven matches, this victory was totally unexpected and although Australia lost the Ashes Test series with England 2-0 that summer, in a 38-match programme, Essex were the only other team to defeat the experienced touring party.

Yorkshire, Surrey, Lancashire and Essex all met the Australians twice during the season but Essex were the only side to dismiss them in all four innings as the County achieved another creditable result later in the season when drawing with the tourists. On that occasion, the effective Tremlin took 10 wickets in the match whilst Buckenham claimed five.

County Championship

Essex v Lancashire

3-day match   **Venue:** County Ground, Leyton **Result:** Essex won by 9 wickets

Following the conclusion of the First World War, cricket decided to experiment with two-day county matches for the 1919 campaign but the experiment was dropped after one season with the high volume of drawn matches dictating the decision to return to three-day cricket. Essex played 18 Championship matches during the season finishing fourteenth after winning two and losing four with the remainder producing stalemates. One of the only two successful results for the Club occurred in their first home match of the season when the game was concluded by lunchtime on the second day.

George Louden: reputedly the best fast bowler in the country

The home ground at Leyton was generally unsuited to two-day matches because of the near-perfect batting pitches although the match against Lancashire proved an exception. In the course of the first day, 395 runs were scored whilst 28 wickets were falling. The visitors batted first and the cross-wind aided paceman Johnny Douglas who took figures of 6-64. He started bowling from the pavilion end but soon switched ends whereupon he met with pronounced success taking three quick wickets. Harry Makepeace was caught in the slips and the bowler then saw Johnny Tyldesley offer a chance in the same area when the batsman had scored two but the opportunity went begging. The home attack continued to pose problems and when left-arm opening bowler Fred Scoulding took the wicket of Charlie Hallows, the visitors were 67-4. John and James Tyldesley carried the score to 110 at lunch but both were then dismissed in one over as Lancashire lost their remaining six wickets in an hour for the addition of 70 runs.

Essex began brightly as Frank Gillingham and C.A.G. 'Jack' Russell posted a brisk 52 in 30 minutes before Gillingham lost his wicket for 25 to start a collapse. The home side recoiled to 78-5 and although Douglas tried to steady the rocking ship, Essex were left trailing by 35 runs on first innings. With play continuing until

George Louden was a stockbroker which restricted his cricket engagements. Standing over six feet, he had a high, easy action and was able to bowl very fast with unerring accuracy. During 1921 and 1923, he performed so well on his limited appearances as to leave little doubt that he was the best bowler in England. Although Louden bowled against the Australians in 1921 and took 13 wickets in two innings, he was not chosen for any Test match. Australian batsman Warren Bardsley thought it ridiculous that, although the England selectors chose fourteen bowlers that series, they never selected the man regarded by the Australians as the best in the country. "All we did was tell the truth," he said later. "We told everybody that Louden was England's best bowler. They thought we were leg-pulling and just didn't pick him!" Louden was fondly remembered by those who played with him as a bowler whose business commitments prevented him from achieving the higher honours he merited.

Toss: Lancashire won the toss and decided to bat.
Umpires: FW Marlow, F Parris

LANCASHIRE

JCHL Hollins	b JWHT Douglas	17	b Louden	14
JWH Makepeace	c Gillingham b JWHT Douglas	16	lbw b JWHT Douglas	2
JT Tyldesley	c Perrin b JWHT Douglas	43	c Williams b Louden	0
GE Tyldesley	b JWHT Douglas	0	b JWHT Douglas	13
C Hallows	c JWHT Douglas b Scoulding	13	b Louden	6
JD Tyldesley	b JWHT Douglas	24	c Gillingham b Louden	9
JS Heap	c Turner b Louden	28	c Scoulding b JWHT Douglas	10
†RA Boddington	c Perrin b JWHT Douglas	2	b Louden	7
*MN Kenyon	c Russell b Scoulding	22	c JWHT Douglas b Louden	5
H Dean	c Waugh b Scoulding	8	not out	27
CS Marriott	not out	0	c and b Louden	6
Extras	(7 lb)	7	(4 lb)	4
Total	**(all out, 66.3 overs)**	**180**	**(all out, 40.2 overs)**	**103**

Fall: 1st inns: 1-19, 2-44, 3-46, 4-67, 5-118, 6-119, 7-129, 8-162, 9-173, 10-180. **2nd inns:** 1-5, 2-10, 3-29, 4-39, 5-39, 6-58, 7-58, 8-70, 9-81, 10-103.
Bowling: 1st inns: JWHT Douglas 23-3-64-6, Scoulding 28.3-3-78-3, Waugh 1-0-2-0, Louden 14-5-29-1.
2nd inns: JWHT Douglas 20-4-53-3, Scoulding 1-0-4-0, Louden 19.2-5-42-7.

ESSEX

FH Gillingham	b JD Tyldesley	25	b JD Tyldesley	60
CAG Russell	c JT Tyldesley b Marriott	30	not out	65
JR Freeman	b JD Tyldesley	8	not out	12
WMF Turner	lbw b Marriott	9	did not bat	
PA Perrin	lbw b JD Tyldesley	0	did not bat	
*JWHT Douglas	c and b Dean	26	did not bat	
HP Waugh	c Boddington b JD Tyldesley	4	did not bat	
CH Douglas	c JT Tyldesley b Marriott	9	did not bat	
†HRH Williams	b Marriott	8	did not bat	
GM Louden	not out	10	did not bat	
FJ Scoulding	b Marriott	2	did not bat	
Extras	(11 b, 2 lb, 1 nb)	14	(3 lb)	3
Total	**(all out, 45.2 overs)**	**145**	**(1 wicket, 34.5 overs)**	**140**

Fall: 1st inns: 1-52, 2-66, 3-76, 4-77, 5-78, 6-90, 7-116, 8-122, 9-135, 10-145. **2nd inns:** 1-114.
Bowling: 1st inns: JD Tyldesley 17-2-54-4, Dean 10-3-25-1, Marriott 18.2-0-52-5. **2nd inns:** JD Tyldesley 12.5-1-65-1, Dean 5-0-19-0, Marriott 12-1-33-0, Hallows 5-0-20-0.

7.30 p.m., Lancashire endured a torrid time in their second innings and by the close, they were 105 runs ahead with only two wickets standing. Despite a brave effort by Harry Dean, who survived for a further 40 minutes the next morning whilst 33 runs were added, the home side were left requiring 139 runs for victory after George Louden provided a defining performance with the ball. Showing fine control, he returned 7-42 to record his career-best figures.

Playing with freedom and confidence, Gillingham and Russell soon removed any thoughts of vagaries in the pitch with an exhilarating and skilful partnership of 114 in an hour and a quarter. Gillingham drove powerfully whilst Russell exhibited a number of well-timed leg side strokes and the liaison was only ended when Gillingham was bowled off his pads. John Freeman joined Russell to secure the remaining runs with play extended beyond the usual luncheon time in order to allow the match to conclude. In front of a small second day attendance, Essex cantered to victory by nine wickets having taken a little over an hour and a half to reach their target.

County Championship

Essex v Middlesex

3-day match   **Venue:** County Ground, Leyton **Result:** Essex won by 4 runs

An estimated 6,000 people were present on the first day of the County's match against a side who arrived as reigning champions. A pitch that had been affected by rain made run-getting a problem with the ball coming on awkwardly to the bat as illustrated by the home side who batted first after winning the toss and were immediately in trouble losing their first four wickets for 24 runs. Half the side were back in the pavilion for 41 before Charles

McGahey and Colin McIver revived matters with a partnership worth 81 runs. The pendulum swung back to favour the visitors once again with the innings being concluded in 25 minutes play after tea whilst only 17 more runs were added. With an hour left, Middlesex reached 57-2 but heavy overnight rain, that continued into the early morning, allowed only 15 minutes play before lunch on day two.

The visitors innings featured an unusual dismissal when Pelham 'Plum' Warner retired on 22 and was adjudged 'retired out' whilst Johnny Douglas also left the field at the same time having only bowled four overs. Both were required to attend a Test selection committee meeting at Lord's. Two long delays due to bad light further restricted play after lunch but with Henry Lee carrying his bat for a determined and well-composed 80, the visitors eventually gained a first innings advantage of 79 runs. Essex were then left with an hour's batting during which time they finished on level terms with their opponents having lost one wicket.

Charles McGahey: top-scored in the Essex first innings

The final day saw the hosts lose Douglas and John Freeman quickly but Percy Perrin and McIver rallied with 48 runs in as many minutes before Harold 'Whiz' Morris joined Perrin taking the score to 163 before he became the fifth wicket to fall as spinner Jack Hearne became increasingly effective. Perrin struggled for subsequent support although he reached a determined half-century before he

In the book *Essex County Cricket Club – The Official History* the concluding segment of the fascinating match involving the legendary Warner and Douglas is wonderfully described. "The battle between Warner and Douglas now took on epic proportions," it states. "Here were the last vestiges of a golden age, now only dimly perceived. This was Plum Warner's last season. Durston defended doggedly and Warner took what runs he could against Douglas. The score mounted but with Warner on 46 and Middlesex five short of victory, Douglas beat the Middlesex captain with a fast yorker and scattered the stumps. The Essex side erupted, caught up in their own captain's joy and enthusiasm. He had dismissed the first seven batsmen on the card without help from the field at a personal cost of 47 runs. He and Warner left the field with their arms around each other's shoulders."

Toss: Essex won the toss and decided to bat.
Umpires: J Blake, FW Marlow.

ESSEX

*JWHT Douglas	c Murrell b Durston	2	c Hearne b Lee	36
CAG Russell	c Lee b Durston	2	b Hearne	26
†JR Freeman	b Haig	3	c Hendren b Durston	8
PA Perrin	lbw b Durston	8	c Hendren b Hearne	50
CD McIver	b Hearne	43	b Hearne	23
HM Morris	b Hearne	3	st Murrell b Hearne	17
CP McGahey	b Hearne	44	c Gunasekera b Hearne	1
JG Dixon	lbw b Lee	1	c Warner b Hearne	0
LC Eastman	c and b Lee	0	st Murrell b Hearne	2
GM Louden	b Lee	2	lbw b Hearne	1
FJ Scoulding	not out	0	not out	0
Extras	(15 b, 10 lb)	25	(24 b, 7 lb, 1 nb)	32
Total	**(all out, 64.2 overs)**	**133**	**(all out, 76.4 overs)**	**196**

Fall: 1st inns: 1-3, 2-4, 3-18, 4-24, 5-41, 6-122, 7-125, 8-131, 9-133, 10-133. **2nd inns:** 1-58, 2-83, 3-83, 4-131, 5-163, 6-169, 7-171, 8-189, 9-195, 10-196.
Bowling: 1st inns: Haig 15-8-15-1, Durston 16-9-16-3, Lee 12.2-3-25-3, Hearne 12-2-33-3, Gunasekera 4-2-2-0, Stevens 5-0-17-0. **2nd inns:** Durston 24-11-37-1, Haig 4-0-20-0, Lee 22-4-58-1, Hearne 26.4-5-49-8.

MIDDLESEX

NE Haig	b Louden	3		b Douglas	6
HW Lee	not out	80		b Douglas	9
JW Hearne	b Eastman	16		lbw b Douglas	6
*PF Warner	retired out	22	(5)	b Douglas	46
EH Hendren	c Louden b Eastman	5	(4)	lbw b Douglas	3
FT Mann	b Louden	0		lbw b Douglas	2
GTS Stevens	c McGahey b Scoulding	36		b Douglas	3
CHL Skeet	run out	2		lbw b Russell	5
CH Gunasekera	b Scoulding	6		b Louden	4
†HR Murrell	b Scoulding	18		lbw b Russell	23
FJ Durston	c Freeman b Eastman	3		not out	1
Extras	(8 b, 13 lb)	21		(4 b, 1 nb)	5
Total	**(all out, 72.3 overs)**	**212**		**(all out, 64.2 overs)**	**113**

Fall: 1st inns: 1-14, 2-40, 3-87, 4-88, 5-156, 6-160, 7-189, 8-207, 9-212. **2nd inns:** 1-15, 2-16, 3-24, 4-27, 5-29, 6-33, 7-50, 8-67, 9-102, 10-113.
Bowling: 1st inns: Douglas 4-2-2-0, Louden 18-6-28-2, Scoulding 19-1-59-3, Eastman 17.3-1-58-3, Russell 14-1-44-0. **2nd inns:** Douglas 24.2-5-47-7, Louden 25-11-32-1, Scoulding 3-0-8-0, Eastman 2-1-5-0, Russell 10-5-16-2.

became one of Hearne's eight wickets as Middlesex were left requiring only 118 runs for victory.

They started disastrously against Douglas who revelled in the challenging situation as he captured the first six wickets with only 33 runs on the board. Three runs later, Warner was dropped by Fred Scoulding at silly mid-on when he had just got off the mark but Churchill Gunasekara joined Warner and stayed with his captain until the total had reached 67 before becoming the eighth wicket to fall. Middlesex still needed 51 runs but Warner, batting with his usual resolution and skill, found a responsible ally in Harry Murrell who batted sensibly. Together they posted 35 runs in 45 minutes before C.A.G. 'Jack' Russell trapped Murrell leg before wicket. In a nail-biting finish, Middlesex now required 16 runs to win with the last pair at the crease. They gradually moved ever-closer but with the total on 113, Warner edged a ball from Douglas onto his stumps to end an innings spanning two and a half hours and give Essex victory by four runs with just 10 minutes remaining. Middlesex soon overcame their disappointment winning their last nine matches on their way to retaining their title.

County Championship
Essex v Derbyshire

3-day match   **Venue:** County Ground, Leyton **Result:** Essex won by an innings and 74 runs

All-rounder Johnny Douglas was one of the true greats of Essex Cricket and it is fascinating that despite his many innings and endless amount of overs in an illustrious career, his personal best performances with both bat and ball came in this memorable match at Leyton. He opened the bowling and after a brief period of resistance, found the breakthrough before running through the visitors batting order returning 9-47 as the innings disintegrated to 114 all out in three hours. Apart from one over, Douglas bowled unchanged. None of the

opposition played him with any confidence as he made the ball swing unnervingly through the air. The majority of the batsmen were unsettled and uncertain with Jim Hutchinson spending an hour at the crease without scoring before he was trapped leg before wicket.

Douglas was then called upon to display his batting proficiency helping his side out of a difficult situation after they had lost five wickets for 37 runs as a series of his colleagues perished chasing deliveries outside the off stump. Aided by Joseph Dixon and Colin McIver and giving an exemplary lesson in foot movement, Douglas arrested a crumbling innings. When the day closed, he had contributed an unbeaten 62 out of 138-7 wickets. McIver soon fell on the resumption of play but debutant and amateur Steriker Hare joined his illustrious colleague at the crease and together they added 148

Steriker Hare: missed a century on debut by just two runs

before lunch with Douglas completing a fine century in two and three-quarter hours. Hare meanwhile looked at ease batting with gusto and produced a number of powerful square cuts and drives to reach a chanceless fifty in 90 minutes. Two interruptions for rain eventually left the hosts 225 runs ahead at the end of the second day.

The pair resumed the following morning with Douglas completing the only

Johnny Douglas captained Essex for 17 years and was a fine all-round sportsman. In addition to winning 23 England Test cricket caps, he also gained amateur international caps in football plus an Olympic Gold medal for boxing in the Middleweight class in 1908. Charles Bray, a subsequent Essex captain and professional journalist wrote of the multi-talented player, "You either liked or respected John Douglas or you loathed him. If the Essex County Cricket Club ever decided to have a Roll of Honour and were foolish enough to place the names in order of merit, there would be much heart-burning, much discussion and, no doubt, much dispute over the one chosen for the top position. It would be a most unenviable task, indeed almost impossible to single out one of the many giants of Essex cricket and say that he was greater than any other. Yet I should be prepared to advance and support the claims of John William Henry Tyler Douglas."

Toss: Derbyshire won the toss and decided to bat.
Umpires: J Blake, WAJ West.

DERBYSHIRE

L Oliver	b Douglas	16	lbw b Lapham	34
WWH Hill-Wood	lbw b Douglas	13	c Dixon b Saint	24
J Bowden	lbw b Douglas	25	b PE Morris	18
JM Hutchinson	lbw b Douglas	0	b Lapham	3
SWA Cadman	c PE Morris b Douglas	26	lbw b Douglas	79
H Storer	b Douglas	10	c Douglas b Dixon	19
A Morton	b Douglas	0	c and b Dixon	0
G Curgenven	b PE Morris	11	c McIver b PE Morris	17
*GM Buckston	b Douglas	5	c Saint b Dixon	1
†H Elliott	not out	1	not out	6
W Bestwick	c Saint b Douglas	0	c Freeman b Douglas	0
Extras	(2 b, 3 lb, 2 nb)	7	(5 b, 2 lb)	7
Total	**(all out, 54.2 overs)**	**114**	**(all out, 68.5 overs)**	**208**

Fall: 1st inns: 1-25, 2-36, 3-48, 4-72, 5-86, 6-86, 7-103, 8-109, 9-114, 10-114. **2nd inns:** 1-54, 2-58, 3-67, 4-104, 5-149, 6-149, 7-176, 8-179, 9-208, 10-208.
Bowling: 1st inns: Douglas 26.2-10-47-9, Dixon 14-2-34-0, PE Morris 13-0-24-1, Lapham 1-0-2-0.
2nd inns: Dixon 18-3-49-3, PE Morris 26-7-58-2, Saint 15-1-62-1, Lapham 7-0-25-2, HM Morris 2-0-7-0, Douglas 0.5-0-0-2.

ESSEX

FH Gillingham	c Morton b Bestwick	13
NH Saint	b Bestwick	5
JR Freeman	c Elliott b Morton	0
GG Farnfield	c Elliott b Bestwick	0
*JWHT Douglas	not out	210
HM Morris	c Storer b Bestwick	4
AWE Lapham	b Bestwick	15
JG Dixon	b Hill-Wood	23
†CD McIver	b Bestwick	15
SN Hare	c Cadman b Morton	98
PE Morris	did not bat	
Extras	(4 b, 8 lb, 1 nb)	13
Total	**(9 wickets, declared, 135.5 overs)**	**396**

Fall: 1st inns: 1-17, 2-18, 3-18, 4-19, 5-37, 6-61, 7-116, 8-145, 9-396.
Bowling: 1st inns: Bestwick 54-16-132-6, Morton 45.5-14-100-2, Hill-Wood 12-0-90-1, Hutchinson 4-1-25-0, Cadman 16-6-32-0, Storer 4-2-4-0.

double-century of his career before Hare was caught at mid-on when just two runs short of a hundred whereupon Douglas declared. The Essex pair had put on 251 for the ninth wicket which remains a county record to this day. With such a sensational start to his career, it was unfortunate that work commitments in South America restricted Hare to only two further appearances for the side.

With Douglas enjoying a well-earned rest from bowling duties, the Derbyshire openers posted a half-century stand but the loss of three quick wickets saw them recoil to 67-3 and then 149-6 before Gilbert Curgenven, attempting to force the pace, was brilliantly caught by McIver in front of the pavilion. Samuel Cadman bravely attempted to halt the decline as the total moved past 200 before a successful appeal for bad light delayed the Essex victory quest for 40 minutes with the hosts 208-8. When play resumed, the refreshed Douglas introduced himself into the attack for the first time in the innings. Taking the new ball, he struck twice in his first over removing the obdurate Cadman with his third delivery and two balls later he accounted for Billy Bestwick to conclude the match and seal victory by an innings and 74 runs.

County Championship
Essex v Somerset

3-day match　**Venue:** County Ground, Chelmsford **Result:** Match tied

The first County Championship match to be staged at Chelmsford was also the first tied match in the Club's history. On a wicket always offering assistance to the bowlers, only Jack MacBryan managed to display the appropriate and effective application and technique. He scored 80 and was the only batsman to record a half-century in the match. Then, apart from John Freeman, the home side also struggled, trailing by 30 runs on first innings after extras had contributed 35 welcome runs, the second highest score of the innings!

John Freeman: made the highest contribution in both Essex innings

Whilst spin had proved the trick for Somerset, their opponents preferred to rely on pace as Stan Nichols and Laurie Eastman stepped forward to boost Essex hopes. Bowling unchanged, they combined to rout Somerset for just 107 to leave the hosts requiring 138 runs for victory on a wicket that was offering increasing assistance to the bowlers. However, rain and the wet state of the wicket delayed the start of play on the final day until shortly before 3.00 p.m. leaving Essex approximately two and three-quarter hours batting time.

Openers Frederick Nicholas and Jim Cutmore gave the innings a solid start posting 27 runs before being parted but warm sunshine began to significantly affect the wicket and the introduction of medium-paced Jimmy Bridges started a decline. Using his off-cutter to good effect, he claimed four wickets to reduce the home side to 60-5 and apart from his continued threat, keen fielding plus a slow outfield and the passing of time began to threaten Essex victory hopes. Nichols and Freeman, who went in at the fall of the fifth wicket, restored belief with a 54 runs stand in 45 minutes and when Nichols departed, only 24 further runs were needed with three wickets standing. With less than a minute remaining, Essex levelled the scores with

This was how *The Times* reported the closing moments of the game. "At Chelmsford yesterday, there was an intensely exciting finish to the match. The home side with a full innings to play had been set 138 runs to win. They had scored 137 of these when Eastman, attempting to run a single was caught. Half a minute then remained for play but as Ridley, the last man, ran to the crease, the bails were removed by the umpires and Mr.Perrin, the Essex captain walked in. Thus the match was drawn with Somerset securing points for a lead on first innings. Before the players left the field, John Daniell, the Somerset captain was apparently calling Mr.Perrin back but the game was not continued. Instructions issued by the MCC state: 'If a wicket falls within two minutes of "time", the umpires should call "time" unless the incoming batsman claims his right to bat for the time remaining.'

Toss: Somerset won the toss and decided to bat.
Umpires: F Chester, J Stone).

SOMERSET

*J Daniell	b Nichols	21	b Nichols		2
A Young	c and b Russell	12	b Nichols		15
MD Lyon	lbw b Russell	15	b Eastman		11
JCW MacBryan	c Perrin b Russell	80	b Eastman		12
JC White	c Ridley b O'Connor	18	c and b Eastman		0
PR Johnson	c O'Connor b Morris	24	b Nichols		0
CCC Case	run out	4	not out		23
GF Earle	c Morris b Nichols	4	b Nichols		15
GE Hunt	run out	0	b Eastman		9
†ML Hill	b Nichols	9	b Eastman		0
JJ Bridges	not out	1	c Nicholas b Eastman		17
Extras	(12 b, 4 lb, 3 nb, 1 w)	20	(1 b, 1 lb, 1 nb)		3
Total	**(all out, 96.5 overs)**	**208**	**(all out, 30 overs)**		**107**

Fall: 1st inns: 1-27, 2-48, 3-57, 4-108, 5-161, 6-190, 7-197, 8-197, 9-197, 10-208. **2nd inns:** 1-3, 2-28, 3-29, 4-29, 5-30, 6-56, 7-56, 8-69, 9-69, 10-107.
Bowling: 1st inns: Nichols 21.5-3-48-3, Eastman 26-9-50-0, Rowley 8-0-26-0, Russell 30-13-39-3, O'Connor 8-1-19-1, Morris 3-1-6-1. **2nd inns:** Nichols 15-2-45-4, Eastman 15-4-59-6.

ESSEX

†JR Freeman	b Earle	43	(7) c Hunt b Bridges	37
JA Cutmore	c Hill b White	13	lbw b White	26
J O'Connor	c White b Hunt	10	c and b White	13
CAG Russell	c Lyon b White	10	b Hunt	4
MS Nichols	c Johnson b Earle	0	(6) b Bridges	23
FWH Nicholas	c Daniell b White	9	(1) b Bridges	13
*PA Perrin	not out	19	(9) not out	15
HM Morris	b Hunt	12	(5) b Hunt	0
GVN Ridley	c White b Hunt	4	did not bat	
LC Eastman	st Hill b White	0	(10) c Earle b Bridges	0
GW Rowley	c Johnson b White	23	(8) b Bridges	0
Extras	(30 b, 5 lb)	35	(1 b, 5 lb)	6
Total	**(all out, 102 overs)**	**178**	**(9 wickets, 58 overs)**	**137**

Fall: 1st inns: 1-55, 2-93, 3-99, 4-99, 5-106, 6-115, 7-137, 8-143, 9-150, 10-178. **2nd inns:** 1-27, 2-55, 3-60, 4-60, 5-60, 6-114, 7-114, 8-133, 9-137.
Bowling: 1st inns: Bridges 15-6-24-0, Earle 7-2-10-2, White 44-21-57-5, Hunt 30-15-42-3, Young 6-2-10-0. **2nd inns:** Bridges 16-4-33-5, Earle 3-1-13-0, White 22-5-49-2, Hunt 17-6-36-2.

eight wickets down and Percy Perrin and Eastman at the crease. Bridges bowled to Eastman who struck out in an attempt to score the winning run but the ball flew into the hands of Guy Earle. Last man Gerald Ridley ran out to the middle but before he could arrive, umpire Frank Chester looked at the clock and promptly removed the bails leaving the scores level.

The ruling of the umpires (Jack Stone was Chester's colleague for this match), was that Somerset should be deemed to have won on first innings.
Essex captain Perrin, at the age of 50 years and leading the side in the absence of Johnny Douglas, had raised no objections when the bails were removed but now challenged the officials interpretation of the points allocation. A request was sent to the MCC for a ruling and the response, after much deliberation, was that the points should be shared. The incident did make the authorities consider the regulations relating to the last over of the match and in due course, it was altered so that the last over must be completed provided it is begun before time, no matter how long it may take.

Tour Match
Essex v New Zealanders

3-day match **Venue:** County Ground, Leyton **Result:** Essex won by 5 wickets

Not only did Essex beat the New Zealand tourists but they also entered broadcasting history when match commentary was relayed on radio for the first time. The transmission was carried out as an exploratory venture and one of the County's players, Reverend Canon Frank Hay Gillingham, was the voice behind the microphone contributing four five-minute spells of commentary. Renowned as a fine preacher and a witty after-dinner speaker, he was also a much-respected member of the Essex team whom he represented for 25 years until retiring in 1928 at the age of 53.

Rev. Frank Gillingham: broadcast match commentary to the nation

The tourists batted sedately on a pitch made for quick scoring and it was only the last two wickets that raised the scoring rate. A stiff breeze enabled Stan Nichols to bowl with more speed and swing than usual and with Jack O'Connor, varying his pace, batting was never straightforward. By tea, the tourists had reached 210-8 but the last two wickets blazed away effectively. Ernest Bernau and Bill Merritt added 54 for the ninth wicket before a highly entertaining 15 minutes produced 41 runs for the last pair as the visitors reached 289 before claiming two Essex wickets for 57 by the close of the opening day. When play resumed, a high percentage of runs were scored between mid-on and square leg as New Zealand, lacking threat, used eight bowlers on a wicket with pace removed by the rain that had fallen the previous evening. O'Connor completed his fifty in 70 minutes figuring in half-century stands with Jimmy Cutmore and Jack Russell, who scored freely with an array of fine drives and leg-side strokeplay. Essex lost three wickets to Herb McGirr with the score on 262 but a last wicket stand between Nichols and George Eastman worth 54 runs gave the County an 84 runs lead.

New Zealand were still 12 runs behind and three wickets down when play ended for the day but heavy overnight rain ensured that proceedings would

The Reverend Canon Frank Hay Gillingham was educated at Durham University and was appointed curate at Leyton which enabled him to qualify for Essex by residence. But for the dual roles of ecclesiastical duties and cricketer, he would have undoubtedly been a prolific batting force in the first-class game but by the time of this match, his cricketing career was drawing to a close. However the task of spreading the gospel of the game to a wider audience from behind the microphone for this fixture was not greatly received. The *Western Daily Press* called it "deadly dull" whilst the *Daily Herald* wondered if "brighter possibilities might be afforded by broadcasts of chess or billiards."

G.D.Martineau in his book *They Made Cricket* described how the wife of a well-known cricketer was led by her enthusiasm into a lapse of curious aptness at Gillingham's memorial service. "It was a wonderful service and we had that lovely chapter out of the Book of Wisden!"

Toss: New Zealanders won the toss and decided to bat.
Umpires: WA Buswell, FH Sugg.

NEW ZEALANDERS

RC Blunt	c GF Eastman b Nichols	1		b O'Connor	21
JE Mills	c Nichols b O'Connor	64		c Douglas b LC Eastman	0
†KC James	b Nichols	4		c Hipkin b O'Connor	26
*TC Lowry	c and b O'Connor	61		st GF Eastman b O'Connor	30
CCR Dacre	c Ashton b LC Eastman	9	(6)	lbw b O'Connor	5
CS Dempster	c GF Eastman b O'Connor	13	(5)	c and b LC Eastman	79
CJ Oliver	lbw b O'Connor	28		c and b LC Eastman	13
HM McGirr	c Ashton b O'Connor	11		lbw b LC Eastman	7
EHL Bernau	lbw b Russell	22		lbw b LC Eastman	0
WE Merritt	not out	49		not out	7
WHR Cunningham	b Meston	23		c Nichols b O'Connor	2
Extras	(2 lb, 1 nb, 1 w)	4		(11 b, 2 lb, 4 nb, 1 w)	18
Total	**(all out, 95 overs)**	**289**		**(all out, 86.4 overs)**	**208**

Fall: 1st inns: 1-2, 2-20, 3-132, 4-133, 5-143, 6-177, 7-194, 8-194, 9-248, 10-289. **2nd inns:** 1-2, 2-46, 3-59, 4-118, 5-126, 6-164, 7-185, 8-189, 9-206, 10-208.
Bowling: 1st inns: Nichols 29-4-111-2, LC Eastman 21-6-34-1, Russell 10-1-37-1, Meston 7-1-13-1, O'Connor 22-2-68-5, Hipkin 6-0-22-0. **2nd inns:** Nichols 12-2-25-0, LC Eastman 20-6-31-5, Russell 4-3-1-0, O'Connor 32.4-7-92-5, Hipkin 14-4-35-0, Douglas 4-2-6-0.

ESSEX

JA Cutmore	c Dacre b Merritt	47		c James b Blunt	18
LC Eastman	lbw b McGirr	30		lbw b Blunt	41
AB Hipkin	run out	0		did not bat	
J O'Connor	lbw b Lowry	65	(3)	st James b Blunt	12
CAG Russell	b McGirr	76	(4)	b Blunt	0
H Ashton	b McGirr	52	(5)	b Merritt	13
*JWHT Douglas	c Dempster b McGirr	0	(6)	not out	19
HM Morris	c Dempster b McGirr	0	(7)	not out	11
MS Nichols	c Lowry b Cunningham	61		did not bat	
AH Meston	b McGirr	0		did not bat	
†GF Eastman	not out	15		did not bat	
Extras	(19 b, 4 lb, 4 w)	27		(1 b, 9 lb, 1 w)	11
Total	**(all out, 107 overs)**	**373**		**(5 wickets, 35.5 overs)**	**125**

Fall: 1st inns: 1-56, 2-56, 3-127, 4-188, 5-262, 6-262, 7-262, 8-319, 9-319, 10-373. **2nd inns:** 1-44, 2-76, 3-76, 4-77, 5-?.
Bowling: 1st inns: Bernau 13-3-47-0, Cunningham 11-0-50-1, McGirr 29-8-77-6, Merritt 21-3-68-1, Blunt 17-2-50-0, Dacre 2-1-8-0, Lowry 12-1-42-1, Oliver 2-0-4-0. **2nd inns:** Cunningham 2-1-1-0, McGirr 7-3-19-0, Merritt 6.5-0-35-1, Blunt 13-4-29-4, Dacre 2-0-10-0, Lowry 3-0-10-0, Oliver 2-0-10-0.

not resume before lunch on day three. Captain Tom Lowry and Stewie Dempster played defensively seeing their side into credit but with the score on 118, Lowry was stumped attempting to drive O'Connor. Ces Dacre was leg before wicket to a full-pitched delivery that he attempted to cut and with half the side dismissed, the lead was just 42 runs. Dempster's superb timing took him to 50 in 100 minutes but his application was not reflected elsewhere in the order and after batting for two and a half hours and striking nine boundaries, he skied a catch and shortly afterwards, the innings ended.

With ample time to score 125 for victory, Cutmore and Laurie Eastman picked off 44 runs before being parted but then O'Connor and Russell both perished in one over to the leg-breaks of Roger Blunt before the same bowler captured Eastman's wicket in his next over as the hosts started to wobble. Claude Ashton offered a difficult chance to Merritt that was spurned but he was out soon after. From thereon Douglas, playing solidly, and 'Whiz' Morris, who quickly settled, took charge with Morris clubbing a six over square leg to hasten a five-wickets victory.

County Championship

Essex v Kent

3-day match   **Venue:** Southchurch Park, Southend-on-Sea **Result:** Kent won by 277 runs

Three individual performances mark this down as one of the 'Classic Matches' in the Club's history. Kent players 'Tich' Freeman and Aidan Crawley made two of the outstanding contributions to the match whilst Ken Farnes gave notice of his prowess as a cricketer of the future. He had been playing for Gidea Park Cricket Club against an Essex Club and Ground XI, captained by Percy Perrin who immediately took note of the tall young fast bowler's potential and invited

him to the County. Standing over 6 feet 5 inches and weighing over fifteen and a half stone, he had a beautiful action and could move the ball both ways off a comparatively short run. This was only the second match that Farnes had played for Essex and he was selected merely because of the unavailability of Arthur Daer but he returned figures of 5-36 in the visitor's first innings including two legendary England batsmen, Frank Woolley and Les Ames, amongst his victims.

Joining the attack as first-change, he had Crawley caught by wicket-keeper Roy Sheffield and soon afterwards added Woolley, who was still to get off the mark. The delighted bowler reflected: "Frank Woolley moved with genteel dignity to the crease and very soon snicked one that left him a bit. Jack Russell (bless him) made a grand catch at second slip, almost brushing aside first slip less he should fumble it in his eagerness to secure the important

Kenneth Farnes: provided an eye-catching demonstration of high-class fast bowling

wicket and I am convinced, to see that I should not be discouraged by a dropped chance off my bowling."

On a green-top, Kent were bowled out for 122 and with the home side moving into the lead with only three wickets down, hopes were high that the County might achieve only their second victory against their old foes since the

---

In the book *Ken Farnes, Diary of an Essex Master* written by David Thurlow, the subject recalled his maiden first-class wicket.

"I bowled calmly with an aim for length which I was allowed to achieve. The Southend air and probably some green in the wicket did the rest. Crawley edged one to Sheffield at the wicket and I had taken my first wicket in first-class cricket – a rather difficult feat to believe at the time. It never occurred to me that there were other things I might do; to play as much as possible seemed the natural and unquestionable thing. Why I had this ardent desire to play could be answered easily, I suppose, by the psychologists but the real significance is that I had a passion – or even a mania – for cricket and first-class cricket was the abstract chief deity. This complete faith in the rightness of my ambition was undoubtedly the driving force that kept me endeavouring to improve."

Toss: Kent won the toss and decided to bat.
Umpires: W Bestwick, WR Parry.

KENT

AM Crawley	c Sheffield b Farnes	25	b O'Connor		175
HTW Hardinge	not out	49	st Sheffield b Palmer		51
FE Woolley	c Russell b Farnes	0	c Franklin b Nichols		16
†LEG Ames	b Farnes	1	b Farnes		35
WH Ashdown	b Palmer	18	c and b Nichols		12
*JL Bryan	b Nichols	6	c Cutmore b Palmer		37
CH Knott	c Nichols b Farnes	2	b O'Connor		28
LJ Todd	lbw b Nichols	10	not out		43
AC Wright	b Nichols	0	st Sheffield b O'Connor		3
AP Freeman	b Farnes	2	run out		4
CW Peach	b Nichols	1	not out		4
Extras	(5 b, 3 nb)	8	(8 b, 4 lb, 1 nb, 1 w)		14
Total	**(all out, 52.4 overs)**	**122**	**(9 wickets, declared, 112 overs)**		**422**

Fall: 1st inns: 1-45, 2-45, 3-49, 4-82, 5-92, 6-95, 7-112, 8-116, 9-119, 10-122. **2nd inns:** 1-186, 2-237, 3-259, 4-294, 5-300, 6-345, 7-386, 8-395, 9-401.
Bowling: 1st inns: Nichols 15.4-5-34-4, Smith 7-1-19-0, Farnes 17-4-36-5, Palmer 11-4-14-1, O'Connor 2-0-11-0. **2nd inns:** Nichols 18-2-65-2, Smith 13-0-76-0, Farnes 29-4-82-1, Palmer 22-0-89-2, O'Connor 29-6-89-3, Franklin 1-0-7-0.

ESSEX

LG Crawley	lbw b Freeman	22	b Wright		8
DF Pope	c Bryan b Freeman	38	lbw b Freeman		3
J O'Connor	lbw b Freeman	19	c Woolley b Freeman		32
CAG Russell	not out	47	c Peach b Freeman		7
JA Cutmore	c Knott b Freeman	6	c Knott b Freeman		9
MS Nichols	st Ames b Freeman	0	lbw b Peach		3
*HWF Franklin	c Bryan b Freeman	1	c and b Freeman		38
†JR Sheffield	st Ames b Freeman	0	c Knott b Freeman		6
K Farnes	b Freeman	1	b Wright		0
TPB Smith	c Woolley b Freeman	1	not out		8
HJ Palmer	b Freeman	0	b Wright		2
Extras	(5 b, 5 lb)	10	(5 b, 1 lb)		6
Total	**(all out, 72.4 overs)**	**145**	**(all out, 59.3 overs)**		**122**

Fall: 1st inns: 1-39, 2-68, 3-113, 4-127, 5-129, 6-137, 7-137, 8-139, 9-145, 10-145. **2nd inns:** 1-8, 2-24, 3-47, 4-56, 5-59, 6-65, 7-93, 8-100, 9-120, 10-122.
Bowling: 1st inns: Wright 13-2-25-0, Ashdown 9-2-23-0, Freeman 30.4-8-53-10, Peach 6-1-14-0, Hardinge 14-6-20-0. **2nd inns:** Wright 15.3-2-49-3, Ashdown 7-2-18-0, Freeman 27-11-41-6, Peach 10-8-8-1.

resumption of the first-class game in 1919 following the end of the First World War. By the end of the first day's exchanges though, Kent had fought back reducing their opponents to 137-7 with prolific spinner Freeman claiming all the wickets. His one-man show with the ball continued the following morning when he added the three further victims to finish with all ten wickets for the second time in his career as the batsmen failed to contend with his wily and clever bowling. His figures of 10-53 beat his previous best of 10-131 and remained a ground record when Essex decided to vacate Southchurch Park after the 2004 season.

Despite having trailed by 23 runs on first innings, Kent dominated the remainder of the match thanks to Crawley, whose cousin Leonard, was playing on the opposite side. The Kent opener made 175 out of 259 in little under three hours with an array of superbly-timed powerful and elegant drives and when his side eventually declared the hosts had been set 400 to win. Perhaps still reeling from Crawley's onslaught, Essex succumbed tamely as Freeman again posed too many questions adding another six victims to his earlier collection allowing his side to achieve a 277 runs success.

County Championship

Essex v Yorkshire

3-day match   **Venue:** County Ground, Leyton **Result:** Yorkshire won by an innings and 313 runs

One of the attractions of the game of cricket is its ability to throw up incongruous situations time after time. This match with the White Rose county was just such an illustration and ended in the most humiliating defeat ever for Essex in the County Championship – a record that still stands although the Australians did invoke a heavier defeat in the tourist match of 1948.

From the moment that Essex stand-in captain Charles Bray lost the toss, a Yorkshire side packed with talented players totally dominated the match. Play

had been in progress for seven hours and 25 minutes before Percy Holmes and Herbert Sutcliffe were parted having posted a world record score for the first wicket. It beat the previous figure of 554 set by another Yorkshire pair, Jack Brown and John Tunnicliffe 34 years earlier. The 45 year-old Holmes had been dropped by wicket-keeper Roy Sheffield off the bowling of Stan Nichols, on three, before runs began to flow with ease. How crucial that error was to prove. The Essex attack were given no further encouragement as the batsmen dictated proceedings so effectively that Bray used eight bowlers in the final session of the day in an unsuccessful bid to unship the openers.

By the close, the total was 423 with plenty more runs to follow. Sutcliffe completed his 1,000 runs for the summer whilst Holmes – for the twelfth time – reached 200. Sutcliffe, had scored 305 of the 547 runs on the scoreboard when he faced the gentle medium-pace

Percy Holmes and Herbert Sutcliffe pictured in front of the scoreboard showing their record-breaking partnership

of Laurie Eastman. The first ball of the over was short-pitched which the batsman swiped to the square leg boundary and two deliveries later, he reached the boundary again with a leg-side blow to set the new record. Facing the very next delivery, he was bowled when he played the ball onto his foot and it went from there onto his wicket at which, Yorkshire captain Brian Sellers immediately declared. The 555 score soon became the subject of much discussion when the two scorers agreed that the total was in fact 554 and the scoreboard reverted to that figure. A lengthy delay followed whilst intense discussions and re-

In an article in *The Cricketer*, Essex captain Charles Bray recounted his version of the instances surrounding the infamous no-ball. "When the board read 555, we all thought the record had been broken, Sutcliffe and Holmes had their photographs taken underneath the score board in traditional fashion. Consternation followed when the scorers maintained the total was 554. I knew little about this until McGahey came bustling into the dressing room where I was trying to get a little rest. 'Sorry to disturb you skip,' said Charles, 'but all hell is going on there, [pointing to the scoreboard]. Bill [Ringrose] and I agree the correct total is 554 not 555 and now they want us to find an extra run to beat the old record. I certainly won't do so without your permission.' "I was tired and depressed and I didn't realise at the time the importance of what was being suggested. 'Find a run for them Charles. They've batted magnificently and more than deserve the record."

Toss: Yorkshire won the toss and decided to bat.
Umpires: EF Field, EJ Smith.

YORKSHIRE

P Holmes	not out	224
H Sutcliffe	b Eastman	313
A Mitchell	did not bat	
M Leyland	did not bat	
W Barber	did not bat	
*AB Sellers	did not bat	
†A Wood	did not bat	
AC Rhodes	did not bat	
GG Macaulay	did not bat	
H Verity	did not bat	
WE Bowes	did not bat	
Extras	(13 b, 3 lb, 2 nb)	18
Total	**(1 wicket, declared, 170.4 overs)**	**555**

Fall: 1st inns: 1-555.
Bowling: 1st inns: Nichols 31-4-105-0, Daer 40-8-106-0, Smith 46-10-128-0, O'Connor 23-5-73-0, Eastman 22.4-2-97-1, Crawley 3-0-7-0, Taylor-4-0-14-0, Bray 1-0-7-0.

ESSEX

			(FOLLOWING ON)	
LG Crawley	b Bowes	0	c Sutcliffe b Bowes	27
DF Pope	c Rhodes b Bowes	6	c Mitchell b Bowes	9
J O'Connor	b Bowes	20	c Rhodes b Bowes	7
JA Cutmore	lbw b Bowes	0	b Verity	1
MS Nichols	b Verity	25	not out	59
LC Eastman	c Sutcliffe b Macaulay	16	c Barber b Verity	19
*C Bray	c and b Verity	1	st Wood b Verity	6
RM Taylor	c Macaulay b Verity	5	c Macaulay b Verity	13
†JR Sheffield	c and b Verity	0	c Sutcliffe b Verity	5
AG Daer	c and b Verity	0	c Verity b Bowes	0
TPB Smith	not out	2	c Rhodes b Bowes	0
Extras	(3 b)	3	(15 b, 1 lb, 2 nb)	18
Total	**(all out, 36.1 overs)**	**78**	**(all out, 78.4 overs)**	**164**

Fall: 1st inns: 1-0, 2-19, 3-19, 4-48, 5-59, 6-60, 7-66, 8-72, 9-74, 10-78. **2nd inns:** 1-38, 2-47, 3-50, 4-50, 5-92, 6-128, 7-148, 8-162, 9-164, 10-164.
Bowling: 1st inns: Bowes 12-1-38-4, Rhodes 10-5-15-0, Macaulay 7.1-2-14-1, Verity 7-3-8-5.
2nd inns: Bowes 23.4-5-47-5, Rhodes 9-5-23-0, Macaulay 16-5-31-0, Verity 30-12- 45-5.

examination of the scorebooks took place before the two scorers, Charlie McGahey and Billy Ringrose, mutually discovered an unaccounted no-ball and the one run was added to the total restoring the new record to the Yorkshire openers.

Against the backcloth of mystery and intrigue, Essex were bowled out within two hours for a miserable 78 having no answer to the pace of Bill Bowes nor Hedley Verity's superbly-flighted bowling. By the close of the second day, the home side were facing certain defeat having slumped to 92-5 and although Stan Nichols battled stoically, Bowes and Verity continued to humble their opponents completing a stunning victory with two sessions of the match remaining. On the day preceding the Yorkshire innings, Surrey had beaten Essex by nine wickets at The Oval where Jack Hobbs and Robert Gregory scored 232 in an unbroken second-wicket stand. The duration of that partnership followed by the Yorkshire first wicket run-fest meant that Essex had fielded for a total of nine hours fifty minutes during which time they conceded 787 runs before taking a wicket.

County Championship
Essex v Kent

3-day match   **Venue:** Old County Ground, Brentwood **Result:** Kent won by an innings and 192 runs

Brentwood had been the County's original home and the return there for the first time since 1922 saw some remarkable cricket and phenomenal scoring. Kent were the first opponents of the new era at the Old County Ground and marked the occasion with a comprehensive innings victory. They won the toss and after Bill Ashdown and Frank Woolley had added 352 for the second wicket with Woolley completing an imperious hundred, they closed the opening day on a phenomenal 623-2 with Ashdown unbeaten on a chanceless 307 and Les Ames 106 not out.

The torrent of runs continued the next day when another 180 were added in an hour and five minutes. Ashdown and Ames extended their third wicket stand to 245 before Ashdown was well caught in the gully and his triple century included one six – an overthrow – and 45 fours. Ian Fleming joined Ames and the pair declined to take any pity on the hapless Essex attack putting on a brisk 96 before the declaration came with Kent 803-4, the third highest total ever recorded in England at that time. Ames was 202 not out having scored an all-run five and 29 boundaries. How Essex must have regretted two particularly costly misses. Woolley was dropped on 2 and Ames on 30 allowing their opponents to record their highest score for 35 years.

By tea, Essex were 201-1 with little sign of the problems that lay ahead. Dudley Pope arrived at his century with a beautiful cover drive to the boundary but immediately afterwards, he was caught at first slip and 11 runs later, Tom Pearce was caught at the wicket. Stan Nichols became the first batsmen in the match to fail to reach double figures and by the end of the day, Essex were 366-7 still needing 287 to avoid the follow-on. At this stage of the match, 1169 runs had been scored for the loss of just 11 wickets. When play resumed the next morning, Jack O'Connor became the fifth

Jack O'Connor: an unbeaten century failed to prevent his side averting the follow-on

Some years later, Kent spinner Doug Wright recalled the game saying, "The pitch was in first-class condition and I remember saying to Arthur Fagg that someone was going to get some "stick" on this wicket. Luckily we batted first and my main interest was the bowling of Peter Smith, the Essex leg-spinner, whom I met at the Faulkner Cricket School. At first, I must admit that I was amused at the treatment Peter received from Ashdown, Frank Woolley and Leslie Ames, but when I heard his analysis, 0-208, I almost felt sorry for him. After 1,200 runs had been scored it is not surprising that the pitch showed some signs of wear although I must say that it did not break up and was a credit to the groundsman. But the ball turned just that little bit more for 'Tich' Freeman who bowled superbly. It was a great game of cricket which I'm sure was appreciated by players and spectators."

Toss: Kent won the toss and decided to bat.
Umpires: W Bestwick, AE Dipper.

KENT

WH Ashdown	c Ashton b Nichols	332
AE Fagg	lbw b R Smith	31
FE Woolley	b Ashton	172
†LEG Ames	not out	202
AE Watt	c R Smith b Ashton	11
IDK Fleming	not out	42
LJ Todd	did not bat	
BH Valentine	did not bat	
*APF Chapman	did not bat	
DVP Wright	did not bat	
AP Freeman	did not bat	
Extras	(8 b, 1 nb, 4 w)	13
Total	**(4 wickets, declared, 146.2 overs)**	**803**

Fall: 1st inns: 1-70, 2-422, 3-667, 4-707.
Bowling: 1st inns: Nichols 20-1-93-1, R Smith 22-1-115-1, Ashton 31-2-185-2, TPB Smith 36-2-208-0, O'Connor 16.2-0-83-0, Cutmore 12-0-63-0, Taylor 7-0-36-0, Pope 2-0-7-0.

ESSEX

				(FOLLOWING ON)	
LC Eastman	c Chapman b Wright	52	(8)	c Woolley b Freeman	4
DF Pope	c Woolley b Valentine	100	(1)	c Ames b Wright	11
*TN Pearce	c Ames b Valentine	79	(4)	c Woolley b Freeman	17
J O'Connor	not out	105	(3)	lbw b Freeman	25
MS Nichols	c Valentine b Wright	3		lbw b Wright	20
JA Cutmore	c Ames b Watt	30	(2)	c Fleming b Wright	0
CT Ashton	st Ames b Freeman	11	(6)	not out	71
RM Taylor	st Ames b Freeman	1		st Ames b Freeman	1
TPB Smith	c Woolley b Freeman	11		c Ashdown b Freeman	0
†JR Sheffield	c Woolley b Freeman	0		c Watt b Ashdown	31
R Smith	b Freeman	0		st Ames b Freeman	1
Extras	(7 b, 8 lb, 1 nb)	16		(14 b, 8 lb)	22
Total	**(all out, 139.5 overs)**	**408**		**(all out, 81.2 overs)**	**203**

Fall: 1st inns: 1-75, 2-231, 3-242, 4-259, 5-333, 6-358, 7-360, 8-394, 9-408, 10-408. **2nd inns:** 1-35, 2-36, 3-42, 4-86, 5-92, 6-97, 7-105, 8-115, 9-201, 10-203.
Bowling: 1st inns: Watt 23-4-85-1, Ashdown 6-2-22-0, Freeman 50.5-15-116-5, Wright 38-9-117-2, Todd 6-0-11-0, Woolley 7-2-10-0, Valentine 9-2-31-2. **2nd inns:** Watt 9-0-20-0, Ashdown 1-1-0-1, Freeman 34.2-13-60-6, Wright 27-12-59-3, Woolley 5-0-26-0, Valentine 5-2-16-0.

batsman to reach three figures but he was unable to find tail-end support having scored an unbeaten 105 out of 408 all out that left the home side trailing by 395 runs.

On a wearing pitch, they followed-on and capitulated to the leg-spin twins of 'Tich' Freeman and Doug Wright. O'Connor was promoted up the order but although he scored 25, he was to become an early wicket for Freeman falling to the bowler's top-spinner. Jimmy Cutmore was caught at mid-wicket off a long-hop and Pope was caught at the wicket to leave Essex in deep trouble at 42-3. Pearce and Nichols doubled the score but then five wickets fell for 29 runs with Freeman exploiting a "spot" on the wicket at one end. Roy Sheffield joined Claude Ashton in an entertaining stand for the ninth wicket with the latter driving superbly to reach a half-century, sweeping Woolley to the square leg boundary and then driving him to the long-on boundary in the same over. Kent though found the breakthrough with the new ball, when Ashdown had Sheffield caught at short leg whilst Ray Smith was stumped shortly afterwards to conclude the match with more than a session to spare.

County Championship
Essex v Surrey

3-day match   **Venue:** Old County Ground, Brentwood **Result:** Essex won by an innings and 192 runs

Comprehensively beaten by Kent in the opening match of the Brentwood Festival, Essex responded in the best possible fashion overcoming Surrey inside two days. Fast bowler, Holcombe Douglas 'Hopper' Read, having only played one match for Essex the previous season without taking a wicket, burst on the scene to claim 7-35 on a good pitch to completely undermine the visitors who were dismissed in 90 minutes. Read was regarded as the fastest bowler in the

world for the brief period he played the first-class game. Tall, well-built, ungainly and erratic in length, he could be devastating on a lively pitch utilising a long run up to generate his explosive pace.

The measure of his speed can be illustrated by the fact that his first ball removed the cap of England and Surrey opening batsman Jack Hobbs whilst the last ball of the over beat the great batsman for pace and bowled him as the visitors were hustled out for 115. Essex soon showed the true quality of the wicket with Jack O'Connor and Claude Ashton combining for a record-breaking fifth wicket stand of 287 runs and when Ashton was dismissed – having scored more than the entire Surrey line-up had managed – Laurie Eastman joined O'Connor in a 142-run alliance. When the declaration came O'Connor, who had batted delightfully for four hours and 25 minutes, had recorded his highest first-class score of 248 before being caught at the wicket.

H.D.'Hopper' Read: startled legendary Jack Hobbs with a delivery that removed the opening batsman's cap

On a bitterly cold second day, Surrey began their second innings again facing Read who, with the score on 9, struck Andy Sandham above the elbow. Upon recovery, the batsman lashed out at a delivery from the ultra-fast bowler and was caught at cover-point. Hobbs perished for 28, Stan Squires went without scoring, Tom Barling was caught at deep square leg off a long hop but Errol Holmes showed a welcome determination for the cause. He hit Read for four

Fifty-three years on when contributing to the *1987 Essex CCC Handbook*, 'Hopper' Read recalled how he came to be selected for the game and his memories of the ground. "I was asked to play for Essex since Nichols and Farnes, their fast bowlers, were on Test Trial duty at Lord's. The previous five days I had been sitting in a hot and stuffy examination room in London, trying to cope with the Final Chartered Accountants examination. And the previous three months, I had been studying hard so I arrived at Brentwood no doubt pent up with energy. I remember finding a lovely hot summer day and a very good and fast wicket on a slight downhill slope. The atmosphere seemed to me more like a Club match [to which I was more accustomed] – a lovely country ground in festive mood with what to me was a big crowd and a mass of school children, and Essex , a most friendly and welcoming side."

Toss: Essex won the toss and decided to field.
Umpires: W Bestwick, AE Dipper.

SURREY

JB Hobbs	b Read	5		c O'Connor b CT Ashton	28
A Sandham	c TPB Smith b Read	10		c O'Connor b Read	3
RJ Gregory	b R Smith	16		run out	67
HS Squires	c and b CT Ashton	24		c H Ashton b CT Ashton	0
HT Barling	c H Ashton b Read	13		c R Smith b Read	1
HM Garland-Wells	b Read	0		c sub b TPB Smith	28
PGH Fender	b Read	9		absent hurt	
*ERT Holmes	b Read	5	(7)	c Eastman b TPB Smith	112
EA Watts	b R Smith	16	(8)	c Pope b CT Ashton	0
†EWJ Brooks	b Read	10	(9)	run out	8
AR Gover	not out	0	(10)	not out	6
Extras	(4 b, 3 lb)	7		(8 b, 2 lb)	10
Total	**(all out, 28.1 overs)**	**115**		**(all out, 71.5 overs)**	**263**

Fall: 1st inns: 1-6, 2-31, 3-33, 4-47, 5-47, 6-59, 7-75, 8-96, 9-110, 10-115. **2nd inns:** 1-9, 2-63, 3-76, 4-77, 5-139, 6-191, 7-199, 8-233, 9-263.
Bowling: 1st inns: Read 9.1-0-35-7, R Smith 11-0-60-2, CT Ashton 4-0-8-1, TPB Smith 4-0-5-0.
2nd inns: Read 18-3-68-2, R Smith 17-2-75-0, CT Ashton 19-3-39-3, TPB Smith 17.5-1-71-2.

ESSEX

JA Cutmore	c Garland-Wells b Gover	50
DF Pope	b Watts	2
*TN Pearce	b Gover	20
J O'Connor	c Brooks b Gover	248
H Ashton	c Brooks b Garland-Wells	22
CT Ashton	c Brooks b Gover	118
LC Eastman	c Garland-Wells b Gregory	85
TPB Smith	not out	9
†TH Wade	b Gregory	4
R Smith	not out	0
HD Read	did not bat	
Extras	(8 lb, 2 nb, 2 w)	12
Total	**(8 wickets, declared, 107 overs)**	**570**

Fall: 1st inns: 1-14, 2-61, 3-82, 4-128, 5-415, 6-557, 7-561, 8-569.
Bowling: 1st inns: Gover 36-5-143-4, Watts 20-2-77-1, Fender 6-1-36-0, Garland-Wells 22-3-135-1, Holmes 15-0-102-0, Gregory 8-1-65-2.

leg-side boundaries and with Robert Gregory took the score to 139 when Holmes called his partner, who was on 67, for a suicidal run to end the resistance. At tea, Surrey were 148-5 but Monty Garland-Wells punished some wayward bowling before holing out to square leg, whilst Eddie Watts was caught off a half-volley and Edward Brooks was run out in a comedy of errors that saw both batsmen standing at the same end. With Percy Fender unable to bat because of a broken hand, last man Alf Gover managed to hang around long enough to allow Holmes to complete a two-hour century, the eighth batsman to reach three-figures in the Brentwood Festival week, before he edged an intended drive to slip.

Essex thus celebrated victory by an innings and 192 runs, just two days after they had been thrashed by Kent by an identical margin! It was suggested that following the Kent match, Frank Woolley had met with Hobbs at Liverpool Street and told the opener, who was seeking the two-hundredth first-class century of his career, to go and help himself to a nice easy ton as the conditions were all in favour of the batsmen.

County Championship
Yorkshire v Essex

Venue: Fartown, Huddersfield **Result:** Essex won by an innings and 204 runs

Star-studded Yorkshire, with eight present or future England players in their side, had not been beaten since August 1934 and lost only one match whilst retaining their title in 1935 winning 19 matches and drawing 10 of their 30 games. Their blemish came at Huddersfield against Essex where play lasted only until 1.00 p.m. on the second day. The hosts were completely undone by the marvellous bowling of Stan Nichols and 'Hopper' Read who ran amok to

dismiss the opposition for 31 runs in an hour with five batsmen failing to score. At one stage, the home side were 9-6 but Arthur Wood scored 13, the only batsman to reach double figures in an innings that spanned just 12 overs and 4 balls to leave Yorkshire reflecting on their lowest total for 26 years.

The initial response by Essex was also beset with problems and half the side were dismissed with just 65 showing on the scoreboard. Frank Rist though proved resolute before Nichols took centre-stage again, this time with the bat. Joined by Oxford Blue and amateur Brian Belle, who played infrequently, 174 runs were added for the sixth wicket that effectively batted Yorkshire out of the game. The brilliant 146 scored by Nichols on a difficult wicket was an extraordinary effort and included two sixes and 16 fours and was to prove more than the two combined totals achieved by the home side.

Nichols then reverted to bowling mode to rip out the home side once again who were unable to cope with the exhilarating pace and accuracy of both he and Read. For the second time in the match, Nichols claimed the wicket of 18 year-old Len Hutton who bagged a "pair" and the bowler, who took his 100th wicket of the season during the game, concluded the match with figures of 11-54 to add to his outstanding batting performance. The visitors left the field to a generous standing ovation from the home crowd and the result allowed Essex to turn the tables on their

Morris Nichols: produced an incredible all-round performance to underpin the comprehensive victory

Wisden described Nichols performance as "the sensation of the season," whilst Charles Bray, who captained the County, offered this praise. "He was a great-hearted player and an indefatigable worker," he stated. "He was a magnificent bowler who had the misfortune to be at his best in an era of fast bowlers in this country. Consequently he did not receive as many representative honours as he would have done had he come to the fore ten years later. With the new ball, he could be deadly. Fast bowlers have bowled faster but few have bowled for such long spells at a time. Often I had to bowl him for well over an hour at a stretch when he looked the only bowler likely to take wickets and he would always continue without complaint. He had many personal triumphs but probably he was most proud of his brilliant hundred against Yorkshire in 1935 at Huddersfield and his 11 wickets for 54 in the same match."

Toss: Yorkshire won the toss and decided to bat.
Umpires: F Chester, FI Walden.

YORKSHIRE

H Sutcliffe	c Sheffield b Nichols	4	c Eastman b Nichols		1
W Barber	c Wilcox b Read	1	b Nichols		18
*AB Sellers	c Wilcox b Read	2	lbw b Nichols		2
M Leyland	b Read	0	b Read		2
PA Gibb	c Rist b Read	0	lbw b Nichols		11
C Turner	c Sheffield b Read	4	b Nichols		13
L Hutton	b Nichols	0	lbw b Nichols		0
†A Wood	c Read b Nichols	13	b Nichols		24
H Fisher	b Read	0	c Rist b Read		2
H Verity	not out	0	c TPB Smith b Read		6
WE Bowes	c Rist b Nichols	4	not out		19
Extras	(1 b, 1 lb, 1 nb)	3	(1 lb)		1
Total	**(all out, 12.4 overs)**	**31**	**(all out, 29.4 overs)**		**99**

Fall: 1st inns: 1-2, 2-6, 3-6, 4-7, 5-9, 6-9, 7-27, 8-27, 9-27, 10-31. **2nd inns:** 1-2, 2-21, 3-22, 4-24, 5-43, 6-48, 7-59, 8-72, 9-78, 10-99.
Bowling: 1st inns: Nichols 6.4-2-17-4, Read 6-1-11-6. **2nd inns:** Nichols 15-3-37-7, Read 11.4-2-51-3, Eastman 3-0-10-0.

ESSEX

†JR Sheffield	b Verity	5
FH Rist	c Gibb b Verity	35
*DR Wilcox	c Wood b Turner	2
JA Cutmore	c Wood b Fisher	2
J O'Connor	b Fisher	0
MS Nichols	c Hutton b Bowes	146
BH Belle	c Verity b Leyland	63
LC Eastman	c Gibb b Bowes	23
TPB Smith	b Bowes	5
R Smith	not out	16
HD Read	st Wood b Verity	0
Extras	(24 b, 13 lb)	37
Total	**(all out, 107.2 overs)**	**334**

Fall: 1st inns: 1-24, 2-30, 3-39, 4-39, 5-65, 6-239, 7-273, 8-287, 9-334, 10-334.
Bowling: 1st inns: Bowes 37-8-77-3, Turner 16-2-41-1, Verity 24.2-4-79-3, Fisher 25-5-62-2, Leyland 5-1-38-1.

opponents following Yorkshire's record breaking first innings partnership three seasons earlier.

Herbert Sutcliffe, having been caught by wicket-keeper Roy Sheffield off the bowling of Nichols is reported to have said, "At least I was good enough to touch it." The tale is also told of a Yorkshire committee member who arrived a little after start of play on the opening day and made enquiries as to the progress of the game. "Thirty for nine," replied the gateman unemotionally. 'Excellent,' responded the committee man, 'and how many wickets has Bowes got?' The gateman replied, "Bowes, he's only just gone in."
Peter Smith also recounted that he fielded the ball just once in the match and that was when he caught Hedley Verity to end the game. In recognition of his outstanding match contribution, the Essex Committee voted to give Nichols an ex-gratia payment of £10. By the end of the season, the prolific all-rounder now 35 years of age, had completed the "double" scoring 1249 runs and claiming 157 wickets in all matches

Essex v South Africans

3-day match **Venue:** Southchurch Park, Southend-on-Sea **Result:** Essex won by 7 wickets

The County rested 'Hopper' Read who had been selected for the forthcoming Fifth Test but the hosts still boasted an effective pace attack. South Africa won the toss and against the fast bowling duo of John Stephenson and Stan Nichols, they were soon in trouble losing their first four wickets for only 23 runs with Stephenson claiming three of the wickets at a personal cost of 11 runs. Jack Siedle and Eric Dalton then revived the innings with a stand of 164 and Dalton went on to complete his first century of the summer before Stephenson returned with the new ball taking the last four wickets to conclude the innings.

The home side then made good progress to reach 139-4 at the close of the opening day and they continued to bat purposefully achieving a lead of 52 runs. That figure became more significant when South Africa again struggled badly succumbing to 20-4 after 40 minutes against the Essex new ball attack. Nichols had Bruce Mitchell caught at the wicket in his second over, then Stephenson, generating excessive swing, spread-eagled the wicket of Eric Rowan before bringing a ball back into Siedle and winning the leg before wicket verdict. Two runs later, he produced another fine delivery that struck Herby Wade on the pads and received further approval from the umpire. At that juncture, the bowler had figures of 3-3 in 4 overs.

John Stephenson: the entertaining and lively medium-pace bowler claimed 10 wickets in the match

Dalton again proved a tough and determined opponent as he attempted to hold the innings together and received solid support from Dudley Nourse, with whom he added 96 runs, before they were parted when a fine return catch by Jack O'Connor removed Nourse who had scored most of his 46 runs on the leg side. Dalton, who had been missed in the slips on 26 but prospered to reach his fifty in an hour,

A defining role in this match was played by John Stephenson who took ten wickets. A serving army officer who had seen service in India before returning to England, he found himself stationed in the garrison town of Colchester and linked up with the County side. A lively medium-paced bowler with boundless enthusiasm and energy for the game, he relished every playing moment but found little time to spare for first-class cricket. Always entertaining, life was never dull when he was on the field. He bowled with a full follow-through and was able to make the ball move both ways; he was also a hard-hitting, free-scoring batsman and excellent fielder. His Essex captain Tom Pearce said: "It is most difficult to write of his cricket because I have never met anybody quite like him. It was nothing to see him running down to third man after he had bowled a batsman out and to return to his position via extra cover."

Toss: South Africans won the toss and decided to bat.
Umpires: JA Newman, CN Woolley.

SOUTH AFRICANS

Batsman	1st innings		Runs	2nd innings		Runs
B Mitchell	b Nichols		0	c Powell b Nichols		3
IJ Siedle	c Sheffield b O'Connor		69	lbw b Stephenson		5
EAB Rowan	lbw b Stephenson		4	b Stephenson		8
AD Nourse	b Stephenson		1	c and b O'Connor		46
*HF Wade	c Sheffield b Stephenson		2	lbw b Stephenson		0
EL Dalton	b Nichols		117	c Sheffield b Evans		65
†RJ Williams	c Nichols b Stephenson		29	c Sheffield b Nichols		46
ACB Langton	b Stephenson		1	c Sheffield b R Smith		34
XC Balaskas	b Stephenson		0	b Nichols		5
RJ Crisp	b Stephenson		12	b Nichols		4
AJ Bell	not out		1	not out		2
Extras	(9 b, 4 lb, 1 nb)		14	(4 lb, 1 nb)		5
Total	**(all out, 77.1 overs)**		**250**	**(all out, 64 overs)**		**223**

Fall: 1st inns: 1-0, 2-15, 3-19, 4-23, 5-187, 6-219, 7-226, 8-226, 9-247, 10-250. **2nd inns:** 1-6, 2-15, 3-18, 4-20, 5-116, 6-141, 7-212, 8-212, 9-216, 10-223.
Bowling: 1st inns: Nichols 21-4-63-2, Stephenson 23.1-2-66-7, R Smith 6-1-24-0, TPB Smith 13-2-35-0, Evans 10-1-36-0, O'Connor 4-0-12-1. **2nd inns:** Nichols 14-135-4, Stephenson 16-2-44-3, R Smith 8-1-41-1, TPB Smith 12-1-50-0, Evans 10-2-36-1, O'Connor 4-0-12-1.

ESSEX

Batsman	1st innings		Runs	2nd innings			Runs
JR Sheffield	c Balaskas b Bell		23		b Bell		13
JA Cutmore	lbw b Crisp		72		not out		59
BH Belle	c Mitchell b Balaskas		11		did not bat		
J O'Connor	c Siedle b Balaskas		16	(5)	not out		13
MS Nichols	run out		1	(4)	b Mitchell		70
*NG Wykes	c Bell b Mitchell		46		did not bat		
JWA Stephenson	c Langton b Mitchell		22		did not bat		
†AG Powell	b Langton		14		did not bat		
TPB Smith	c Dalton b Crisp		21		did not bat		
R Smith	st Williams b Balaskas		43		did not bat		
VJ Evans	not out		7	(3)	b Langton		8
Extras	(19 b, 5 lb, 2 nb)		26		(6 b, 2 lb, 1 nb)		9
Total	**(all out, 95.4 overs)**		**302**		**(3 wickets, 46 overs)**		**172**

Fall: 1st inns: 1-45, 2-66, 3-108, 4-109, 5-163, 6-208, 7-215, 8-246, 9-258, 10-302. **2nd inns:** 1-20, 2-33, 3-133.
Bowling: 1st inns: Crisp 26-8-86-2, Bell 13-2-24-1, Langton 23-4-75-1, Balaskas 25.4-5-62-3, Mitchell 8-0-29-2. **2nd inns:** Crisp 14-2-57-0, Bell 4-2-10-1, Langton 12-1-23-1, Balaskas 8-0-39-0, Mitchell 7-0-30-1, Dalton 1-0-4-0.

eventually departed for a battling 65 although the home side's attempts to wrap up the innings were frustrated by Robert Williams and Arthur Langton. It took a couple of fine slip catches by Roy Sheffield to account for the pair but once they were out, Nichols wasted little time in removing the tail.

Needing 172 for victory, Essex lost Sheffield before the close but when the third day started, they only needed another 148 runs with nine wickets standing. Although they soon lost nightwatchman Victor Evans and were twice forced off the field in the opening hour because of bad light, conditions improved to allow Jimmy Cutmore and Stan Nichols to build a defining partnership. They took the total into three figures and soon after, Nichols struck Xen Balaskas for two boundaries to complete his fifty out of 76 made in an hour. The partnership had put on exactly 100, when a few minutes before lunch, Nichols played around an off-break and was bowled. That left Cutmore to complete his fifty and shortly afterwards, he struck the winning runs to see his side to a memorable seven wickets victory.

County Championship

Essex v Glamorgan

3-day match

Venue: Vista Road Recreation Ground, Clacton-on-Sea **Result:** Essex won by an innings and 87 runs

Kenneth Farnes was one of the best fast bowlers to pull on an Essex sweater although his appearances were intermittent because of his duties as a schoolmaster at Worksop College whilst England Test calls also denied the County use of his services. Some of his best performances for the County came at Vista Road Recreation Ground, Clacton-on-Sea and this match was just such an occasion. Against Glamorgan, Farnes overwhelmed the men from the Principality returning his best-ever match haul of 15 wickets. The pitch, which had been covered overnight, had sweated and left several damp spots and Glamorgan were soon in all sorts of trouble having won the toss and elected to bat.

Generating top speed throughout, Farnes bowled unchanged in both Glamorgan innings and with the pitch progressively breaking up and causing the ball to constantly kick up off a good length, the bowler was virtually unplayable. That the Welsh county made 150 in their first innings was thanks to a spirited effort from Cyril Smart who made a half-century despite being struck painfully by a Farnes delivery. A second wicket partnership of 152 between Denys Wilcox and Reg Taylor dominated the Essex reply although the visitors fielded badly allowing a number of Essex batsmen to receive at least one "life" and by the close on the opening day, the home side were already 170 runs ahead. The most expensive error was to allow Wilcox to survive two dropped chances when he had scored 30 but he took full advantage to reach 89 in an hour and a half stay at the crease during which

Denys Wilcox: figured in a defining second-wicket partnership

time he struck 12 boundaries. A number of his runs were gained from steering deliveries from the slow bowlers down to the vacant third man boundary.

Rain had got under the covers overnight and a declaration followed first thing in the morning although the start was delayed for 30 minutes. Farnes, now bowling from the opposite end to that of the first innings, retained his fearsome pace and was destined to repeat his one-man show as the hapless Glamorgan batsmen

---

Essex captain of the time, Tom Pearce who shared those duties with Denys Wilcox during the 1938 season, stated of Farnes: "He was one of the most delightful of men and regarded by us all as a gentle giant. We often thought we ought to kick him in the shins as we went out on the field to get him a little angry. He was a really fast bowler of some 6ft 7ins in height, who could certainly move the ball and vary its pace as well as make it rise sharply."

Farnes earned this tribute from celebrated cricket journalist E.W.Swanton: "At his best, he was a high class bowler. I saw some of the fastest bowling I have ever seen in this country in the Gentlemen v Players match of 1938. I do not think I have ever seen faster bowling, not by an Englishman in this country. He had a good action with his arm right at the top."

Toss: Glamorgan won the toss and decided to bat.
Umpires: LC Braund, JA Newman.

GLAMORGAN

AH Dyson	c Wilcox b R Smith	3	b Nichols		23
DE Davies	lbw b Nichols	17	c Wade b Farnes		0
TL Brierley	c Farnes b R Smith	0	c Taylor b Farnes		15
D Davies	c and b Farnes	11	c Pearce b Farnes		3
*MJL Turnbull	c Taylor b Farnes	11	b Farnes		3
CC Smart	c and b Farnes	54	c and b Farnes		4
RG Duckfield	b Farnes	5	c Wilcox b Farnes		17
PB Clift	b Farnes	5	c Nichols b TPB Smith		1
†HG Davies	b Farnes	34	b Farnes		0
DA Davies	not out	4	c and b Farnes		7
J Mercer	c Pearce b Farnes	0	not out		1
Extras	(3 b, 2 lb, 1 w)	6	(3 b, 6 lb)		9
Total	**(all out, 44.5 overs)**	**150**	**(all out, 20.5 overs)**		**83**

Fall: 1st inns: 1-3, 2-5, 3-18, 4-39, 5-61, 6-68, 7-84, 8-129, 9-150, 10-150. **2nd inns:** 1-1, 2-39, 3-43, 4-43, 5-51, 6-56, 7-57, 8-58, 9-82, 10-83.
Bowling: 1st inns: Farnes 22.5-4-75-7, R Smith 7-1-24-2, Nichols 15-1-45-1. **2nd inns:** Farnes 10.5-0-38-8, Nichols 7-0-29-1, TPB Smith 3-1-7-1.

ESSEX

DR Wilcox	b Mercer	89
AV Avery	lbw b Mercer	5
RM Taylor	lbw b Clift	53
J O'Connor	lbw b Mercer	38
TPB Smith	c Smart b Mercer	35
MS Nichols	c Dyson b Mercer	0
*TN Pearce	c DA Davies b Smart	17
N Vere Hodge	st HG Davies b DE Davies	8
R Smith	c D Davies b DA Davies	29
†TH Wade	not out	18
K Farnes	did not bat	
Extras	(21 b, 7 lb)	28
Total	**(9 wickets, declared, 69.5 overs)**	**320**

Fall: 1st inns: 1-12, 2-164, 3-176, 4-223, 5-225, 6-262, 7-262, 8-288, 9-320.
Bowling: 1st inns: Mercer 27-2-106-5, D Davies 12-3-38-0, DE Davies 14-1-67-1, Smart 10-0-54-1, DA Davies 3.5-0-18-1, Clift 3-1-9-1.

formed a constant procession from and back to the pavilion. His fifth delivery of the innings popped up alarmingly causing Emrys Davies to edge the ball into the gloves of wicket-keeper Tom Wade. Both Arnold Dyson and Tom Brierley were dropped but neither mistake proved too costly as the visitors found themselves 43-4 and on the road to defeat. Taylor produced a stunning catch to dismiss Brierley for 15 when he ran backwards for a considerable distance from slip almost to the boundary to take a skier. Although Dyson and Dick Duckfield took 28 runs off his bowling, their colleagues were so helpless against Farnes that the bowler only conceded 10 other runs in taking eight wickets and his match figures of 15-113 represented a career-best.

Glamorgan were routed by an innings and 87 runs after being bowled out for 83 inside 21 overs in 75 minutes and the match was over by lunchtime on the second day. A year later, Farnes was again grabbing the headlines at the seaside town where he took a hat-trick against Nottinghamshire accounting for the impressive trio of George Hearne, Joe Hardstaff and George Gunn.

County Championship
Derbyshire v Essex

3-day match | **Venue:** Queen's Park, Chesterfield **Result:** Essex won by 5 wickets

Derbyshire started the match in third position in the County Championship table and were indebted to Alan Townsend who helped them recover from a poor start to reach 223. His effort appeared altogether more noteworthy when mid-table Essex lost their ninth wicket with 199 runs on the board. Enter Peter Smith to join the gritty fighter Frank Vigar and begin a partnership that transformed the match. At first, Vigar tried to protect his partner but soon realised that he was playing with a lot of confidence and assurance and let the tail-ender 'have his head.' Smith was the dominant partner with 163 runs as the duo put on 218 for the last wicket, making Essex only one of three first-class teams in the world to have scored over 200 for every wicket.

Their partnership lasted for 150 minutes with Smith, in his Benefit year, clubbing three sixes and 22 fours as he recorded the highest score made by a number eleven batsman. In an exceptional innings, he did offer two difficult chances but punished Eric Marsh for 22 in one over.

Peter Smith (top) and Frank Vigar: featured in a double-century partnership for the 10th wicket that still remains a County record

In contrast, Vigar was a model of patience batting five hours for his 114 not out. He had gone into bat with the score on 33-3 and saw the innings continue to falter onto 104-7 before orchestrating the revival that saw 313 runs added for the final three wickets.

Vigar was a tall, Somerset-born leg-spinner who became one of the County's most reliable batsmen in the decade after the war. The year 1947 proved a golden one for the player who made 1,735 runs with five hundreds and he also took 64 wickets. Trevor Bailey remembered him as, "a very unusual mix – a very sound batsman, solid and stubborn, and a useful leg-spinner." In this match, the Essex late order consisted of Bailey at number 8, Doug Insole at nine and Ray Smith at 10, hardly

Recalling the match some years later, Frank Vigar stated, "My main concern when Peter joined me with my score standing somewhere in the 80's was to keep him away from the bowling so I could reach my century. I am still not certain who obtained it first! Peter, coming in at No. 11, says much for the standard of the Essex batting order in this match, as he was no 'rabbit' with the bat. When I saw the mood Peter was in, I was determined not to throw my wicket away [as though I ever did] and to give him as much of the bowling as possible. Which reminds me of the Derbyshire attack – it contained in Copson, Pope and Gladwin, probably the most feared attack in the country. When Peter was eventually bowled, we had broken the Essex last wicket stand and also turned what looked like certain defeat into a remarkable victory."

Toss: Derbyshire won the toss and decided to bat.
Umpires: N Harris, D Hendren.

DERBYSHIRE

AF Townsend	b TPB Smith	86		b R Smith	1
CS Elliott	b R Smith	2		run out	68
TS Worthington	c TPB Smith b Bailey	0		b Bailey	9
D Smith	run out	10		b R Smith	35
GH Pope	c Insole b Bailey	5	(8)	c Dodds b Bailey	11
†AE Alderman	b Bailey	20	(6)	c Insole b Bailey	27
FE Marsh	c Crabtree b TPB Smith	24	(7)	c Horsfall b Bailey	4
AEG Rhodes	c Insole b TPB Smith	4	(5)	c Horsfall b R Smith	0
*EJ Gothard	not out	24		b R Smith	40
C Gladwin	c Insole b Bailey	27		c Wilcox b Bailey	52
WH Copson	b Bailey	0		not out	38
Extras	(16 b, 4 lb, 1 nb)	21		(9 b, 8 lb, 1 nb, 1 w)	19
Total	**(all out, 62.2 overs)**	**223**		**(all out, 106.5 overs)**	**304**

Fall: 1st inns: 1-8, 2-9, 3-39, 4-45, 5-89, 6-153, 7-162, 8-167, 9-223, 10-223. **2nd inns:** 1-2, 2-22, 3-83, 4-85, 5-146, 6-150, 7-155, 8-170, 9-242, 10-304.
Bowling: 1st inns: Bailey 24.2-1-83-5, R Smith 18-3-50-1, TPB Smith 18-2-59-3, Vigar 2-0-10-0.
2nd inns: Bailey 30.5-6-92-5, R Smith 49-14-122-4, TPB Smith 22-6-53-0, Vigar 5-0-18-0.

ESSEX

TC Dodds	lbw b Copson	20		c Townsend b Copson	23
SJ Cray	b Copson	11		b Pope	9
AV Avery	c Pope b Copson	0	(4)	lbw b Pope	0
HP Crabtree	lbw b Pope	2	(5)	c Worthington b Gladwin	30
FH Vigar	not out	114	(6)	not out	40
R Horsfall	b Pope	8	(7)	not out	3
*DR Wilcox	b Gladwin	9		did not bat	
TE Bailey	b Worthington	19		did not bat	
†DJ Insole	b Copson	48		did not bat	
R Smith	c Marsh b Pope	21		did not bat	
TPB Smith	b Worthington	163	(3)	c Worthington b Copson	4
Extras	(1 b, 1 nb)	2		(5 lb)	5
Total	**(all out, 126.5 overs)**	**417**		**(5 wickets, 37.1 overs)**	**114**

Fall: 1st inns: 1-30, 2-30, 3-33, 4-33, 5-51, 6-65, 7-104, 8-160, 9-199, 10-417. **2nd inns:** 1-32, 2-36, 3-36, 4-36, 5-103.
Bowling: 1st inns: Copson 36-8-117-4, Pope 27-8-73-3, Gladwin 13-3-54-1, Worthington 21.5-1-90-2, Rhodes 18-4-44-0, Marsh 11-3-37-0. **2nd inns:** Copson 14-3-36-2, Pope 15-5-39-2, Gladwin 3.1-0-15-1, Rhodes 5-0-19-0.

a typical lowly line-up! When Derbyshire batted again, the still bemused home side lost eight wickets before clearing the arrears of 194 runs until they too were galvanised by the late order with Edward Gothard, Cliff Gladwin and Bill Copson all scoring freely to add 134 runs for the remaining two wickets.

Needing 111 for victory, Essex comfortably accomplished their task with five wickets to spare although promoted Peter Smith fell cheaply. Vigar though was again unbeaten, this time scoring 40 not out to secure the win. *Wisden* stated that the first innings stand between Vigar and Smith, "completely altered the course of the game, for when they came together, Essex were 24 behind." *The Essex CCC Year Book* of 1948 summarising the match stated, "A truly remarkable game, the highlight of which was an Essex record last wicket stand. For No.11 to score a century is unusual enough but the way in which Smith hit the bowling of three England bowlers, Copson, Pope and Gladwin, was even more surprising. Vigar gave solid support, R.Smith reached his 1,000 runs and Bailey took 10 wickets in the match but Essex had to fight hard to win."

Tour Match

Essex v Australians

3-day match

Venue: Southchurch Park, Southend-on-Sea **Result:** Australians won by an innings and 451 runs

Of all the matches to be included under the heading of 'Classic' Essex encounters, this particular game would surely be at the forefront. The all-conquering Australians under the captain Donald Bradman arrived at Southchurch Park in glorious Whit weekend sunshine to entertain crowds estimated to number 16,000 on each of the two days it took to complete the match. The tourists had won five consecutive matches, four by an innings, before this fixture and the crowds flocked to the venue seeking entertainment of the richest order. They were not to be disappointed as the Australians made hay in the Saturday sun after winning the toss.

Tom Pearce: Essex Captain in the record-breaking match at Southend

By lunch, they had reached 202 for the loss of one wicket after openers Sid Barnes and Bill Brown had realised 145 in 95 minutes and in the next 90 minutes, Bradman and Brown struck out to gather a whirlwind 219 runs before Brown was caught off the bowling of Trevor Bailey. With the score 364-2, Aussie Golden-Boy of the time, charismatic Keith Miller was bowled first ball by Bailey but hopes of a hat-trick were thwarted by Ron Hamence. When Bradman finally departed for a regal 187 that included 32 fours and one five and having scored at the rate of 90 runs per hour, the visitors continued to thrash the Essex attack with Sam Loxton and wicket-keeper Ron Saggers putting on another 166 runs in 65 minutes.

By the close, the Australians had reached 721, the highest total ever recorded in a single day's first-class cricket. But as Essex captain Tom Pearce cheerfully claimed, Essex had become the first county in 1948 to bowl the Australians out in a day! Whilst Australia could boast four century-makers in their innings, there were also four centurions amongst the Essex side although not with the bat as four members of the attack conceded 100 runs or more. Facing their opponents mammoth score,

In his book *Wickets, Catches and the Odd Run*, Trevor Bailey admits that his admiration for the Australian team was "enormous" and he further recalls the occasion of this famous match. "There were several intriguing features about that Southchurch massacre," he wrote. "First – the Australians never accelerated – they kept plodding along at just under 250 runs per session. Second, I bowled Keith Miller for nought first ball with an absolutely straight ball. I remarked to Don [Bradman] that Keith had not appeared interested to which he replied with the cryptic, 'he'll learn.' Third although the attendance of 32,000 for the two days was easily a ground record, I have met subsequently at least one million people who claim to have been present. Finally, we managed somehow to bowl 129 overs, which was remarkable in six hours of play considering the amount of time spent retrieving the ball from the boundary."

Toss: Australians won the toss and decided to bat.
Umpires: WH Ashdown, D Hendren.

AUSTRALIANS

SG Barnes	hit wkt b R Smith	79
WA Brown	c Horsfall b Bailey	153
*DG Bradman	b TPB Smith	187
KR Miller	b Bailey	0
RA Hamence	c TPB Smith b R Smith	46
SJE Loxton	c Rist b Vigar	120
†RA Saggers	not out	104
IWG Johnson	st Rist b TPB Smith	9
DT Ring	c Vigar b TPB Smith	1
WA Johnston	b Vigar	9
ERH Toshack	c Vigar b TPB Smith	4
Extras	(7 b, 2 nb)	9
Total	**(all out, 129 overs)**	**721**

Fall: 1st inns: 1-145, 2-364, 3-364, 4-452, 5-498, 6-664, 7-686, 8-692, 9-716, 10-721.
Bowling: 1st inns: Bailey 21-1-128-2, R Smith 37-2-169-2, TPB Smith 38-0-193-4, Price 20-0-156-0, Vigar 13-1-66-2.

ESSEX

				(FOLLOWING ON)	
TC Dodds	c Ring b Miller	0		b Toshack	16
SJ Cray	b Miller	5		b Johnson	15
AV Avery	b Johnston	10		c Brown b Johnson	3
FH Vigar	c Saggers b Miller	0		c Johnson b Toshack	0
R Horsfall	b Toshack	11		b Johnson	8
*TN Pearce	c Miller b Toshack	8		c and b Johnson	71
R Smith	c Barnes b Toshack	25		c Ring b Johnson	0
TPB Smith	b Toshack	3		lbw b Barnes	54
†FH Rist	c Barnes b Toshack	8		b Johnson	1
EJ Price	not out	4		not out	4
TE Bailey	absent hurt			absent hurt	
Extras	(2 b, 6 lb, 1 nb)	9		(6 b, 3 lb, 6 nb)	15
Total	**(all out, 36.5 overs)**	**83**		**(all out, 78.4 overs)**	**187**

Fall: 1st inns: 1-0, 2-13, 3-13, 4-19, 5-30, 6-47, 7-63, 8-74, 9-83. **2nd inns:** 1-24, 2-32, 3-35, 4-36, 5-46, 6-46, 7-177, 8-183, 9-187.
Bowling: 1st inns: Miller 8-3-14-3, Johnston 7-1-10-1, Toshack 10.5-2-31-5, Ring 11-4-19-0.
2nd inns: Miller 2-1-4-0, Loxton 12-3-28-0, Johnston 10-4-26-0, Toshack 17-2-50-2, Johnson 21-6-37-6, Barnes 9.4-5-11-1, Ring 7-3-16-0.

Essex were then shot out for 83 by Ernie Toshack and Miller when play resumed on the Monday although Bailey, destined to become one of England's greatest all-rounders, had broken a finger on the first day and was unable to bat in either innings. Bradman dismissed the theory that his side had been fortunate to bat on a gem of a pitch. "Let me dispose of that by saying it was just as good on Monday when Essex batted," he insisted. "It was all a question of comparative skill."

For the second time before lunch on the second day, spectators witnessed the Essex openers emerging from the pavilion to face the new ball and the home side appeared to be heading for another dismal score when they slumped to 46-6 but Pearce and Peter Smith put on 131 for the seventh wicket to prolong the entertainment for the crowd and add some much-needed substance to the total. The margin of defeat though was still an Essex record of an innings and 451 runs. At least the County experienced some welcome consolation with the record attendance of 32,000 providing record receipts of £3,482 for Southchurch Park.

County Championship
Essex v Lancashire

3-day match   **Venue:** Vista Road Recreation Ground, Clacton-on-Sea **Result:** Lancashire won by 10 wickets

Only twice in the history of Essex County Cricket Club has one of their bowlers taken all 10 wickets in a first-class innings and this match saw Trevor Bailey become the second player to achieve this distinction. The opposition's previous fixture had been at Liverpool and the gruelling journey south meant that they arrived in the Essex seaside resort at 3.00 a.m. so it was with some relief for them that they won the toss and elected to bat on a good wicket on a hot day.

They made sound progress with the first three wickets posting just over 100 runs and a further 140 were added between lunch and tea including a fourth wicket stand of 124 between Geoff Edrich and Nigel Howard. The sixth wicket went down with the score on 264 just before tea and Bailey had accounted for each dismissal. Shortly after the resumption, the all-rounder claimed another two victims and when he added a ninth, captain Tom Pearce sent down his only four overs of the season in a bid to give him the opportunity of all ten wickets. The ploy was successful with Bailey taking the tenth and final wicket when he bowled Alfred Barlow.

Bailey had used his away swinger to such telling effect that with the ball moving late, six of his victims were either caught by the wicket-keeper or in the slip region. Three others were bowled. By the close, Essex had reached 32-1 but any fears of weariness amongst the visitors attack were soon dispelled the following morning when the fast bowling of John Deighton caused

Trevor Bailey: 10 wickets in an innings but still finished on the losing side

problems a-plenty for the home side. Only Frank Vigar, who batted two hours and twenty minutes for 53, and Pearce showed the right qualities putting on 63 for the fifth wicket. Essex were forced to follow-on after conceding a first innings lead of 167 runs but on a wearing wicket, they again batted disappointingly with left-arm spinner Bill Roberts proving destroyer-in-chief with six wickets.

In his book *Wickets, Catches and the Odd Run*, Trevor Bailey recalls his outstanding achievement of taking all ten wickets. "At lunch, I was pleased at having taken three wickets and even more satisfied to have six when we came in for tea. It was not until two more had come my way that I realised I had a chance. But I could never have captured the final two wickets without the active co-operation of Tom Pearce who in the closing stages, used two non-bowlers including himself whose purpose was not to get a wicket. The fact that the Lancashire tail scored rather more than they should have done he regarded as immaterial.

"It was a generous typically pre-war approach but I am sure that I would never have taken all ten if Tom's successor, Doug Insole, had been captain. Doug believed that records were of no importance and had to occur within the strict context of the game."

Toss: Lancashire won the toss and decided to bat.
Umpires: K McCanlis, CN Woolley.

LANCASHIRE

C Washbrook	c Wade b Bailey	18	did not bat	
JT Ikin	b Bailey	42	did not bat	
W Place	c Wade b Bailey	28	did not bat	
GA Edrich	c Vigar b Bailey	82	did not bat	
KJ Grieves	c Wade b Bailey	11	did not bat	
*ND Howard	c Vigar b Bailey	66	did not bat	
P Greenwood	c Vigar b Bailey	2	did not bat	
JHG Deighton	c Pearce b Bailey	1	did not bat	
R Tattersall	not out	34	(2) not out	3
WB Roberts	b Bailey	15	did not bat	
†A Barlow	b Bailey	12	(1) not out	0
Extras	(10 b, 9 lb, 1 w)	20		0
Total	(all out, 106.4 overs)	331	(no wicket, 0.3 overs)	3

Fall: 1st inns: 1-26, 2-84, 3-104, 4-228, 5-256, 6-264, 7-265, 8-268, 9-297, 10-331. **2nd inns:** 1-20, 2-63, 3-85, 4-143.
Bowling: 1st inns: Bailey 39.4-9-90-10, R Smith 33-8-107-0, TPB Smith 12-3-26-0, Vigar 7-1-27-0, Price 8-1-29-0, Morris 3-1-12-0, Pearce 4-0-20-0. **2nd inns:** Wade 0.3-0-3-0.

ESSEX

			(FOLLOWING ON)	
TC Dodds	c Grieves b Deighton	11	b Greenwood	37
SJ Cray	c Ikin b Deighton	10	(6) b Deighton	6
FH Vigar	c Barlow b Grieves	53	(3) c Deighton b Roberts	10
R Horsfall	c Edrich b Greenwood	11	b Greenwood	19
TE Bailey	c Ikin b Greenwood	10	c Barlow b Tattersall	28
*TN Pearce	run out	28	(2) b Roberts	12
WB Morris	c Edrich b Deighton	13	c Ikin b Roberts	15
R Smith	c Ikin b Greenwood	6	st Barlow b Roberts	20
TPB Smith	c Barlow b Deighton	0	b Roberts	7
†TH Wade	c Barlow b Deighton	1	b Roberts	0
EJ Price	not out	3	not out	1
Extras	(7 b, 7 lb, 4 nb)	18	(13 b, 1 lb)	14
Total	(all out, 79 overs)	164	(all out, 69.4 overs)	169

Fall: 1st inns: 1-23, 2-39, 3-52, 4-75, 5-138, 6-138, 7-144, 8-151, 9-153, 10-164. **2nd inns:** 1-44, 2-64, 3-69, 4-87, 5-111, 6-140, 7-140, 8-148, 9-148, 10-169.
Bowling: 1st inns: Greenwood 24-4-38-3, Deighton 24-3-53-5, Tattersall 7-1-15-0, Roberts 16-7-18-0, Grieves 8-2-22-1. **2nd inns:** Greenwood 19-5-47-2, Deighton 11-2-30-1, Tattersall 9-2-27-1, Roberts 22.4-8-29 6, Grieves 8-3-22-0.

Opener Dickie Dodds dominated a first wicket partnership of 44 with stand-in opener Pearce who replaced Stan 'Chick' Cray who had been forced to retire hurt during his first innings although he did return. Dodds hit six boundaries in his 37 but the remaining batsmen had little answer to the problems posed by Roberts who was getting significant turn whilst also flighting the ball deceptively. Towards the latter stages of the game, a sea mist obscured parts of the ground adding to the difficulties of the batsmen. In the course of the second day's play, Essex feebly lost 19 wickets whilst scoring 301 runs and Lancashire were left requiring just three runs for victory. They sent in two tail-enders and victory was accomplished in just three deliveries off the bowling of regular wicket-keeper Tommy Wade achieving a 10-wickets win with more than a day to spare. Incredibly, it was the second time that an Essex bowler had taken all ten wickets in an innings yet finished on the losing side! The feat of taking all ten wickets in an innings was subsequently acknowledged by a formal presentation from the Club Committee to Bailey of the ball mounted and suitably inscribed.

County Championship
Essex v Lancashire

3-day match   **Venue:** Old County Ground, Brentwood **Result:** Match tied

The tied match was the County's third such outcome since joining the first-class ranks. In a fascinating encounter between two closely-matched teams, Lancashire started well reaching a cautious 153-2 in rather indifferent light with Alan Wharton batting stylishly together with Winston Place who had just returned from a fractured thumb. Then Ken Preston and Ray Smith got to work as the visitors lost their last eight wickets for just 113 runs with the former

claiming 5-8 in his final spell. The home side found scoring difficult against an opposition attack that bowled with commendable accuracy and nagging length. At the end of the second day, the hosts were trailing by six runs with one wicket standing.

Having captured the remaining wicket shortly after play resumed, Lancashire batted enterprisingly scoring 226-7 in three hours and twenty minutes with the innovative Geoff Edrich hitting 69 before being stumped by stand-in wicket-keeper Doug Insole whilst Malcolm Hilton made his highest score of the season when reaching an unbeaten 48 before the declaration came to set up an enthralling conclusion. Smith's six wickets haul gave him match figures of 11-227 and he was then to make a telling contribution with the bat in the run-chase that ensued.

Dickie Dodds: launched the Essex second innings with a 4 then 6 off successive deliveries in the first over

Set 232 to win in two hours and twenty minutes, the scintillating Dickie Dodds was soon into his stride. Renowned as the fastest scoring opener in the country with an average rate throughout the season of more than 40 runs per hour, his unwavering philosophy was to attack the bowling from the start. On more than one occasion, he would launch the ball over the boundary for a six in the first over of the innings.

This match against Lancashire was one such example as he struck England Test opening bowler Brian Statham for four and six in the opening over as 33

In reviewing the 1952 season, the *Essex CCC Year Book* reported that "there had been a universal demand for more entertaining cricket and Essex responded by heading the News Chronicle Fast Scoring Table." All-rounder Trevor Bailey acknowledged the achievement by highlighting three individual performers amongst his colleagues that helped the team carry off the title. "Firstly there was Dickie Dodds who so often led the onslaught on the opposition and besides being the fastest opening bat in the country, was also one of the most attractive to watch," he wrote. "Secondly, there was Colin Griffiths who, besides registering the quickest century of the season, also collected his runs at an average of 48 per hour throughout the season. Finally there was Doug Insole who was never happier than when chasing runs and who also imbued the whole of his team with his own happy approach to the game."

Toss: Lancashire won the toss and decided to bat.
Umpires: TW Spencer, CH Welch.

LANCASHIRE

Batsman	1st innings		2nd innings	
A Wharton	lbw b Smith	85	c Avery b Smith	16
JG Lomax	c Gibb b Smith	10	c Bailey b Greensmith	47
GA Edrich	c Insole b Smith	35	st Insole b Smith	69
W Place	c Avery b Preston	63	did not bat	
KJ Grieves	b Preston	34	(4) c and b Smith	0
*ND Howard	c Avery b Preston	0	(5) b Smith	5
P Greenwood	b Smith	14	(6) b Smith	8
MJ Hilton	b Preston	8	(7) not out	48
R Tattersall	b Smith	1	(9) not out	7
JB Statham	b Preston	1	(8) c Greensmith b Smith	15
†A Wilson	not out	0	did not bat	
Extras	(10 b, 3 lb, 2 nb)	15	(9 b, 1 nb, 1 w)	11
Total	**(all out, 108.3 overs)**	**266**	**(7 wickets, declared, 70 overs)**	**226**

Fall: 1st inns: 1-20, 2-111, 3-153, 4-237, 5-237, 6-240, 7-255, 8-265, 9-266, 10-266. **2nd inns:** 1-32, 2-103, 3-104, 4-114, 5-138, 6-175, 7-208.
Bowling: 1st inns: Bailey 21-6-44-0, Preston 20.3-2-49-5, Smith 39-5-105-5, Greensmith 24-12-30-0, Insole 4-0-23-0. **2nd inns:** Bailey 14-3-34-0, Preston 11-2-26-0, Smith 33-4-122-6, Greensmith 12-5-33-1.

ESSEX

Batsman	1st innings		2nd innings	
TC Dodds	c Howard b Lomax	46	c Tattersall b Lomax	26
AV Avery	c Wilson b Lomax	41	(9) st Wilson b Hilton	4
†PA Gibb	c Edrich b Hilton	13	(6) c Grieves b Tattersall	33
R Horsfall	c Edrich b Hilton	3	(3) lbw b Statham	10
*DJ Insole	b Lomax	2	(2) b Statham	18
TE Bailey	c Wharton b Hilton	34	(8) c Howard b Hilton	52
R Smith	run out	27	(4) c Wharton b Tattersall	48
FH Vigar	not out	25	(11) not out	1
C Griffiths	c Edrich b Tattersall	6	(5) c Wilson b Tattersall	19
WT Greensmith	b Statham	56	(7) b Statham	5
KC Preston	b Statham	1	(10) c Grieves b Tattersall	10
Extras	(4 b, 2 lb, 1 nb)	7	(3 b, 2 lb)	5
Total	**(all out, 144.4 overs)**	**261**	**(all out, 46.4 overs)**	**231**

Fall: 1st inns: 1-86, 2-89, 3-92, 4-104, 5-111, 6-164, 7-181, 8-187, 9-259, 10-261. **2nd inns:** 1-33, 2-50, 3-61, 4-89, 5-150, 6-156, 7-167, 8-183, 9-206, 10-231.
Bowling: 1st inns: Statham 24.4-3-50-2, Lomax 21-4-37-3, Tattersall 25-5-46-1, Hilton 37-15-47-3, Grieves 22-7-44-0, Wharton 3-0-11-0, Greenwood 12-4-19-0. **2nd inns:** Statham 12-1-59-3, Lomax 3-0-14-1, Tattersall 18-3-61-4, Hilton 10.4-0-69-2, Greenwood 3-0-23-0.

were collected in the first 14 minutes and the run-rate was maintained with the first 100 raised in 50 minutes although four wickets had been lost at that point. The next 50 took another half-hour with five wickets down at that stage after Ray Smith and Paul Gibb added 61 in half an hour. The next four wickets added 56 runs with Bailey attempting to anchor the victory quest but when the ninth wicket fell, 26 runs were needed with 12 minutes remaining. Frank Vigar had been held back in the order and strode to the wicket to join Bailey and with five minutes to go, 12 runs were required but when the last over commenced, Essex were still nine runs from victory. Hilton was entrusted with the final over of the match and from his first delivery, Bailey straight drove a six to raise the tension. He was then dropped in the deep off the next ball by Wharton and compounded the fielder's misery by taking two runs to level the scores. Bailey defended the third ball without scoring but then attempted the winning hit off the next delivery and saw Lancashire skipper Nigel Howard take the catch at deep mid-off leaving the match tied with the visitors taking eight points (including the four points for first innings lead) and their opponents four points.

County Championship

Essex v Nottinghamshire

3-day match

Venue: Southchurch Park, Southend-on-Sea **Result:** Nottinghamshire won by 2 wickets.

In what had proved to be a poor season of results for the County, this final fixture of the season provided one of the most absorbing conclusions to a game. Both sides struggled to score freely on a slow wicket in their first innings before conditions improved enabling some fine entertainment to be produced. Failing to take advantage of winning the toss, Essex were bowled out for 191 with seven batsmen contributing a meagre collective amount of just nine runs. Thankfully, dependable all-rounder Trevor Bailey was again in magnificent form with both the bat and ball and his first innings half-century at least allowed the home side some modicum of respectability. He then turned his attentions to bowling issues enduring long spells of action as he accounted for half the Nottinghamshire side who were in trouble at 137-7. Gamini Goonesena came to the rescue with an unbeaten 66 in almost two hours to guide his side to a first innings lead after they had occupied the crease for five hours and forty minutes.

Trevor Bailey *(left)* and Doug Insole: both scored centuries before lunch

By the close of the second day, Essex were 92 runs ahead having lost three second innings wickets and the match was nicely poised. However, Bailey surpassed his first innings achievement, this time hitting 114 not out during a fourth wicket partnership with his captain Doug Insole who also scored an unbeaten 114. The pair reached their respective centuries before lunch, as they added an unbroken 239 in three hours for the fourth wicket to record the highest Essex stand of the season. They were also the only pair of batsmen in the County's history to have jointly achieved a century apiece before lunch. This was against conventional bowling and without needing to resort to "feeding runs" in order to set-up a declaration. Insole called a halt to the Essex innings at lunch on day three.

Nottinghamshire were set a demanding challenge of 311 in two sessions but they immediately took up the challenge. They scored briskly to maintain the required run-rate but Essex retained interest taking wickets at regular intervals

The fourth wicket partnership between Doug Insole and Trevor Bailey carried these comments in the *1956 Essex CCC Year Book*. **"These two redoubtable personages proceeded to make the biggest Essex stand of the season, both being undefeated for 114 when the innings was declared."** The same publication also acknowledged the performance of captain Insole throughout the season. **"All too often, Essex batting was literally Douglas Insole, who enjoyed a fabulous summer and, in a year when the ball very much dominated the bat, scored nine centuries, not only considerably more than anyone else in the country but only one Essex player has ever made as many,"** it stated. **"It seems strange that a player in such wonderful form who made so many of his runs against strong bowling sides, including two hundreds against Yorkshire and one off the South Africans, should only once find favour with the [Test] selectors and then, despite doing rather better than most people, be once again cast aside."**

Toss: Essex won the toss and decided to bat.
Umpires: D Davies, TW Spencer.

ESSEX

Batsman	1st innings		2nd innings	
TC Dodds	c Rowe b Jepson	32	b Dooland	44
G Barker	lbw b Jepson	2	c Clay b KJ Poole	2
†PA Gibb	run out	2	c Stocks b Goonesena	40
*DJ Insole	lbw b Goonesena	37	not out	114
TE Bailey	c Stocks b Dooland	54	not out	114
MJ Bear	c Clay b Dooland	0	did not bat	
WT Greensmith	lbw b Goonesena	46	did not bat	
GJ Smith	c Stocks b Dooland	3	did not bat	
R Smith	lbw b Dooland	2	did not bat	
LHR Ralph	not out	0	did not bat	
KC Preston	b Dooland	0	did not bat	
Extras	(8 b, 2 lb, 2 nb, 1 w)	13	(11 b, 5 lb)	16
Total	(all out, 79.3 overs)	191	(3 wickets, declared, 92 overs)	330

Fall: 1st inns: 1-5, 2-36, 3-36, 4-109, 5-114, 6-181, 7-189, 8-190, 9-191, 10-191. **2nd inns:** 1-18, 2-91, 3-91.
Bowling: 1st inns: Jepson 17-5-30-2, KJ Poole 12-2-44-0, Smales 16-7-37-0, Dooland 17.3-4-34-5, Goonesena 17-6-33-2. **2nd inns:** Jepson 26-2-67-0, KJ Poole 14-1-62-1, Smales 8-2-39-0, Dooland 29-8-92-1, Goonesena 15-2-54-1.

NOTTINGHAMSHIRE

Batsman	1st innings		2nd innings		
*RT Simpson	c Gibb b Bailey	8		c Preston b Greensmith	39
JD Clay	c Bear b Ralph	18		c Bailey b Preston	6
RJ Giles	c and b Insole	55		b R Smith	77
†EJ Rowe	b Bailey	4		did not bat	
FW Stocks	c Ralph b Bailey	2	(4)	c Ralph b R Smith	7
CJ Poole	b Bailey	13	(5)	b R Smith	59
KJ Poole	c Gibb b Bailey	13	(6)	lbw b Preston	58
G Goonesena	not out	66	(7)	st Gibb b Greensmith	5
B Dooland	c Preston b Greensmith	14	(8)	c GJ Smith b Preston	35
K Smales	c Barker b Greensmith	6	(9)	not out	11
A Jepson	run out	7	(10)	not out	0
Extras	(3 b, 1 lb, 1 nb)	5		(6 b, 9 lb, 2 nb)	17
Total	(all out, 89.3 overs)	211		(8 wickets, 72 overs)	314

Fall: 1st inns: 1-22, 2-36, 3-51, 4-65, 5-87, 6-105, 7-137, 8-187, 9-193, 10-211. **2nd inns:** 1-9, 2-88, 3-105, 4-181, 5-210, 6-227, 7-296, 8-310.
Bowling: 1st inns: Bailey 31-6-68-5, Preston 13-2-32-0, R Smith 20-5-34-0, Ralph 11-2-33-1, Insole 3-0-9-1, Greensmith 11.3-2-30-2. **2nd inns:** Bailey 8-0-33-0, Preston 11-1-42-3, R Smith 26-5-97-3, Ralph 2-0-14-0, Insole 8-0-32-0, Greensmith 17-0-79-2.

although Ron Giles proved difficult to dislodge batting for two and three-quarter hours for 77 whilst Cyril Poole took just 75 minutes to score 59 with these two contributions providing the impetus Nottinghamshire were seeking. Needing a further 100 runs to clinch victory, the visitors still had five wickets in hand but when the sixth wicket fell with 84 runs still required and only 40 minutes remaining, a draw looked the most likely outcome.

Bruce Dooland and Ken Poole then produced a defining partnership adding 69 in 35 minutes before Poole was trapped in front of his stumps by Ken Preston. When the final over arrived, Nottinghamshire had reduced the target to six runs with three wickets in hand and Preston was charged with the responsibility of sending down the last six balls. Five runs were gleaned from the first four deliveries to level the scores before Dooland drove the ball into the hands of Geoff Smith at mid-off. Amidst great tension, last man Arthur Jepson, a tail-ender not noted for his batting skills, arrived at the crease and he proved up to the immediate task driving the last delivery of an enthralling match to the boundary for the winning runs.

County Championship

Essex v Hampshire

3-day match   **Venue:** Gidea Park Sports Ground, Romford **Result:** Essex won by 46 runs

The *Romford Times* reported that the festival was nearly abandoned because of wilful damage. 'A few weeks before the festival, vandals almost brought disaster to Romford Cricket Week,' it reported. 'The square was in perfect condition when hooligans broke into the ground at night and tore holes in the pitch with a spike believed to have been taken from nearby Romford Golf Course. Luckily the ground was soft and groundsman Jack Parker, with the help of staff, was able to replace divots and patch-up other problem areas. The pitch was tended and repaired to a satisfactory condition allowing the game to go ahead."

If there had been a man-of-the-match award made for this contest, then there would have only been one nomination – Trevor Bailey. Despite being

Essex CCC team 1957

inconvenienced by a cracked knuckle bone in his right hand sustained in the previous match against Derbyshire, the Westcliff-on-Sea born all-rounder completely dominated the fixture played at the Gallows Corner venue and was on the field for all but an hour and a half of the match. The visitors boasted a fine opening attack in Derek Shackleton and Vic Cannings who knew how to exploit favourable conditions to the full. However, Bailey served notice of his authority contributing 59 of the 130 runs scored by Essex in their first innings made on a typical green Romford pitch before he followed up with an unbeaten 71 out of 141 in the second innings.

Bailey protected that modest first innings total taking 6-32 as the visitors were hustled out for 109 and they only reached that figure thanks to a number of lusty and fortuitous blows from cavalier Colin Ingleby-Mackenzie. Having gained a slender but valuable first innings lead of 21 runs, Essex started their second innings disastrously as Hampshire's new ball pair claimed the first three Essex wickets without a run on the board. Bailey arrived at the crease and

Revisiting the match in the *Essex CCC Handbook 1984*, Trevor Bailey wrote: "Nobody could describe the Romford ground at Gallows Corner as attractive. Nevertheless, I looked forward to playing there for the good reason that the pitches frequently suited both my batting and bowling. On this occasion, as on so many park pitches in Essex, the ball moved disconcertingly, sometimes alarmingly, off the seam which made batting a challenge but not an impossible exercise. My first ambition was my survival, my second to get off the mark and my third to reach double figures. After that, it was a combination of head down, hope, nick and very occasionally reach the boundary. Although not unfamiliar with Essex collapses, I was still surprised to find myself walking out to the middle at number 5 with the scoreboard reading 0-3 in the second innings. Our eventual total of 141 meant that Hampshire had to make the highest score of the match to win which, on that pitch, was never really on."

Toss: Essex won the toss and decided to bat.
Umpires: P Corrall, N Oldfield.

ESSEX

G Barker	lbw b Cannings	5	b Shackleton		0
RE Evans	b Shackleton	4	b Cannings		0
†B Taylor	lbw b Heath	35	run out		17
*DJ Insole	b Heath	14	b Shackleton		0
TE Bailey	b Heath	59	not out		71
MJ Bear	b Cannings	2	c Sainsbury b Shackleton		1
GJ Smith	c Harrison b Shackleton	5	lbw b Shackleton		4
AW Durley	b Heath	4	c Eagar b Cannings		11
LHR Ralph	b Sainsbury	1	b Sainsbury		16
KC Preston	b Sainsbury	1	b Shackleton		0
IM King	not out	0	c Eagar b Heath		9
Extras		0	(5 b, 7 lb)		12
Total	(all out, 80.2 overs)	**130**	(all out, 75.4 overs)		**141**

Fall: 1st inns: 1-9, 2-9, 3-40, 4-87, 5-94, 6-105, 7-117, 8-118, 9-120, 10-130. **2nd inns:** 1-0, 2-0, 3-0, 4-37, 5-44, 6-48, 7-75, 8-105, 9-112, 10-141.
Bowling: 1st inns: Shackleton 16-6-37-2, Cannings 16-10-15-2, Sainsbury 24-10-41-2, Heath 24.2-9-37-4.
2nd inns: Shackleton 26-6-47-5, Cannings 27-14-30-2, Sainsbury 4-3-4-1, Heath 18.4-1-48-1.

HAMPSHIRE

RE Marshall	b Bailey	4	c Taylor b Bailey		6
JR Gray	lbw b Bailey	2	c King b Bailey		40
H Horton	run out	1	c Taylor b Bailey		7
PJ Sainsbury	b Ralph	5	lbw b Preston		3
HM Barnard	c King b Insole	26	b Bailey		15
ACD Ingleby-Mackenzie	not out	37	c Taylor b Bailey		23
†L Harrison	b Insole	8	b Bailey		5
*EDR Eagar	c Taylor b Bailey	0	c Insole b King		3
D Shackleton	lbw b Bailey	5	not out		7
VHD Cannings	b Bailey	7	b Bailey		2
MB Heath	c Insole b Bailey	0	c Taylor b Bailey		0
Extras	(4 b, 10 lb)	14	(4 b, 1 lb)		5
Total	(all out, 47 overs)	**109**	(all out, 58.5 overs)		**116**

Fall: 1st inns: 1-5, 2-8, 3-9, 4-27, 5-72, 6-82, 7-83, 8-89, 9-109, 10-109. **2nd inns:** 1-6, 2-26, 3-34, 4-62, 5-95, 6-100, 7-103, 8-103, 9-116, 10-116.
Bowling: 1st inns: Bailey 17-5-32-6, Preston 14-5-30-0, Ralph 9-2-19-1, Insole 7-1-14-2.
2nd inns: Bailey 23.5-7-49-8, Preston 17-6-31-1, Ralph 8-1-21-0, Insole 4-1-3-0, King 6-3-7-1.

immediately provided a stubborn and effective obstacle to the opposition's hopes of improving further their situation by contributing more than half of his side's second innings total and being still unbeaten when the tenth wicket fell.

Hampshire needed 163 to win but soon after they began their pursuit, Bailey removed opener Roy Marshall and Henry Horton to inspire the home side although Jimmy Gray put up a brave fight and was 30 not out with Hampshire 61-3 at the close of the second day. Bailey though was determined to ensure his personal efforts underpinned victory for his side and he capped a wonderful performance by taking another six wickets for 28 more runs on the final day to finish with 8-49 leading his side to victory by 46 runs. The match was completed before lunch on the third day and upon its conclusion, the all-rounder strode through a lane of applauding players from both sides. The match generated £539 10s 6d (£539.52p) in gate receipts with an attendance of 4,292 present on the first day (Saturday), 1,964 on Monday and only 295 paying customers on Tuesday – the third and final day

County Championship
Essex v Surrey

Venue: Vista Road Recreation Ground, Clacton-on-Sea **Result:** Essex won by 2 wickets

Surrey were the elite side of the fifties and had already retained their County Championship crown for the seventh successive season by the time they arrived at the Vista Road ground. Both teams were lacking an England international player with Peter May missing from the Surrey team whilst Trevor Bailey was an absentee from the Essex side. The visitors showed their quality when, after declaring on 367-7, they gained a first innings lead of 133 runs by

tea on the second day. Against a Surrey attack that was the most potent in the county game and included pace men Alec Bedser and Peter Loader plus leading spinners Jim Laker and Tony Lock – all England Test players – Essex had still wanted 86 to make their opponents bat again when the sixth wicket fell but Bill Greensmith and Geoff Smith added 46 before Roy Ralph joined Greensmith to avert the follow-on.

Just after tea on the second day, Surrey began their second innings but facing some lively bowling from Ken Preston supported by good fielding, they were given a jolt losing half their side for 49 runs in 85 minutes with Preston taking 4-24, the last three in 11 balls without cost. By the close the champions were 61-5 and they failed to show any marked improvement the following morning after leg-spinner Greensmith removed the hitherto resilient Arthur McIntyre with the last three wickets falling for six runs to leave Essex a challenging 253 runs for victory.

Bill Greensmith: claimed vital wickets with his leg-spin and contributed useful runs towards his side's victory

The omens for the home side were not promising when the new ball pair of Loader and Bedser struck early to reduce the hosts to 22-3 with defeat apparently beckoning. However, Doug Insole, cutting and driving forcefully, redeemed the parlous situation combining in a fourth wicket partnership with Les Savill that produced 81 runs in 85 minutes before Bedser broke the stand when he struck Savill on his pads. Greensmith contributed useful runs to keep the victory hopes alive but it was after Insole teamed-up with left-hander Mickey Bear for a sixth wicket stand that yielded 82 runs in three-quarters of

Writing about the match in the *Essex CCC Handbook 1971*, Doug Insole recalled: "I choose this from a whole lot of enjoyable and memorable matches because I regard it as perhaps the most meritorious victory by an Essex team during my time as a player. Wisden calls it "this remarkable victory," and it was certainly nothing less. Two important wickets by Bill Greensmith, together with a couple of smart run outs, helped to get rid of Surrey for 119, leaving us to score 253 to win in just under four hours. I witnessed the winning hit and was delighted to watch a mixture of hats, scorecards, year books and other miscellaneous objects go into the air when the deed was done. It was a match in which every one of our players made a worthwhile contribution and on this kind of occasion, there is in the dressing room a particular and almost indescribable brand of quiet elation which is in its way unforgettable."

Toss: Surrey won the toss and decided to bat.
Umpires: WE Phillipson, W Place.

SURREY

MJ Stewart	c King b Insole	66	c Taylor b Ralph	8
TH Clark	c Taylor b Preston	17	c Taylor b Preston	0
B Constable	c Savill b Preston	105	lbw b Preston	19
KF Barrington	not out	129	c Taylor b Preston	16
DGW Fletcher	c Taylor b Preston	13	c Ralph b Preston	0
EA Bedser	b Ralph	13	b Ralph	15
†AJW McIntyre	run out	5	c Preston b Greensmith	41
GAR Lock	c sub b Ralph	0	run out	1
JC Laker	not out	4	not out	13
PJ Loader	did not bat		c King b Greensmith	0
*AV Bedser	did not bat		run out	0
Extras	(5 b, 9 lb, 1 w)	15	(1 b, 5 lb)	6
Total	**(7 wickets, declared, 125 overs)**	**367**	**(all out, 51.3 overs)**	**119**

Fall: 1st inns: 1-29, 2-143, 3-260, 4-304, 5-327, 6-345, 7-346. **2nd inns:** 1-0, 2-18, 3-42, 4-44, 5-49, 6-67, 7-68, 8-113, 9-119, 10-119.
Bowling: 1st inns: Preston 36-5-88-3, Ralph 36-6-122-2, Insole 18-4-31-1, King 22-8-52-0, Greensmith 13-0-59-0. **2nd inns:** Preston 25.3-6-59-4, Ralph 18-3-48-2, Insole 5-3-3-0, Greensmith 3-2-3-2.

ESSEX

TC Dodds	run out	21	c Lock b Loader	8
G Barker	b Laker	66	c Laker b Loader	2
†B Taylor	b AV Bedser	10	c Barrington b AV Bedser	7
*DJ Insole	c Stewart b Laker	21	b AV Bedser	115
LA Savill	c Barrington b Laker	6	lbw b AV Bedser	32
WT Greensmith	c Barrington b AV Bedser	43	c Lock b Laker	18
MJ Bear	lbw b AV Bedser	1	c Fletcher b Loader	41
GJ Smith	c Fletcher b Lock	25	c McIntyre b AV Bedser	3
LHR Ralph	c Fletcher b AV Bedser	22	not out	2
KC Preston	b AV Bedser	8	not out	8
IM King	not out	1	did not bat	
Extras	(3 b, 6 lb, 1 nb)	10	(6 b, 14 lb)	20
Total	**(all out, 90.3 overs)**	**234**	**(8 wickets, 65.5 overs)**	**256**

Fall: 1st inns: 1-35, 2-49, 3-103, 4-124, 5-129, 6-132, 7-178, 8-224, 9-225, 10-234. **2nd inns:** 1-9, 2-16, 3-22, 4-103, 5-149, 6-231, 7-245, 8-245.
Bowling: 1st inns: Loader 16-2-48-0, AV Bedser 25.3-7-49-5, Lock 23-5-79-1, Laker 20-7-38-3, EA Bedser 6-3-10-0. **2nd inns:** Loader 17.5-3-60-3, AV Bedser 21-2-61-4, Lock 12-1-54-0, Laker 14-2-54-1, EA Bedser 1-0-7-0.

an hour that really raised the hopes. Insole hit a superb 115 and was sixth out with Essex needing 22 more runs but the loss of two wickets with the score on 245 left the match tantalisingly poised. However, 32 year-old Preston and 37 year-old Roy Ralph called on their experience remaining unruffled and victory was secured with two wickets and 20 minutes to spare when Preston produced a flashing cover drive off Loader that raced to the boundary.

The win was greeted enthusiastically by members with car hooters and vociferous celebrations heralding the unexpected but welcome triumph. The victory left Essex in an acceptable final position of fifth in the Championship table having won 11 of their 28 matches although Surrey were runaway winners of the competition with a massive 312 points after 21 victories and just three defeats. Pleasingly, Essex had provided plenty of entertainment during the summer as they continued their nomadic existence taking the game around the county. The two matches at each of the Romford, Brentwood, Colchester and Clacton festivals all finished with victories for the home side.

County Championship

Essex v Gloucestershire

3-day match **Venue:** County Ground, Leyton **Result:** Match tied

Opening bowler Ken Preston chose this game as his Benefit match and could not have scripted a more enthralling outcome. Disappointingly, he was forced to miss the fixture due to injury although he did appear as a substitute fielder. Gloucestershire's prolific England batsman Tom Graveney was also an absentee but the visitors arrived at the County Ground enjoying a good run of form. Essex were captained by Doug Insole, who had taken over from Tom Pearce in 1951 and under his stewardship, the County played highly attractive cricket during the fifties and won the trophy for the fastest scoring rate on two occasions. Their reputation as an excellent fielding side also prospered.

Although the outfield was rough and bumpy, the Leyton pitch was good offering a bit of pace and even bounce. Insole provided the defining contribution with a quite brilliant unbeaten 177, the fiftieth first-class century of his career and he was accompanied by Trevor Bailey in a fourth wicket partnership of 175 runs. Insole was able to declare before the close of play allowing Barry Knight to remove prolific Martin Young as Gloucestershire reached 31-1.

Essex continued to enjoy the better of the next day's action gaining a 35 runs advantage on first innings after the visitors lower order managed to add just over 100 runs. Insole again dominated the play in the home side's second innings with 90 out of 176 whilst the next highest contribution came from Bill Greensmith who scored 28 not out. After discussions between the two captains during lunch on the third day, Essex declared for the second time in the match setting their opponents 212 in 170 minutes and the target looked highly unlikely when the West Country outfit slumped to 131-8. However, Tony Brown chose the moment to surpass his previous highest first-class score hitting 91 in 85 minutes including four sixes and ten fours. He and Barrie Meyer put on 78 runs that took Gloucestershire to

Ken Preston: the beneficiary could not have scripted a more thrilling finish to the match

Gloucestershire's Tony Brown recalled the closing stages of the match when contributing to the *Essex CCC Yearbook 1989*. "Wickets went down regularly until Barrie Meyer came in," he wrote. "I had been having a bit of a dart at Bill Greensmith with fortuitous effect so Barrie said, 'You keep slogging, I'll block and we'll run for everything.' That tactic worked quite well and we put on 50 or 60 in quick time. The match was nicely poised. Trevor Bailey then bowled me a shortish, wide ball. I could see the winning four written all over it but in attempting to smash it past cover, all I did was nick it to 'Tonker' Taylor. I was upset with myself for getting out when victory was in sight. Bemoaning my stupidity as I drove the baggage van back to Gloucestershire, Arthur Milton, my co-driver consoled me by saying, 'Don't worry about it. Just think what a fine game it was; too good a match for either side to win or lose.'"

Toss: Essex won the toss and decided to bat.
Umpires: AE Fagg, TW Spencer.

ESSEX

LA Savill	c Brown b Allen	25		b Brown	10
G Barker	c Mortimore b Brown	6		did not bat	
†B Taylor	c Brown b Allen	74	(4)	b Brown	6
*DJ Insole	not out	177	(5)	c Cook b Brown	90
TE Bailey	c Meyer b Bernard	50	(6)	c Milton b Bernard	10
CCP Williams	b Brown	3	(7)	c Meyer b Smith	1
J Milner	c Milton b Brown	6	(2)	c Meyer b Brown	11
BR Knight	not out	17		c Meyer b Smith	0
LHR Ralph	did not bat		(3)	b Bernard	13
WT Greensmith	did not bat			not out	28
A Hurd	did not bat			did not bat	
Extras	(5 lb, 1 nb)	6		(2 b, 2 lb, 3 nb)	7
Total	**(6 wickets, declared, 118 overs)**	**364**		**(8 wickets, declared, 62.5 overs)**	**176**

Fall: 1st inns: 1-16, 2-101, 3-114, 4-289, 5-305, 6-325. **2nd inns:** 1-21, 2-22, 3-31, 4-59, 5-82, 6-83, 7-109, 8-176.
Bowling: 1st inns: Smith 23-2-86-0, Brown 24-4-66-3, Milton 2-0-13-0, Cook 20-11-38-0, Mortimore 28-7-82-0, Allen 8-4-6-2, Bernard 13-1-67-1. **2nd inns:** Smith 22-8-44-2, Brown 18.5-2-60-4, Cook 8-1-22-0, Allen 6-0-20-0, Bernard 8-1-23-2.

GLOUCESTERSHIRE

DM Young	b Knight	14		c Ralph b Bailey	0
*CA Milton	c Ralph b Knight	99		run out	23
RB Nicholls	c Taylor b Hurd	64		c Milner b Knight	41
JB Mortimore	c Taylor b Hurd	30		c Williams b Ralph	12
D Carpenter	c and b Greensmith	1		b Greensmith	13
AS Brown	b Knight	35		c Taylor b Bailey	91
JR Bernard	c Insole b Bailey	9	(8)	b Knight	1
DA Allen	c Bailey b Greensmith	37	(9)	lbw b Knight	5
DR Smith	c Williams b Knight	1	(7)	c Taylor b Greensmith	6
†BJ Meyer	c Taylor b Greensmith	21		not out	13
C Cook	not out	0		c Milner b Knight	0
Extras	(3 b, 12 lb, 3 nb)	18		(4 lb, 1 nb, 1 w)	6
Total	**(all out, 125.2 overs)**	**329**		**(all out, 46.4 overs)**	**211**

Fall: 1st inns: 1-19, 2-133, 3-199, 4-211, 5-238, 6-263, 7-267, 8-276, 9-326, 10-329. **2nd inns:** 1-0, 2-61, 3-73, 4-82, 5-104, 6-110, 7-111, 8-131, 9-209, 10-211.
Bowling: 1st inns: Bailey 29-5-74-1, Knight 25-4-69-4, Ralph 23-6-56-0, Greensmith 30.2-4-80-3, Hurd 18-6-32-2. **2nd inns:** Bailey 14-1-46-2, Knight 17.4-2-64-4, Ralph 7-1-30-1, Greensmith 8-1-65-2.

within three runs of victory with two wickets standing and at that juncture, and with a last throw of the dice, Essex took the new ball.

It provided the breakthrough that they were desperately seeking. Bailey sent down a short and wider delivery to Brown who attempted to drive it past cover for the winning runs but only succeeded in nicking the ball off the toe end of the bat to Brian Taylor behind the stumps. Amidst great tension, Bailey then sent down a wide to last batsman Sam Cook before his final delivery of the over had the batsman groping at a perfect away swinger that missed everything. Meyer then edged the first ball of Knight's over to Alan Hurd at third man where the fielder, on the poor outfield, did well to prevent a second run. With pressure high and the scores level, Knight produced a good length inswinger to Cook that lifted onto the batsman's glove and bat handle. Joe Milner, one of three short leg fielders, dived forward to complete a wonderful left-handed catch and the match was tied. Both teams earned 6 points for the result but Essex received two further points allocated at that time for first innings lead.

County Championship
Essex v Middlesex

3-day match **Venue:** Old County Ground, Brentwood **Result:** Essex won by 10 wickets

A recruit to the County this season was former England off-spin bowler Jim Laker. He had retired from the Surrey staff at the end of the 1959 season and went off to play for Norton in the North Staffordshire and District League. Now 40 years of age, he had intimated that he would enjoy a return to the first-class game and Essex were able to negotiate a deal with the legendary bowler that would see him play as an amateur. It was to prove a successful relationship between club and player with Laker heading the bowling averages at the end of the season with 51 wickets to finish sixth in the national averages and higher than any of his off-spin successors in the England team.

However, he was not to prove influential in this match when Essex were led by Ken Preston, deputising for Trevor Bailey who had split a finger when taking a catch in the previous match at Derby. Middlesex had won the toss and elected to bat but the fast pitch offering bounce caused all manner of problems for the visiting batsmen with the last six wickets realising only 37 runs against the lively Barry Knight and medium-pacer Brian Edmeades. Seven batsmen were dismissed for single figure scores whilst only Fred Titmus managed to exceed 16 runs for the discomforted visiting side as Knight took his tally of first-class wickets for the season to 50 when taking his fifth wicket.

Barry Knight: underpinned the win with a century and 7 wickets

The home side started their reply soon after lunch on the opening day and passed the Middlesex score with only three wickets down. Geoff Smith made a painstaking half-century that helped lay the foundations for a winning total but Essex then faltered to 162-5 before Knight again took centre-stage. Timing the ball to perfection and driving with impressive authority, he set a new personal best score and together with Roger Luckin, who also reached a career-best, the pair posted 206 for the sixth wicket to equal the record figure set by J.W.H.T. Douglas and Jack O'Connor against Gloucestershire in 1923. Luckin was a youngster from Felsted School and showed

Highlighting the record equalling partnership between Barry Knight and Roger Luckin, *The Times* correspondent stated, "This was gay adventurous cricket and a crowd firmly behind Essex on the loveliest of grounds absorbed it all to the full stroke by stroke. It was a magnificent innings by Knight during which he collared all of the Middlesex bowlers in turn, none of whom will want to have too much to do with bowling figures. He hit 3 sixes and 24 fours in just under 3 hours. He is an invigorating cricketer because he plays his shots all the time and misses his fair share but as likely as not, he will hit the next ball for 4 or even 6 with considerable power and the highest degree of technical skill and beauty. One flashing cut was reminiscent of the flexible wrists of L.Constantine. In this frame of mind, bowlers had no idea where to bowl to him."

Toss: Middlesex won the toss and decided to bat.
Umpires: HG Baldwin, HE Hammond.

MIDDLESEX

RA Gale	lbw b Knight	6	b Greensmith	29
WE Russell	b Preston	0	st Taylor b Greensmith	80
SEJ Russell	c Taylor b Knight	10	c Smith b Laker	6
RW Hooker	b Knight	6	b Knight	102
FJ Titmus	c Taylor b Edmeades	48	lbw b Greensmith	0
RA White	c Greensmith b Edmeades	16	lbw b Greensmith	1
MJ Smith	c Knight b Edmeades	8	c and b Greensmith	41
†JT Murray	b Knight	2	c Taylor b Greensmith	32
D Bennett	not out	14	not out	24
*PI Bedford	b Knight	1	c Taylor b Greensmith	4
AE Moss	c Preston b Knight	4	c Edmeades b Greensmith	2
Extras		0	(10 b, 3 lb)	13
Total	**(all out, 42.4 overs)**	**115**	**(all out, 114.4 overs)**	**334**

Fall: 1st inns: 1-6, 2-14, 3-16, 4-41, 5-78, 6-86, 7-95, 8-109, 9-111, 10-115. **2nd inns:** 1-76, 2-91, 3-152, 4-222, 5-228, 6-230, 7-296, 8-310, 9-320, 10-334.
Bowling: 1st inns: Knight 17.4-3-50-6, Preston 15-2-42-1, Edmeades 10-1-23-3. **2nd inns:** Knight 21-3-78-1, Preston 13-1-45-0, Edmeades 7-1-10-0, Greensmith 39.4-8-116-8, Laker 34-5-72-1.

ESSEX

G Barker	c Murray b Moss	25	not out	11
MJ Bear	c White b Titmus	27	not out	15
GJ Smith	c Murray b Bennett	56	did not bat	
BEA Edmeades	c Hooker b Titmus	11	did not bat	
†B Taylor	c Murray b Hooker	25	did not bat	
BR Knight	c White b Smith	165	did not bat	
RAG Luckin	c Murray b Moss	82	did not bat	
PA Spicer	not out	27	did not bat	
WT Greensmith	not out	1	did not bat	
JC Laker	did not bat		did not bat	
*KC Preston	did not bat		did not bat	
Extras	(2 b, 4 lb)	6	(1 lb)	1
Total	**(7 wickets, declared, 137 overs)**	**425**	**(no wicket, 6.3 overs)**	**27**

Fall: 1st inns: 1-42, 2-67, 3-87, 4-136, 5-162, 6-368, 7-424. **2nd inns:** 1-45, 2-114, 3-139, 4-160, 5-203.
Bowling: 1st inns: Moss 33-6-71-2, Bennett 17-3-56-1, Hooker 33-5-110-1, Titmus 26-7-72-2, Smith 19-7-59-1, Bedford 9-2-51-0. **2nd inns:** Gale 3.3-1-16-0, Smith 3-0-10-0.

superb technique with a penchant to play on the front foot and his contribution allowed the home side to declare with a lead of 310 runs and all recorded on the new mobile scoreboard which was to become a feature on all Essex festival grounds in the ensuing years.

Middlesex proved doughty fighters but leg-spinner Bill Greensmith was to grab the plaudits for his exploits during the visitors second innings. He wheeled away to telling effect mixing his leg breaks and googlies to claim eight wickets for 116 that included his fiftieth first-class victim for the season whilst Laker managed just one wicket in 34 overs. At one stage, Middlesex were 222-3 but Greensmith produced an incisive spell of three wickets for 5 runs removing Mike Smith, Fred Titmus and Bob White to reduce the visitors to 230-6. At lunch they had moved onto 270-6 but Knight ended the valiant resistance of Ron Hooker, who had scored 102, when he was bowled although useful contributions elsewhere in the order ensured that the home side would need to bat again. Requiring only 25 runs for victory, Essex completed the task inside seven overs without losing a wicket and facing an old ball.

Tour Match

Essex v Australians

Venue: Southchurch Park, Southend-on-Sea **Result:** Essex won by 6 wickets

Sixteen years after the famous match at Southchurch Park featured earlier in this book, the Australians, who were to prove the masters of England in the Ashes Series during the summer, returned to the same seaside venue no doubt expecting another rewarding experience. Instead, they were defeated when the County produced a magnificent performance to overturn their elitist opponents. In blistering hot temperatures that soared into the nineties, on a low and slow wicket, 1,065 runs were scored in the match for a total of 30 wickets, with the impressive Essex attack accounting for 20 victims.

Paddy Phelan: claimed 10 wickets with his off-breaks that spurred his side towards a memorable victory

Captained by Trevor Bailey, Essex won the toss and enjoyed a wonderful opening day with Gordon Barker and Keith Fletcher recording fine centuries and combining for a superb third-wicket partnership worth 184 runs with Barker consistently earning runs with the "lap-shot" against the Aussie spinners. Later John Wilcox, son of former Essex captain Denys Wilcox, and Brian Edmeades added an unbroken 83 for the seventh wicket before the declaration came at the overnight 425-6.

The second day saw the home side again rule proceedings, this time with the ball. Bailey had the obdurate Bill Lawry caught by wicket-keeper Brian Taylor cheaply and although eight of the Aussie batsmen played themselves in, none reached a score of 40 as spinner Paddy Phelan provided plenty of problems whilst the economic Ken Preston also took three wickets to give the home side a first innings lead of 207 runs. Bailey immediately enforced the follow-on but there was a more solid application from the tourists second time around. Three batsmen reached half-centuries although Essex retained the upper hand with the Aussies losing six wickets before the arrears had been cleared. An entertaining innings from Graham McKenzie, who launched three sixes and four other boundaries before falling one run short of his half-century, added some substance to the total although

Quoted in the *1988 Essex Handbook*, Brian Booth, captaining Australia in this match recalled, "When Trevor Bailey and his team celebrated their well deserved victory in 1964, I did not fully realise the true significance of the occasion at the time. As the crowd gathered enthusiastically around the pavilion and Trevor Bailey and others spoke, I sensed at the time more than joy over beating the Australian tourists of 1964. Other county sides had already done this earlier in the tour and under my captaincy! I knew it was sweet revenge for the heavy defeat suffered by Essex in 1948. What I did not know at the time was that this was the first win by Essex over Australia since 1905. I have fond memories of a picturesque ground, the friendliness of the crowd, the double-decked pavilion, walking out to toss with Trevor Bailey and a pitch conducive to spin. I also recall a competitive game of cricket played in a marvellous sporting spirit."

Toss: Essex won the toss and decided to bat.
Umpires: AE Fagg, WFF Price.

ESSEX

G Barker	b McKenzie	123	c Booth b Cowper		9
MJ Bear	b Connolly	2	run out		26
†B Taylor	b Connolly	29	lbw b Potter		33
KWR Fletcher	b Cowper	125	not out		19
*TE Bailey	c Sellers b O'Neill	22	st Grout b Booth		15
BR Knight	b Martin	15	not out		4
JWT Wilcox	not out	46	did not bat		
BEA Edmeades	not out	53	did not bat		
PJ Phelan	did not bat		did not bat		
RNS Hobbs	did not bat		did not bat		
KC Preston	did not bat		did not bat		
Extras	(9 b, 1 lb)	10	(3 lb)		3
Total	**(6 wickets, declared, 113 overs)**	**425**	**(4 wickets, 30 overs)**		**109**

Fall: 1st inns: 1-6, 2-42, 3-226, 4-257, 5-301, 6-342. **2nd inns:** 1-9, 2-67, 3-74, 4-105.
Bowling: 1st inns: McKenzie 22-6-62-1, Connolly 17-3-68-2, Cowper 18-6-61-1, Martin 17-2-78-1, Sellers 19-1-75-0, O'Neill 14-1-52-1, Potter-6-1-19-0. **2nd inns:** McKenzie 3-0-12-0, Connolly 6-2-18-0, Cowper 8-2-35-1, O'Neill 6-1-19-0, Potter 5-1-13-1, Booth 2-0-9-1.

AUSTRALIANS

			(FOLLOWING ON)	
WM Lawry	c Taylor b Bailey	6	b Phelan	52
RM Cowper	b Hobbs	39	c Fletcher b Phelan	28
NCL O'Neill	c Hobbs b Preston	26	c Fletcher b Phelan	52
J Potter	b Phelan	19	lbw b Phelan	8
*BC Booth	c Barker b Phelan	28	c and b Preston	95
PJP Burge	b Phelan	27	c Knight b Phelan	0
†ATW Grout	c Edmeades b Phelan	17	c Knight b Hobbs	4
JW Martin	b Preston	18	c Taylor b Knight	19
GD McKenzie	c Barker b Phelan	22	c Bear b Hobbs	49
RHD Sellers	c Bailey b Preston	4	not out	0
AN Connolly	not out	0	c Preston b Hobbs	1
Extras	(7 b, 3 lb, 2 nb)	12	(5 lb)	5
Total	**(all out, 73.2 overs)**	**218**	**(all out, 92.4 overs)**	**313**

Fall: 1st inns: 1-9, 2-51, 3-80, 4-116, 5-126, 6-146, 7-187, 8-206, 9-218, 10-218. **2nd inns:** 1-69, 2-114, 3-119, 4-155, 5-179, 6-194, 7-238, 8-312, 9-312, 10-313.
Bowling: 1st inns: Knight 15-3-30-0, Bailey 16-6-37-1, Preston 11-2-27-3, Phelan 22.2-1-94-5, Hobbs 9-3-18-1.
2nd inns: Knight 6-2-11-1, Bailey 12-1-30-0, Preston 12-0-40-1, Phelan 36-4-154-5, Hobbs 26.4-8-73-3.

Phelan continued to trouble the visitors adding another five-wicket haul to mirror his first innings achievement whilst leg-spinner Robin Hobbs weighed in with three wickets.

Needing only 107 for victory in two hours and five minutes, Essex lost Barker with nine runs on the board but Taylor produced a tenacious innings, cutting and hooking freely that saw him collect seven boundaries in his 33 out of the 58 runs achieved a second wicket partnership with Mickey Bear spanning 45 minutes. By tea, only 28 further runs were required and Fletcher and Bailey quickly collected five boundaries between them before Bailey was stumped with two runs needed. Barry Knight immediately launched the winning blow and Essex were able to celebrate their first victory over Australia in almost 60 years. The result avenged the heavy defeats suffered by the County against the tourists at the same venue in 1948, 1953 and 1956 and the only consolation for their skipper Brian Booth was his dismissal of Bailey with an off-break, his only wicket of the tour. "Although I did not manage quantity with my bowling, I like to think that in gaining Trevor's wicket, I at least gained quality," the bowler said afterwards.

Tour Match

Essex v New Zealanders

3-day match **Venue:** Chalkwell Park, Westcliff-on-Sea **Result:** Essex won by 15 runs

Spin held sway in this tourist match at Westcliff as the County became the only team to beat the New Zealanders in a first-class game outside the Test series (which England won 2-0). Twenty-five victims were claimed by the slow bowlers on either side as Essex ran out narrow winners despite setting the opposition little over 100 to win in the last innings. New Zealand dominated on day one, dismissing the hosts for 121 and then equalling their total by the close for the loss of just three wickets. Ray East then began what turned into a fine all-round display when the left-arm spinner bowled unchanged on day two for figures of 19-9-23-4 to finish with 6-49. Leg-spinner Robin Hobbs also caused considerable trouble to the tourists but his figures were spoiled by Dick Motz, who swung lustily to take the tourists past the 200-mark.

New Zealand's ascendancy had started to recede from the off on the second day as skipper Graham Dowling, who was on 61 overnight, added only four runs in 45 minutes before falling to East. All the remaining batsmen found themselves bewitched by the Essex spinners, save for the big-hitting Motz, who struck Hobbs for four sixes and two fours in rapid succession. As Hobbs recalls, "I was hit for the biggest six of my career in that game by Dick Motz – it was enormous, soaring down the road towards Hadleigh!"

Ray East:
outstanding
all-round display

New Zealand had a capable slow bowler of their own in the shape of Hedley Howarth, and the left-armer seemingly turned the game decisively in his team's favour when he picked up five wickets for six runs in nine overs on the final day. In all, Howarth returned career-best – at the time – figures of 7-43 from 44 overs to leave the tourists needing only 113 for victory. However, even that meagre total was manna from heaven to the home side as they had led by only 22 runs with eight second-innings wickets down until East struck a career-

In a match full of twists and turns, there remained time for a lighter moment when Robin Hobbs suffered the ignominy of being given out by the umpire standing at square-leg. The leg-spinner recalls: "Arthur Jepson had the habit [when standing at the non-striker's end] of raising his finger at the end of every over after he tossed the last stone from one hand to the other. Hedley Howarth bowled the last ball, it hit me on the pad well outside the line and I assumed Arthur's finger went up as a matter of habit at the end of the over. I asked their wicketkeeper [Barry Milburn] if the ball was going to hit and he said it was missing another set of stumps. But when Arthur took his place at square-leg, at the start of the next over, he raised his finger again and said 'hey, you're out, get out!'. Ray East, who was batting at the other end and always the joker, joined in the chorus and was also shouting at me, 'go on, away you go, stop cheating!'. It was quite extraordinary really."

Toss: Essex won the toss and decided to bat.
Umpires: A Jepson, AEG Rhodes.

ESSEX

B Ward	lbw b Collinge	26	c Burgess b Cunis		33
BEA Edmeades	c Milburn b Collinge	0	c Turner b Howarth		43
G Barker	c Congdon b Cunis	6	c Cunis b Howarth		3
KWR Fletcher	c Collinge b Motz	8	c Hastings b Howarth		6
BL Irvine	c Hastings b Burgess	31	c Congdon b Howarth		4
KD Boyce	c Milburn b Collinge	19	c Burgess b Cunis		2
*†B Taylor	c Milburn b Motz	26	c Turner b Howarth		1
RNS Hobbs	c Dowling b Burgess	0	lbw b Howarth		6
RE East	c Milburn b Motz	0	c Dowling b Howarth		58
JK Lever	b Motz	0	c Congdon b Collinge		20
DL Acfield	not out	2	not out		7
Extras	(2 lb, 1 nb)	3	(1 b, 6 lb, 2 nb)		9
Total	**(all out, 56.5 overs)**	**121**	**(all out, 121 overs)**		**192**

Fall: 1st inns: 1-9, 2-16, 3-37, 4-53, 5-77, 6-117, 7-118, 8-119, 9-119, 10-121. **2nd inns:** 1-62, 2-67, 3-82, 4-89, 5-94, 6-94, 7-95, 8-102, 9-160, 10-192.
Bowling: 1st inns: Collinge 15 3-56-3, Cunis 18-9-20-1, Motz 13.5-2-29-4, Howarth 4-1-10-0, Burgess 6-3-3-2. **2nd inns:** Collinge 23-8-28-1, Cunis 19-5-35-2, Motz 20-6-42-0, Howarth 44-25-43-7, Burgess 15-3-35-0.

NEW ZEALANDERS

*GT Dowling	c Fletcher b East	65	c Acfield b Lever		2
GM Turner	lbw b Boyce	18	b Acfield		11
BE Congdon	b East	21	c Acfield b East		1
MG Burgess	lbw b East	4	c East b Hobbs		13
BF Hastings	lbw b Hobbs	17	c Irvine b Acfield		17
KJ Wadsworth	c Barker b East	7	b Acfield		4
RC Motz	c Hobbs b Boyce	40	c Fletcher b Hobbs		0
RS Cunis	st Taylor b East	9	lbw b Hobbs		8
RO Collinge	b East	7	b East		15
HJ Howarth	st Taylor b Hobbs	2	c Boyce b Hobbs		1
†BD Milburn	not out	0	not out		17
Extras	(4 b, 4 lb, 3 nb)	11	(5 b, 2 nb, 1 w)		8
Total	**(all out, 86.1 overs)**	**201**	**(all out, 40 overs)**		**97**

Fall: 1st inns: 1-46, 2-86, 3-92, 4-128, 5-137, 6-142, 7-182, 8-190, 9-201, 10-201. **2nd inns:** 1-5, 2-10, 3-24, 4-34, 5-38, 6-40, 7-56, 8-60, 9-61, 10-97.
Bowling: 1st inns: Boyce 17-5-36-2, Lever 13-4-24-0, East 32-13-49-6, Edmeades 5-0-24-0, Hobbs 19.1-8-57-2.
2nd inns: Boyce 3-2-1-0, Lever 2-1-1-1, East 7-2-19-2, Hobbs 12-3-31-4, Acfield 16-3-37-3.

best at the time of 58. With plenty of time to knock off the runs, there seemed little prospect of Essex claiming their first win over a New Zealand touring side for 42 years. Yet after John Lever made the initial breakthrough, spin was introduced into the attack after five overs and remained the effective order of the day until the close.

With wickets falling at regular intervals, Essex's chances improved rapidly but, as Hobbs recalled in the *1985 Essex Handbook*, the match was still in the balance while his first-innings nemesis was at the crease: "I can remember being very apprehensive when Dick Motz came in...He was the one man on the New Zealand side who could change the course of the match within the space of just two overs. This time his luck was out, he took a great heave at a wide leg-spinner which Keith Fletcher caught at slip. From then on we were in the driving seat qnd although, the last wicket put on 30-odd runs, we never felt in danger of losing the match." East fittingly claimed the last wicket to crown a remarkable final day when 18 wickets went down for an aggregate of 211 runs.

John Player League
Lancashire v Essex

40-overs match | **Venue:** Old Trafford, Manchester **Result:** Essex won on faster scoring rate (Run rate)

Essex's best one-day bowling figures – a performance that remained in place at the end of the 2010 season – were recorded as far back as 1971. West Indian overseas pace bowler Keith Boyce may have had the elements to thank in part

Keith Boyce: lethal bowling performance

for his feat but that would be to denigrate unduly a devastating spell of hostile bowling. With the intervention of Manchester rain always a possibility at some point, Lancashire captain Jack Bond did his side no favours by electing to field after winning the toss. Even in an uninterrupted innings allowing the full schedule of overs, the Essex total of 216-4 – only the third of more than 200 against Lancashire in the competition up to that point – would have represented a testing target for the reigning champions. Australian batsman Bruce Francis underpinned the Essex batting effort with 107 – sharing in stands of 85 with Brian Taylor and 112 with Gordon Barker. Francis began scratchily – making just two in the first six overs out of a total of 19 – but of the next 40 his share was 33. The right-hander's effort was punctuated by square cuts and pulls along the way to a maiden limited-overs century for the County that included one six and 13 other boundaries. Robin Hobbs, whose impact on this match was limited by the weather, recalls that Essex's Aussie import played an increasingly influential role in the team during his two seasons with the County (1971 and 1973). When Bruce Francis arrived at Essex he looked like he couldn't play," Hobbs admits. "But, in the last month before he left, he scored almost 1,000 runs and he looked like a high-class batsman by the end of his time with Essex.

Essex leg-spinner Robin Hobbs concedes the one-day laws of the time improved the team's chances of victory as they were able to keep their most potent bowling weapon in the attack for longer than would have been the case under today's rules. "I think we got too many runs anyway but then they ended up needing a crazy reduced target – certainly in those days. The reduction in overs worked very much in our favour. Our captain Brian Taylor had a theory in rotating his bowlers in the Sunday League which he stuck to every game. I remember a game against Northants at Ilford [the week after the Lancashire match] when Keith Boyce and John Lever had them at 11-5. A few of us said to Brian to keep them on for another over each but Brian, who was not very good at maths, had a 4-4-8-8 policy where he bowled the openers for four overs each and then the next two bowlers for eight overs straight. In that match at Lancashire the regulations worked in our favour because it meant that Keith could bowl straight through [at this time the number of overs per bowler were not restricted when the total overs were reduced]."

Toss: Lancashire won the toss and decided to field.
Umpires: A Jepson, AEG Rhodes.

ESSEX

		Runs
BC Francis	c Hughes b Wood	107
*†B Taylor	c and b Hughes	45
G Barker	b Shuttleworth	41
KWR Fletcher	not out	7
KD Boyce	b Lever	4
S Turner	not out	6
GJ Saville	did not bat	
RNS Hobbs	did not bat	
RE East	did not bat	
JK Lever	did not bat	
DL Acfield	did not bat	
Extras	(3 b, 3 lb)	6
Total	**(4 wickets, 38 overs)**	**216**

Fall: 1st inns: 1-85, 2-197, 3-198, 4-203
Bowling: Lever 8-1-41-1, Shuttleworth 7-1-29-1, CH Lloyd 7-0-54-0, Wood 8-0-50-1, Hughes 8-0-36-1.

LANCASHIRE

		Runs
†FM Engineer	b Boyce	7
KL Snellgrove	b Boyce	6
H Pilling	b Lever	10
CH Lloyd	c Hobbs b Boyce	9
J Sullivan	c Fletcher b Lever	19
D Lloyd	c East b Boyce	6
*JD Bond	b Boyce	1
B Wood	c Taylor b Boyce	2
DP Hughes	not out	10
P Lever	b Boyce	2
K Shuttleworth	c Taylor b Boyce	4
Extras	(11 lb)	11
Total	**(all out, 16.4 overs)**	**87**

Fall: 1st inns: 1-11, 2-20, 3-28, 4-52, 5-54, 6-58, 7-70, 8-72, 9-83, 10-87.
Bowling: Boyce 7.4-0-26-8, Lever 8-0-38-2, Turner 1-0-12-0.

He always detested fielding though!" Essex's trump bowling card, Boyce, then set to work by clean bowling Lancashire openers Farokh Engineer and Ken Snellgrove early on in the reply. Lancashire were already in trouble at 20-2 after 6.2 overs when the rain began. Following the loss of an hour's play, the umpires decided there was time for another 10.4 overs. Essex had averaged 5.684 runs per over so to win, Lancashire therefore, needed another 77 runs from the remaining overs (to eclipse Essex's rate over the whole of their innings). John Sullivan (19) briefly threatened to pull off an unlikely victory but when he was caught at long-on by Keith Fletcher – one of six Essex fielders guarding the boundaries – the match swung inexorably towards the fielding side. Twenty three were needed off the last two overs and 14 off the last – at which point nine fielders were positioned on the boundary rope. Off the first ball of the last over, Peter Lever was bowled and then Boyce wrapped up the game off the fourth when Ken Shuttleworth provided wicket-keeper Taylor with his second skier. Boyce became the first bowler to take eight wickets in a John Player League innings and Essex had won for the fifth time in five Sunday matches that season, ending the day joint top with Leicestershire.

Tour Match

Essex v Australians

3-day match

Venue: County Ground, Chelmsford **Result:** Australians won by 98 runs

As with a number of other heroic feats in the County's annals, the batting fireworks provided by Robin Hobbs against the touring Australians of 1975 were unable to prevent an Essex defeat. To make the achievement even more poignant, this was to be the veteran leg-spinner's last home first-class appearance for the Club. Australia entered the match leading 1-0 in their series with England, with the last Test due to start just two days later at the Oval. Seven of the team that would go on to draw the final Test featured at Chelmsford with Rick McCosker, the Chappell brothers and Dennis Lillee given a rest. Alan Turner and Bruce Laird justified the tourists' stand-in captain Rodney Marsh's decision to bat first. Laird went on to reach three figures along with Ross Edwards as the home bowlers were made to toil. Essex reached 75-2 at the close of day one but not out batsman Keith Fletcher was unable

Robin Hobbs:
big hitter

to resume his innings on Monday due to a bruised left shoulder sustained when struck by a ball from Hampshire fast bowler Andy Roberts in the previous day's John Player League match. Graham Gooch joined Ken McEwan in his place and the pair made 75 in 50 minutes. The latter was then bowled middle stump trying to drive Max Walker after hitting 71 in 92 minutes (with 13 fours). Gooch continued to prosper and reached a half-century in 75 minutes which included one six and 10 fours. He was eventually smartly stumped by Richie Robinson off Ashley Mallett, a rare moment of triumph for the off-spinner in a match to forget. Keith Boyce and Neil Smith then compiled a half-century stand in 36 minutes after lunch – Smith hitting 18 off an over by Mallett. The Essex wicket-keeper hit 46 at a run-a-minute (8 x 4) before he was another stumping victim off Mallett. Boyce was run out in the same over in which he hit Mallett for two sixes, putting an end to an innings of 79 made in 88 minutes with three 6's and 10 other boundaries. Essex declared 27 runs behind the tourists having batted for 35 fewer overs as bat continued to dominate ball. The Australians began their second innings with the best opening partnership of the tour, Turner and Laird putting on 185 runs in 147 minutes. Turner, who made his century in 134 minutes (15 x 4) was missed at slip on one but gave no more chances as he reached 116 not out by the close. The left-hander added just two on the final day – David Acfield taking a smart catch at mid-off – but Ross Edwards and Doug Walters then put on 55 in 42 minutes. Walters went on to complete a 50 in 75 minutes (1 x 6, 7 x 4) and was ably supported by Marsh in

Robin Hobbs may have delighted the Chelmsford public on that famous day in 1975 but, as he recalls, his efforts couldn't entirely satisfy everyone: "Off-spinner Ashley Mallett was bowling from the Tom Pearce End and was tearing his hair out, getting increasingly annoyed. But the quicker he bowled the more I deposited him over the boundary. By contrast, Jim Higgs was treating it like a Benefit game and bowling gentle leg-spin. So it was friendly at one end and not so friendly at the other. When I reached my century Marsh said to me 'Ok mate, you've had your fun now get out'. I took that as a sign that he was going to bring Thommo [fast bowler Jeff Thomson] back on so I promptly skied a catch next ball. I got a right dressing-down from [Essex Chairman of the time] Doug Insole when I returned to the dressing-room, saying to me 'well played but you've let your mate down there' [referring to Brian Hardie who was eventually left stranded on 88 not out]."

Toss: Australians won the toss and decided to bat.
Umpires: A Jepson, PB Wight.

AUSTRALIANS

A Turner	lbw b Hobbs	33		c Acfield b Turner	118
BM Laird	c Edmeades b Lever	127		c Smith b Turner	72
*RW Marsh	lbw b Acfield	30	(6)	not out	39
R Edwards	run out	101		c and b Acfield	19
GJ Gilmour	b Lever	2		did not bat	
KD Walters	c Hardie b Hobbs	10	(5)	not out	61
†RD Robinson	not out	39		did not bat	
MHN Walker	not out	4	(3)	lbw b Lever	1
JR Thomson	did not bat			did not bat	
JD Higgs	did not bat			did not bat	
AA Mallett	did not bat			did not bat	
Extras	(2 b, 11 lb, 6 nb)	19		(2 b, 6 lb, 7 nb)	15
Total	**(6 wickets, declared, 101 overs)**	**365**		**(4 wickets, declared, 83 overs)**	**325**

Fall: 1st inns: 1-103, 2-169, 3-243, 4-247, 5-289, 6-350. **2nd inns:** 1-185, 2-192, 3-202, 4-257.
Bowling: 1st inns: Boyce 8-0-39-0, Lever 12-2-35-2, Acfield 31-7-96-1, Turner 11-0-38-0, Edmeades 6-1-22-0, Hobbs 33-5-116-2. **2nd inns:** Lever 17-6-48-1, Acfield 22-4-86-1, Turner 20-3-62-2, Hobbs 11-0-73-0, Gooch 13-2-41-0.

ESSEX

BEA Edmeades	lbw b Walker	15		absent ill	
BR Hardie	b Thomson	8	(1)	not out	88
KS McEwan	b Walker	71		hit wkt b Thomson	3
*KWR Fletcher	retired hurt	24		absent hurt	
GA Gooch	st Robinson b Mallett	68	(4)	lbw b Walker	0
S Turner	b Walker	9	(5)	c Turner b Walker	11
KD Boyce	run out	79	(6)	c Robinson b Walker	11
†N Smith	st Robinson b Mallett	46	(2)	c Higgs b Thomson	24
RNS Hobbs	c Gilmour b Higgs	5	(7)	c Laird b Higgs	100
JK Lever	not out	1	(8)	c Thomson b Higgs	0
DL Acfield	did not bat		(9)	st Robinson b Mallett	10
Extras	(2 lb, 10 nb)	12		(4 lb, 2 nb, 1 w)	7
Total	**(8 wickets, declared, 66 overs)**	**338**		**(all out, 39.4 overs)**	**254**

Fall: 1st inns: 1-15, 2-23, 3-150, 4-194, 5-212, 6-279, 7-324, 8-338. **2nd inns:** 1-42, 2-58, 3-65, 4-95, 5-109, 6-242, 7-243, 8-254.
Bowling: 1st inns: Thomson 12-1-64-1, Walker 19-3-61-3, Higgs 15-1-103-1, Gilmour 2-0-9-0, Mallett 18-2-89-2. **2nd inns:** Thomson 7-0-35-2, Walker 12-2-45-3, Higgs 13-0-91-2, Mallett 7.4-0-76-1.

another half-century stand as the declaration neared. Requiring 353, Essex were hampered in their pursuit by the loss through injury of Fletcher (still absent with his shoulder injury) and Brian Edmeades (illness). The home team's slim victory hopes looked even less likely once pace bowlers Jeff Thomson and Walker reduced them to 109-5. Thereupon Hobbs joined opening batsman Brian Hardie in a sixth-wicket stand of 133 in 44 minutes, the last 26 balls accruing 88 runs including 27 in one Mallett over. Hobbs, whose bowling was his strongest suit, was responsible for 100 runs of the partnership, his contribution equalling his previous highest career score made against Glamorgan in 1968. The right-hander's effort saw him record the sixth fastest century in first-class cricket at the time with Percy Fender's all-time record of 35 minutes for Surrey v Northants in 1920 leading the way. Hobbs's first 50 came up in 32 minutes while his second 50 required just 12 minutes before he was caught in the deep. His 46-ball innings contained seven 6's and 12 other boundaries with his last 50 runs coming off 15 balls, a sequence that ran as follows: 6, 6, 1, 4, 6, 6, 0, 6, 1, 2, 1, 0, 6, 1, 4. Hardie batted throughout the innings of 254 for his 88 not out in 136 minutes (2 x 6, 7 x 4) but he was denied a century when the last three wickets fell in a cluster.

Benson and Hedges Cup, Final

Essex v Surrey

55-overs match **Venue:** Lord's Cricket Ground, St John's Wood **Result:** Essex won by 35 runs

Whilst there were a number of strong candidates that missed the cut for this book, it would have been sacrilegious to omit the match that saw all the ghosts of so many glorious failures of the past finally exorcised. Essex went into the 1979 season on the back of a previous campaign that had maintained their reputation for near-misses – second place in the Championship and a narrow Gillette Cup semi-final loss to Somerset – as they continued to search for a first trophy in their 103 years of existence. As a result, a renewed show of fortitude was required by captain Keith Fletcher to once again rally the troops after a season of 'so near but yet so far'. An impressive start meant Essex travelled to Lord's with a 53-point cushion at the top of the Championship table (with a game in hand on second-placed Somerset). But the three-day game

Thumbs up: Stuart Turner *(left)* and Mike Denness with the Benson & Hedges Cup

could wait as hordes of Essex supporters converged on the home of cricket for the Club's first appearance in a knockout final. Despite still searching for that elusive first piece of silverware, Essex went into the final as favourites against their more exalted opponents – particularly so with West Indian pace bowler Sylvester Clarke out of the game and fellow paceman Robin Jackman restricted by a calf injury. In fact Surrey were odds of 33-1 to win the tournament back in April but, under the management of Mickey Stewart and the captaincy of Roger Knight, their fortunes were improving. Furthermore, up to that point, Surrey had played Essex six times in the B & H Cup and won every match – including the contest on May 7 that year by seven runs. What followed on a balmy July day at Lord's would go down in Essex folklore as the County's openers, Mike Denness and Graham Gooch, took to the field to rapturous applause from an expectant support. After Denness helped Gooch put on 48 in good time, Ken McEwan then joined the latter to add 128 runs in 28 overs. Gooch, who had warmed up with 83 in England's innings and 83-run win against India at Edgbaston, went on to 120 – the highest individual score in the first eight B & H Finals. Treating all bowlers

Essex's centurion Graham Gooch enjoyed numerous matches to remember during a glittering career for Club and country but the triumph over Surrey continues to hold a notable place in his heart: "That was a very special day," Gooch explains. "Most of the players had come through an era with a lot of near misses – second spot in the Championship, seconds in the JPL, cup semi-finals. We were always the bridesmaids so to get home at Lord's in front of a full house – most of the crowd seemed to be supporting Essex – was easily one of the greatest days of my cricket career. Lord's was a good ground to me over my career and that was the start of it. The ovation that myself and Mike Denness received as we came out to bat was a moment I will never forget and to influence the match with a century and bat for a while with Kenny McEwan in a pivotal stand was the icing on the cake for me."

Toss: Surrey won the toss and decided to field.
Umpires: HD Bird, BJ Meyer.

ESSEX

		Runs	Balls	Mins	4s	6s	S-Rate
MH Denness	c Smith b Wilson	24	36	43	4	-	66.67
GA Gooch	b Wilson	120	141	203	11	3	85.11
KS McEwan	c Richards b Wilson	72	99	96	10	-	72.73
*KWR Fletcher	b Knight	34	30	37	3	-	113.33
BR Hardie	c Intikhab Alam b Wilson	4	6	14	-	-	66.67
KR Pont	not out	19	13	19	3	-	146.15
N Phillip	c Howarth b Jackman	2	6	5	-	-	33.33
S Turner	not out	1	2	5	-	-	50.00
†N Smith	did not bat						
RE East	did not bat						
JK Lever	did not bat						
Extras	(3 b, 8 lb, 2 nb, 1 w)	14					
Total	**(6 wickets, 55 overs)**	**290**					

Fall: 1st inns: 1-48, 2-172, 3-239, 4-261, 5-273, 6-276.
Bowling: Jackman 11-0-69-1, Wilson 11-1-56-4, Knight 11-1-40-1, Intikhab Alam 11-0-38-0, Pocock 11-0-73-0.

SURREY

		Runs	Balls	Mins	4s	6s	S-Rate
AR Butcher	c Smith b Lever	13	22	20	2	-	59.09
MA Lynch	c McEwan b East	17	32	53	2	-	53.12
GP Howarth	c Fletcher b Pont	74	99	131	6	-	74.75
*RDV Knight	c Smith b Pont	52	64	66	8	-	81.25
DM Smith	b Phillip	24	34	45	2	-	70.59
GRJ Roope	not out	39	32	64	2	1	121.88
Intikhab Alam	c Pont b Phillip	1	5	9	-	-	20.00
RD Jackman	b East	1	5	3	-	-	20.00
†CJ Richards	b Turner	1	5	5	-	-	20.00
PI Pocock	b Phillip	7	17	21	1	-	41.18
PHL Wilson	b Lever	0	1	3	-	-	0.00
Extras	(4 b, 16 lb, 5 nb, 1 w)	26					
Total	**(all out, 51.4 overs)**	**255**					

Fall: 1st inns: 1-21, 2-45, 3-136, 4-187, 5-205, 6-219, 7-220, 8-226, 9-250, 10-255.
Bowling: Lever 9.4-2-33-2, Phillip 10-2-42-3, East 11-1-40-2, Turner 11-1-47-1, Pont 10-0-67-2.

with equal disdain, the opener played what David Lemmon described in 'Great One-Day Cricket Matches' as "an innings of magnitude, personality and power. It had the strength of a century by Wally Hammond and a range of shots that defies comparison."

Facing the daunting prospect of chasing 291 for victory, Surrey went about their task vigorously despite the loss of the openers with just 45 on the scoreboard. Knight and New Zealander Geoff Howarth added 91 in 17 overs and then Howarth and David Smith put on 51 in eight overs to leave the batting side on 187-3 with 16 overs left. Just before, Denness had set Essex hearts-a-fluttering when he dropped Howarth at long-leg off John Lever on 69. Fortunately, for all concerned of an Essex hue, the reprieve was only temporary as the Kiwi rashly hit Keith Pont to Fletcher at mid-wicket five runs later. Essex ultimately held their nerve – and their remaining catches – as Surrey's challenge faltered from that point. Lever comprehensively bowled youngster Hugh Wilson to complete Essex's maiden triumph with 20 balls to spare but it had not been without its worrying moments – a Club's history encapsulated in one fine day.

Schweppes County Championship

Northamptonshire v Essex

3-day match **Venue:** County Ground, Northampton **Result:** Essex won by 7 wickets

Essex may have broken their trophy duck earlier that summer with the Benson & Hedges Cup but for Captain Keith Fletcher, the County Championship was the title he coveted most. A nucleus of players who had been together for approaching a decade were hitting their peak around the same time as the 1979 campaign began. Such was Essex's dominance of the three-day season that year, the County found themselves on the verge of their first Championship with five games remaining. Second-placed Worcestershire had failed to close the gap in the previous match so Essex went to Northampton knowing a maximum 20-point haul would see them take the title. As it transpired, any victory would suffice as Worcester failed to claim victory in their controversial game against Derbyshire in the corresponding round of fixtures. Opener bowlers John Lever and Norbert Phillip vindicated Fletcher's decision to bowl first with three wickets

in the first half-hour but Peter Willey rallied the home side in a three hours and 30 minute stay at the crease that brought him 131 runs. Essex reached the close trailing by 142 with nine wickets in hand so entered day two in the ascendancy. Pakistan quick bowler Sarfraz Nawaz – who picked up Championship best figures for the season of 6-60 – then took advantage of humid conditions and a damp pitch to instigate a slide from 118-1 to 199 all out on day two. It could have been even worse for the visitors as Fletcher was dropped on 0 before batting through to 52 not out. Allan Lamb – second in the national averages at the time and to be a frequent scourge of Essex over his career – dug in during Northants' second innings but they too suffered a collapse. Stuart Turner – in his Benefit Year – nipped out two late wickets off successive deliveries to leave the hosts on 174-8 when poor light halted play just before the close. Overnight rain had slowed the pitch on day three so the final Northants wickets took some time to shift before Essex were set the task of making 229 in five hours. The champions elect were boosted in their run-chase by the absence of Sarfraz for most of the innings after the paceman suffered back trouble in his first spell. Opening pair Brian Hardie and Mike Denness got Essex off to a solid beginning with a 103-run stand before the latter, having just reached 50, cut against the spin of Richard Williams and

A title secured: Brian Hardie *(facing the camera)* and Keith Pont complete victory at Northampton

Essex Captain Keith Fletcher had made his first-class debut for the County in 1962 so this victory was particularly significant for him. Fletcher would go on to lead the side to another two Championships in 1983 and 1984 before playing under Graham Gooch in the 1986 title success and coaching the side to victory in 1991 and 1992. Although he also led the side to a number of one-day triumphs, it was in the longer form that Fletcher took most pride in achieving success. He told the press soon after clinching this first Championship title: "This is the one you want to win most. The Benson & Hedges Cup is the cream of the cake but this Championship is what matters...the big thing is for a side to know how to win. I can't explain it, but it takes time to get this into a side. We go out to win from the first morning and of course this is a wonderful moment."

Toss: Essex won the toss and decided to field.
Umpires: KE Palmer, PB Wight.

NORTHAMPTONSHIRE

G Cook	lbw b Turner	32	b Turner	38
W Larkins	lbw b Lever	0	lbw b Lever	17
RG Williams	b Phillip	1	lbw b Lever	1
AJ Lamb	c Hardie b Phillip	2	lbw b Phillip	66
P Willey	lbw b Turner	131	lbw b Turner	2
TJ Yardley	b Turner	1	c Denness b Phillip	24
†G Sharp	lbw b Lever	9	lbw b Turner	2
*PJ Watts	c Fletcher b Turner	12	not out	25
Sarfraz Nawaz	b Turner	5	lbw b Turner	0
TM Lamb	not out	3	b Turner	2
BJ Griffiths	c Smith b Phillip	3	lbw b Lever	2
Extras	(4 b, 12 lb, 7 nb, 2 w)	25	(2 b, 13 lb, 8 nb, 1 w)	24
Total	**(all out, 69.4 overs)**	**224**	**(all out, 64.3 overs)**	**203**

Fall: 1st inns: 1-1, 2-7, 3-9, 4-71, 5-83, 6-149, 7-205, 8-212, 9-219, 10-224. **2nd inns:** 1-35, 2-41, 3-104, 4-106, 5-161, 6-166, 7-174, 8-174, 9-195, 10-203.
Bowling: 1st inns: Lever 22-4-77-2, Phillip 17.4-6-35-3, Turner 17-2-70-5, Acfield 13-4-17-0.
2nd inns: Lever 22.3-4-71-3, Phillip 15-2-52-2, Turner 25-2-56-5, East 2-2-0-0.

ESSEX

BR Hardie	lbw b Sarfraz Nawaz	11	not out	103
MH Denness	c Yardley b Sarfraz Nawaz	31	b Williams	51
KS McEwan	lbw b Sarfraz Nawaz	70	lbw b Willey	11
*KWR Fletcher	not out	52	c Yardley b Larkins	39
KR Pont	c Yardley b Griffiths	6	not out	8
S Turner	lbw b Griffiths	6	did not bat	
N Phillip	b Sarfraz Nawaz	2	did not bat	
†N Smith	b Sarfraz Nawaz	0	did not bat	
RE East	c Yardley b Sarfraz Nawaz	3	did not bat	
JK Lever	run out	1	did not bat	
DL Acfield	c Sharp b Griffiths	0	did not bat	
Extras	(1 b, 6 lb, 8 nb, 2 w)	17	(1 b, 16 lb)	17
Total	**(all out, 79.4 overs)**	**199**	**(3 wickets, 95.3 overs)**	**229**

Fall: 1st inns: 1-22, 2-118, 3-121, 4-143, 5-157, 6-165, 7-169, 8-183, 9-187, 10-199. **2nd inns:** 1-113, 2-132, 3-210.
Bowling: 1st inns: Sarfraz Nawaz 27-7-60-6, Griffiths 23.4-6-65-3, TM Lamb 19-6-35-0, Willey 10-4-22-0.
2nd inns: Sarfraz Nawaz 7-2-23-0, Griffiths 21-5-55-0, TM Lamb 12-4-23-0, Willey 28-7-42-1, Williams 15, Larkins 7-3-15-1, Watts 5-1-22-0, Yardley 0.3-0-3-0.

played on. By tea, the County had reached 165-2 with Fletcher now offering Hardie excellent support. The Essex skipper was caught at slip with 20 needed but Hardie moved serenely on, and it was the right-hander who stroked the winning runs off Jim Yardley, shortly after reaching three figures, with 9.3 overs still remaining. Essex completed their victory at 5.30pm but the champagne – which Secretary Peter Edwards had packed in his car before setting off for Northampton – was kept on ice until the conclusion of the match between Derbyshire and Worcestershire. The visitors bowled Derby out in their second innings in the 19th over of the last hour, leaving the visitors with 10 minutes to score 25 runs for victory. Worcester had been under the impression they were due four overs but, having reached 17-1 after two, the match was concluded with time having run out. Worcester captain Norman Gifford then held a conversation with the Test and County Cricket Board (TCCB) Secretary Donald Carr in an attempt to extend the innings but could not reverse the decision. Eventually, at 6pm, there were no more obstacles in Essex's way and the Championship pennant was finally winging its way to Chelmsford. A period of unprecedented glory had well and truly begun.

John Player League

Surrey v Essex

40-overs match, reduced to 39-overs

Venue: Kennington Oval **Result:** Essex won by 21 runs

Essex all-rounder Norbert Phillip may have been forgiven for wishing the 1981 season away when he fluffed a run out opportunity off his own bowling to gift Derbyshire victory in the NatWest Trophy semi-final of mid-August. The West Indian was made of sterner stuff however and played a pivotal role in Essex claiming their first Sunday League title in the final match at The Oval a month later. Essex had developed an affinity with the 40-overs game, since its 1969 inception, but three second-placed finishes was the best they could show for their efforts. In this 1981 season, the County moved to the top of the table on July 19 since when they had only suffered one defeat – to Hampshire – by the time they came to visit Surrey. Victory would assure the visitors of the title but

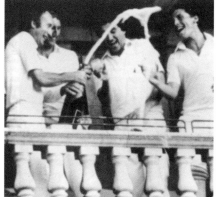

any slip-up could let in Warwickshire, who met Somerset at Taunton. Play started six minutes late due to rain – a delay that was to play a significant part in the match later on – as Essex were put into bat. Veteran spinner Pat Pocock was the pick of the Surrey bowlers as Essex struggled to dominate in difficult batting conditions.

To the victor the spoils: *(left to right)* Keith Fletcher, John Lever, Brian Hardie and David East toast the JPL title at the Oval

Keith Fletcher and Philip added 53 in eight overs to advance the score to 127-3 before Pocock struck twice in quick succession to remove the Essex skipper and Alan Lilley. It fell to Phillip and Stuart Turner to galvanise the innings and they did so providing a flourishing climax with 51 runs added in seven overs. Eighteen runs were taken off the 38th over – bowled by Robin Jackman – at which point the players left the field with Essex's innings seemingly at an end. Fletcher then reminded the umpires that time lost in a delayed match is 'shared' between the sides, in which case each team was due to receive 39 overs. The teams thus marched out for another over and Phillip hit 19 off Roger Knight's over including a six over long-on and another over mid-wicket that sailed out of the ground.

Even 30 years on, those blows from Phillip live in the memory of the hordes of Essex supporters who had converged on the Oval in expectant mood. Those 37

"It was fantastic to come onto the Essex staff in April but I couldn't have dreamed I would make my debut in July and then continue in the side after that" said Essex wicket-keeper David East. He marked his first season at the Club by tasting success in the John Player League and recalls the impact that Norbert Phillip made in the final game, just weeks after blowing his lines against Derbyshire: "If there was one particular memory I have about that match at the Oval it was the six that Norbert Phillip hit that almost went over the top of the pavilion," East remembers. "'Nobby' was a great trier and a great asset to the side. Nobody blamed him for that incident at Derby [in the NatWest Trophy semi-final earlier in the season when he missed a run-out] because he made a major contribution getting us there in the first place. It showed the strength of his character that he could put us into a winning position at the Oval. It was a very close squad in the early '80s and it was great as a youngster to come into such a unified bunch."

Toss: Surrey won the toss and decided to field.
Umpires: RS Herman, D Shackleton.

ESSEX

		Runs	Balls	Mins	4s	6s
GA Gooch	c Richards b Jackman	8	8	8	1	-
BR Hardie	c Richards b Mackintosh	33	54	47	1	-
KS McEwan	b Pocock	18	40	57	-	-
*KWR Fletcher	c Jackman b Pocock	27	40	45	1	1
N Phillip	not out	80	67	60	3	5
AW Lilley	c Mackintosh b Pocock	1	6	7	-	-
S Turner	run out	23	23	20	3	-
DR Pringle	run out	0	-	1	-	-
RE East	not out	0	-	2	-	-
†DE East	did not bat					
JK Lever	did not bat					
Extras	(4 b, 9 lb)	13				
Total	**(7 wickets, 39 overs)**	**203**				

Fall: 1-12, 2-57, 3-74, 4-127, 5-133, 6-184, 7-189.
Bowling: Jackman 8-0-46-1, Monkhouse 8-0-33-0, Mackintosh 8-1-34-1, Knight 7-0-56-0, Pocock 8-2-21-3.

SURREY

		Runs	Balls	Mins	4s	6s
AR Butcher	b RE East	19	34	47	1	-
DB Pauline	c DE East b Turner	18	43	42	2	-
MA Lynch	c DE East b Pringle	4	14	16	-	-
*RDV Knight	st DE East b RE East	29	33	35	2	-
DM Smith	c and b Phillip	24	40	62	1	-
†GRJ Roope	not out	60	55	55	3	1
CJ Richards	not out	14	16	17	-	-
KS Mackintosh	did not bat					
RD Jackman	did not bat					
G Monkhouse	did not bat					
PI Pocock	did not bat					
Extras	(1 b, 9 lb, 1 nb, 3 w)	14				
Total	**(5 wickets, 39 overs)**	**182**				

Fall: 1-40, 2-44, 3-48, 4-84, 5-140.
Bowling: Lever 8-0-30-0, Phillip 8-0-38-1, Turner 8-0-45-1, RE East 8-1-21-2, Pringle 7-0-34-1.

runs from the final 12 deliveries – with Phillip responsible for 34 off his bat – were decisive in swinging the game in the away side's favour. Essex reduced Surrey to 48-3 in reply but then stands of 36 and 56 for the fourth-wicket and fifth-wicket respectively gave the hosts hope. The hosts wanted 71 from the last seven overs but, as the light faded, they were unable to find their answer to Phillip.By this stage, a Viv Richards-inspired Somerset were well on the way to defeating Warwickshire but Essex's support were keen to see their side win the trophy in style – with victory against their near-neighbours.

John Lever – Essex's leading wicket-taker in the competition – fittingly bowled the last over as the County ultimately ran out comfortable winners. The Oval became Essex territory for one day as the balcony celebrations were greeted rapturously by the visiting masses. All those near-misses in the 40-overs game were long forgotten as the County went on to lift the Sunday League trophy three times between 1981 and 1985 to make Fletcher and company the indisputable one-day kings of the age.

Schweppes County Championship
Essex v Surrey

3-day match **Venue:** County Ground, Chelmsford **Result:** Draw

Records are there to be broken but whether Essex will ever bowl a side out so cheaply or Surrey will be shot out for so few as during an astonishing May late afternoon in 1983 is extremely unlikely. Even with heightened coverage in that era, it was still a rare event for a county cricket match to make the front page of The Times. When a professional team is bowled out for 14 it makes the recognition a little more understandable. Day one of the Championship match at Chelmsford had been washed out, so by the time Monday arrived there was little prospect of an outright result. With Essex stretching their first innings beyond 5pm in making 287 – Captain Keith Fletcher compiling a dogged 110 – there was even less hope of either side snatching victory. For Surrey to have been dismissed for 14 by the close in 14.3 overs it required several factors – firstly that Essex's opening bowlers Neil Foster and Norbert Phillip would take the utmost advantage of any assistance

Arch destroyers:
Neil Foster *(left)* and
Norbert Phillip

offered by overhead conditions and movement off the seam. Secondly, any catching opportunities that went the way of the Essex fielders had to be taken. Finally, Surrey's batsmen needed to have a collective off-day where they contrived all sorts of ways to prematurely exit the crease. As chance would have it, all key elements came together in one crazy hour as everything that could go wrong for Surrey did go wrong. The dismissal of opener Alan Butcher illustrated the away side's batting effort when he was caught down the leg-side off an intended hook to give wicketkeeper David East the first of two such catches. Foster then claimed his first wicket when he beat Andy Needham's indecisive forward push before Surrey captain Roger Knight was trapped leg before by Phillip shuffling across his crease. Monte Lynch went the same way before opener Graeme Clinton was another victim caught down the leg-side to a Foster bouncer. Clinton's dismissal was the second of five wickets to fall with the score on eight as Jack Richards, Dave Thomas and Ian Payne all perished without scoring. Graham Monkhouse edged just short of Ray East at slip to provide him with his two runs as Surrey moved into double figures. Sylvester Clarke then heaved a boundary to mid-wicket before he was yorked by Foster. Phillip immediately wrapped things up at the other end by trapping Monkhouse lbw. Surrey's paltry total remains the fifth lowest in first-class cricket and is the most meagre since 1901, only Oxford

An opposition perspective of the devastating bowling efforts of Neil Foster and Norbert Phillip were provided by Surrey captain Roger Knight in the *1995 Essex Yearbook*: "It was difficult to make any constructive comments that evening in the hotel. Shock affects people in different ways. Some wanted to forget the last 70 minutes of the day. Others felt the urge to giggle and one or two tried to analyse what happened. There is no doubt that the bowlers had made the ball swing quite considerably. Every time they bowled it straight we appeared to miss it and every time they bowled it off the stumps we nicked it to the wicket-keeper or slips. In the total of 14, there were 7 ducks and a 0 not out. One always says that it only takes 10 deliveries to bowl out a team. We obviously had the 10 early in our innings on that occasion."

Toss: Surrey won the toss and decided to field.
Umpires: WE Alley, JW Holder.

ESSEX

GA Gooch	b Thomas	1
BR Hardie	b Clarke	16
*KWR Fletcher	c Lynch b Monkhouse	110
KS McEwan	c Lynch b Knight	45
KR Pont	b Pocock	12
N Phillip	b Pocock	8
S Turner	c and b Knight	20
RE East	c Lynch b Clarke	19
†DE East	c Butcher b Pocock	17
NA Foster	not out	19
DL Acfield	run out	0
Extras	(4 b, 10 lb, 6 nb)	20
Total	**(all out, 89.5 overs)**	**287**

Fall: 1st inns: 1-1, 2-27, 3-113, 4-156, 5-179, 6-222, 7-238, 8-252, 9-276, 10-287.
Bowling: 1st inns: Clarke 20-3-58-2, Thomas 20-2-78-1, Monkhouse 13-2-49-1, Knight 17-6-33-2, Pocock 19.5-6-49-3.

SURREY

			(FOLLOWING ON)		
AR Butcher	c DE East b Phillip	2	c Gooch b Foster		5
GS Clinton	c DE East b Foster	6	not out		61
A Needham	b Foster	0	lbw b Phillip		4
*RDV Knight	lbw b Phillip	0	not out		101
MA Lynch	lbw b Phillip	0	did not bat		
†CJ Richards	c Turner b Phillip	0	did not bat		
DJ Thomas	lbw b Foster	0	did not bat		
IR Payne	b Phillip	0	did not bat		
G Monkhouse	lbw b Phillip	2	did not bat		
ST Clarke	b Foster	4	did not bat		
PI Pocock	not out	0	did not bat		
Extras		0	(1 b, 8 lb, 3 nb, 2 w)		14
Total	**(all out, 14.3 overs)**	**14**	**(2 wickets, 78 overs)**		**185**

Fall: 1st inns: 1-2, 2-5, 3-6, 4-8, 5-8, 6-8, 7-8, 8-8, 9-14, 10-14. **2nd inns:** 1-11, 2-18.
Bowling: 1st inns: Phillip 7.3-4-4-6, Foster 7-3-10-4. **2nd inns:** Phillip 13-2-39-1, Foster 13-2-33-1, Turner 7-3-16-0, Gooch 22-6-45-0, Acfield 17-7-23-0, RE East 1-0-5-0, Pont 5-1-10-0.

University and Northamptonshire (12) and Auckland and Nottinghamshire (13) scoring less. Phillip, who said after the innings that he had "just made a point of keeping the ball up and letting it do the rest" claimed his six wickets in the space of 39 deliveries for three runs. Meanwhile, Foster, who was returning to action following a year out with a back injury, took four wickets in the space of 24 balls for nine runs. Overnight rain delayed Essex's attempts to inflict further misery on the opposition until 12.30pm on the final day. By then, batting conditions appeared somewhat more favourable with sunshine the order of the day. Foster and Phillip still used the new ball well, however, to leave Surrey on 20-2 by lunch. Clinton batted for four hours and found himself a reliable partner in Knight – who survived a close leg before early in his innings – as the third-wicket pair batted out the remainder of the day. Despite their humbling experience, Surrey picked up only three less points than their opponent and would even exact their revenge with a seven-wicket victory later in the season in the corresponding fixture at The Oval. However it was Essex who were to take the most satisfaction as they finished the campaign with smiles on their faces when they secured their second-ever Championship title in the final round of matches.

Britannic Assurance County Championship

Somerset v Essex

3-day match   **Venue:** County Ground, Taunton **Result:** Essex won by 7 wickets

Despite a second-day wash-out, Essex's trip to Taunton in 1985 will be fondly remembered by several participants for their outstanding personal achievements. With Viv Richards, Ian Botham and Graham Gooch in the batting line-ups it was always likely to be a match where the bowlers needed to be wary. So it came to pass that Botham and Gooch produced stunning displays of hitting to light up days one and three in between a second day where the weather held the upper hand. Yet this match also went down as a notable one for the Essex wicket-keeper and a rookie fast bowler. Ian Pont was handed his first-team debut while Don Topley was making only his second Championship appearance for the Club with John Lever and Neil Foster both out injured. Pont joined his brother Keith in the side and made an immediate impact as he registered figures of 3-15 at one point. David East was

**David East:
day to remember**

the grateful recipient of edges proffered by Nigel Popplewell, Peter Roebuck and Richards to leave the home side on 56-3. The dismissal of Richards brought to an end a terrific duel between Essex's tyro pace bowler and the legendary West Indian. Building up a fine head of steam, Pont unseated Richards with a fearsome early bouncer before the batsman responded with a fierce square-driven four – a shot that Gooch noted in his autobiography was the hardest he had ever seen hit. As Gooch acknowledged, he feared the worst from his vantage point at slip after being on the wrong end of several explosive innings from the right-hander in the past. On this occasion, however, the debutant out-foxed his worthy opponent with a slower ball as he got a thin edge to East. Nick Felton and Julian Wyatt added 92 for the fourth-wicket before Keith Pont ended the resistance with East claiming another victim. Wyatt then became the first of three victims for Derek Pringle to bring up East's five-catch haul. Botham had joined the fray by this point and he ensured that East and Pont would have to share the stage on a first day that was anything but dull. Keith Pont dropped the Somerset captain on 64 and the batsman made the visitors suffer with a vintage innings of 152 off 121 balls that included 16 fours and four sixes. Pont's younger brother finally accounted for the England all-rounder – naturally caught behind for East's seventh catch – but the damage had been done. There was still time in the day for East to claim his eighth catch when Mark Davis nicked Pringle to equal Wally Grout's record. Pont bowled Colin Dredge to complete his five-wicket haul

Essex wicket-keeper David East had a season to remember in 1985 when he contributed hugely to the team's success with both gloves and bat. East's highlight came at Taunton with his world record-equalling eight catches. It wasn't all good news for the man behind the stumps, however: "It cost me a fortune behind the bar!," he remembers. "A couple of catches was not unusual with the quality of seamers we had – I expected between two and four in most innings – but they just kept on coming on this particular day. [Captain] Keith Fletcher said 'well done' as we came off the field but followed that by saying his daughter could have caught those with one hand tied behind her back – and he wasn't wrong, most of them were comfortable takes. But it was nice to achieve and nice to equal the record."

Toss: Essex won the toss and decided to field.
Umpires: KJ Lyons, R Palmer.

SOMERSET

(INNINGS FORFEITED)

NFM Popplewell	c East b IL Pont	27	did not bat
PM Roebuck	c East b IL Pont	17	did not bat
NA Felton	c East b KR Pont	49	did not bat
IVA Richards	c East b IL Pont	5	did not bat
JG Wyatt	c East b Pringle	50	did not bat
*IT Botham	c East b IL Pont	152	did not bat
VJ Marks	c East b Pringle	17	did not bat
†T Gard	not out	27	did not bat
MR Davis	c East b Pringle	7	did not bat
CH Dredge	b IL Pont	1	did not bat
J Garner	not out	4	did not bat
Extras	(4 lb, 2 nb, 1 w)	7	
Total	**(9 wickets, declared, 100 overs)**	**363**	

Fall: 1st inns: 1-36, 2-45, 3-56, 4-148, 5-162, 6-246, 7-343, 8-352 9-353.
Bowling: 1st inns: Pringle 30-2-90-3, IL Pont 24-2-103-5, Topley 24-3-86-0, KR Pont 11-0-45-1, Acfield 11-1-35-0.

ESSEX

GA Gooch	c Gard b Wyatt	19	not out	173
BR Hardie	not out	25	b Dredge	20
PJ Prichard	not out	18	b Dredge	44
KS McEwan	did not bat		lbw b Dredge	0
DR Pringle	did not bat		not out	45
*KWR Fletcher	did not bat		did not bat	
KR Pont	did not bat		did not bat	
†DE East	did not bat		did not bat	
TD Topley	did not bat		did not bat	
DL Acfield	did not bat		did not bat	
IL Pont	did not bat		did not bat	
Extras	(4 lb, 2 w)	6	(11 lb, 3 nb)	14
Total	**(1 wicket, declared, 13 overs)**	**68**	**(3 wickets, 69 overs)**	**296**

Fall: 1st inns: 1-25. **2nd inns:** 1-84, 2-165, 3-165.
Bowling: 1st inns: Garner 1-1-0-0, Wyatt 6-0-40-1, Roebuck 6-0-24-0. **2nd inns:** Wyatt 3-0-18-0, Botham 8-0-61-0, Davis 16-2-65-0, Dredge 22-0-82-3, Marks 18-2-48-0, Popplewell 2-0-11-0.

and, in the process, deny East the chance of a clean sweep. Botham's declaration after 100 overs also scuppered the Essex gloveman's hopes of surpassing Grout's effort. Negotiations took place before play on day three between respective captains Botham and Fletcher in an attempt to generate a positive result out of the truncated match. Roebuck and Wyatt sent down some friendly overs of declaration bowling before Essex were set 296 in 90 overs or by half past six. Newspaper reports at the time criticised Botham for what they perceived to be an overly generous run-chase while Gooch recalled in his autobiography how Fletcher hoodwinked his opposite number into believing the pitch was cracking up. If it was, Gooch did not read the script as he set about the victory charge with gusto. Botham's opening four overs were hammered for 41 as Essex got off to a flying start. The Essex opener made light of the loss of Paul Prichard and Ken McEwan in quick succession during the afternoon to reach his century and victory was achieved with 21 overs to spare. Gooch finished with 173 not out off 190 balls and was well supported by Pringle in an unbeaten fourth-wicket stand of 131. Essex may have relinquished their Championship title by the end of the year but they continued to entertain wherever they went.

60-overs match   **Venue:** Lord's Cricket Ground, St John's Wood **Result:** Essex won by 1 run

Championship, 55-overs and 40-overs glory had all come Essex's way after breaking their trophy duck in 1979. Just one tournament remained elusive but they were finally in sight of a clean-sweep when reaching the 60-overs NatWest Trophy Final in 1985. When Nottinghamshire began the last over still 18 runs short of victory, it looked even more likely that Essex skipper Keith Fletcher would become the first cricketer to lead a County to all four domestic titles. Of course, the path to success never did run smoothly for Essex and so it was over the course of the last six deliveries. As was par for the course with 10.30am September starts, Notts had earlier put their opponents into bat after winning the toss. True to form, Essex

One-day kings: man-of-the-match Brian Hardie *(left)* and captain Keith Fletcher with the NatWest Trophy

openers Graham Gooch and Brian Hardie found the going tough with New Zealand fast bowler Richard Hadlee's first three overs all maidens. But around 11am the sun came out and the County's first-wicket pair made hay. Hardie reached his 100 (off 136 balls) out of 175 in the 44th over along the way to an opening stand of 202 – the highest ever made for any wicket in a one-day final at Lord's. The right-hander's cover drive was particularly effective on a rare day when Gooch – who was dropped twice – was overshadowed by his fellow opener. Nonetheless, the England legend still compiled 91 off 142 balls before he was bowled through the gate by Andy Pick. Hardie was run out by a smart pick up and throw from Eddie Hemmings but third-wicket pair Ken McEwan – in his last season with the County – and Derek Pringle added an unbeaten 77. A final flourish of 44 from the last four overs allowed Essex to register a daunting 280-2 from their 60 overs. It was imperative that Notts' England openers Tim Robinson and Chris Broad got their side off to a decent start in reply. How well they responded! The pair posted 143 runs and it became increasingly difficult to gauge how they might be parted. As it transpired it needed a run-out to split the duo when young fast bowler Ian Pont – in for the sick Neil Foster – delivered an arrow-like return from the boundary into the hands of wicket-keeper David East with Broad short of his crease. Stuart Turner made a crucial double strike as both Robinson and Notts' captain Clive Rice picked out Hardie. Hadlee upped the tempo but when Pont bowled the left-hander, as he backed away and missed a drive, it seemed the game was swinging decisively towards Essex. Derek Randall's innings started slowly as he regularly picked out the fielders and, with 53 off five overs needed, the match

Paul Prichard did not bat or bowl in the 1985 NatWest Trophy Final but he still had a significant part to play in Essex's victory, catching Derek Randall off the last ball when the Nottinghamshire batsman was on the verge of winning his team the game. Prichard recalls: "I was at mid-wicket and remember Alan Lilley, who was fielding behind me, shouting at me to tell him which way the ball was going if it came his way – because it was pitch black by that time. I was standing a bit out of position – in between saving a single and on the edge of the ring – but luckily Pring [Derek Pringle] bowled a good ball on [Derek] Randall's legs and he flipped it straight to me at head height. Then the celebrations began!"

Toss: Nottinghamshire won the toss and decided to field.
Umpires: DJ Constant, BJ Meyer

ESSEX

		Runs	Balls	Mins	4s	6s	S-Rate
GA Gooch	b Pick	91	142	169	8	1	64.08
BR Hardie	run out (Hemmings)	110	149	176	15	-	73.83
KS McEwan	not out	46	39	47	4	1	117.95
DR Pringle	not out	29	30	40	2	-	96.67
PJ Prichard	did not bat						
*KWR Fletcher	did not bat						
AW Lilley	did not bat						
†DE East	did not bat						
S Turner	did not bat						
IL Pont	did not bat						
JK Lever	did not bat						
Extras	(1 b, 3 lb)	4					
Total	**(2 wickets, 60 overs)**	**280**					

Fall: 1-202, 2-203
Bowling: Hadlee 12-4-48-0, Cooper 9-3-27-0, Saxelby 12-0-73-0, Rice 7-0-38-0, Pick 8-0-36-1, Hemmings 12-1-54-0.

NOTTINGHAMSHIRE

		Runs	Balls	Mins	4s	6s	S-Rate
RT Robinson	c Hardie b Turner	80	142	149	4	1	56.34
BC Broad	run out (Pont->East)	64	107	137	6	-	59.81
*CEB Rice	c Hardie b Turner	12	19	26	1	-	63.16
DW Randall	c Prichard b Pringle	66	54	72	6	-	122.22
RJ Hadlee	b Pont	22	17	20	2	1	129.41
DJR Martindale	not out	20	22	33	-	-	90.91
†BN French	did not bat						
EE Hemmings	did not bat						
RA Pick	did not bat						
K Saxelby	did not bat						
KE Cooper	did not bat						
Extras	(14 lb, 1 nb)	15					
Total	**(5 wickets, 60 overs)**	**279**					

Fall: 1-143, 2-153, 3-173, 4-214, 5-279.
Bowling: Lever 12-2-53-0, Pont 12-0-54-1, Turner 12-1-43-2, Gooch 12-0-47-0, Pringle 12-1-68-1.

appeared even more likely to go in the favour of the fielding side. Youngster Duncan Martindale helped Randall advance the total by another 35 from the next four overs but, with 18 needed off the last six balls, Essex's vociferous supporters were upbeat. Pringle was to prove himself a highly capable 'death' bowler before and after this match but, on this occasion, Randall almost got the better of him. Driving repeatedly to the off-side, the right-hander rattled off a sequence of 2, 4, 2, 4, 4 to bring the equation down to just two needed from the last delivery. Pringle revealed after the match that "leg stump or just outside" was Captain Fletcher's instructions as he thought Randall would move to the leg-side again. Had Randall stayed in his initial position the delivery might have been called a wide but he once more shuffled outside his leg-stump. Cramped for room, the batsman chipped to the on-side, where Paul Prichard plucked out a catch at mid-wicket. Having snatched defeat from the jaws of victory in a number of other Lord's Finals, losing under these circumstances would have been particularly hard to bear for Essex. On this occasion however, a format that deals in fine margins came down in the County's favour and Hardie's outstanding effort with the bat – for which he was named the man-of-the-match – was duly rewarded.

Britannic Assurance County Championship
Somerset v Essex

3-day match

Venue: County Ground, Taunton **Result:** Essex won by 9 runs

On August 5, Gloucestershire held a 54-point lead over Essex at the top of the table. In the six matches that followed, the West Country county managed only 22 points against the 85 achieved by Essex. With just one game left for Gloucestershire, their challenge was effectively over and the title was heading to Chelmsford. Yet everything had seemed so different when Essex stood on the verge of defeat in the final session of their match with Somerset at Taunton. There are positions of strength and then there is an equation whereby Somerset required 20 runs with 18 overs left and Ian Botham at the crease. If ever a champion county was to prove its worth, by snatching victory from the jaws of defeat, the moment had come.

John Childs:
last-gasp hero

The Somerset captain's dismissal – having risen from his sickbed to smash 41 off 29 balls – triggered a collapse whereby the last five wickets toppled for 10 runs in 40 minutes. The hosts had earlier been left to make 273 in 250 minutes or a minimum of 68 overs – a target, according to reports at the time that appeared generous but, with an uncertain forecast and two games in hand, the gamble seemed worth it. By tea, Somerset needed another 121 with six wickets left on a dry pitch that was playing more easily than at any other time in the match. At that stage it was Viv Richards – in his last season at the Club after it was decided both he and fellow West Indian Joel Garner would not return in 1987 – who looked capable of winning the match off his own bat. The legendary right-hander and Vic Marks added 88 in 17 overs before Richards pulled John Lever to Brian Hardie at mid-wicket for 94. Marks then proved a capable ally for Botham as the sixth-wicket pair added 55 before the match was turned on its head. Derek Pringle removed Trevor Gard in the next over and then bowled Marks for 56. Mark Harman was run out trying to snatch a single after Colin Dredge drove a ball near Keith Fletcher at backward point. Ten tense minutes followed before Childs had Nick Taylor leg before and Essex had won with 8.5 overs in hand. The visitors went into the game trailing Gloucestershire by 10 points but their prospects of closing the gap had looked slim on day one when they were dismissed for 129. Botham and Taylor bowled unchanged until lunch either side of a 35-minute interruption for rain, taking advantage of seam movement and unpredictable bounce. Essex wicket-keeper

The six County Championship titles won by Essex were founded on the ability to never know when they were beaten. As spinner John Childs, who claimed the final wicket, recounts, the victory at Somerset encapsulated this 'never-say-die' attitude: "We had self-belief and we knew how to win games," he explained. "We felt once we won that game it [the title] was very much in our hands after that. It was more a case of them losing it but us still having the belief that anything was possible. I remember the celebrations at the end of the match [after Childs trapped Nick Taylor] because it was a very important win. By the time of the last wicket, it was a case of building up pressure because they were never going to win but it was a question of could we get them out in the time required. Taylor was a genuine number 11 so it was just a matter of time."

Toss: Essex won the toss and decided to bat.
Umpires: Essex won by 9 runs.

ESSEX

*GA Gooch	c Richards b Botham	0		lbw b Taylor	38
JP Stephenson	c Botham b Taylor	0		c Gard b Taylor	11
PJ Prichard	c Richards b Taylor	1		c Hardy b Marks	38
BR Hardie	c Roebuck b Taylor	18		not out	113
KWR Fletcher	c Roebuck b Botham	7		c Harden b Marks	28
DR Pringle	lbw b Botham	2		run out	21
†DE East	not out	58	(8)	c Roebuck b Harman	41
NA Foster	c Gard b Taylor	14	(9)	not out	0
JK Lever	c Harman b Dredge	18	(7)	b Dredge	38
JH Childs	c Botham b Dredge	7		did not bat	
DL Acfield	c Gard b Dredge	0		did not bat	
Extras	(2 lb, 2 nb)	4		(6 b, 9 lb)	15
Total	**(all out, 41.3 overs)**	**129**		**(7 wickets, declared, 131.3 overs)**	**343**

Fall: 1st inns: 1-0, 2-0, 3-2, 4-29, 5-29, 6-36, 7-57, 8-109, 9-129, 10-129. **2nd inns:** 1-32, 2-64, 3-115, 4-163, 5-207, 6-259, 7-343.
Bowling: 1st inns: Botham 21-5-77-3, Taylor 15-5-40-4, Dredge 5.3-1-10-3. **2nd inns:** Botham 7-2-32-0, Taylor 25-9-58-2, Dredge 21-6-51-1, Marks 39-10-99-2, Harman 39.3-11-88-1.

SOMERSET

NA Felton	c Prichard b Childs	10		lbw b Lever	6
*PM Roebuck	b Childs	10		lbw b Foster	24
JJE Hardy	run out	11		c Pringle b Foster	19
IVA Richards	c Fletcher b Gooch	53		c Hardie b Lever	94
RJ Harden	c Fletcher b Childs	14		c Fletcher b Foster	4
IT Botham	c Foster b Lever	67	(7)	c Stephenson b Childs	41
†T Gard	c Lever b Childs	0	(8)	lbw b Pringle	0
VJ Marks	run out	4	(6)	b Pringle	56
CH Dredge	c East b Foster	24		not out	4
MD Harman	not out	4		run out	0
NS Taylor	b Foster	2		lbw b Childs	2
Extras	(1 lb)	1		(5 b, 7 lb, 1 nb)	13
Total	**(all out, 63.3 overs)**	**200**		**(all out, 59.1 overs)**	**263**

Fall: 1st inns: 1-16, 2-21, 3-72, 4-96, 5-133, 6-133, 7-150, 8-194, 9-196, 10-200. **2nd inns:** 1-30, 2-38, 3-100, 4-110, 5-198, 6-253, 7-254, 8-259, 9-261, 10-263.
Bowling: 1st inns: Lever 21-7-59-1, Foster 26.3-7-62-2, Childs-8-0-27-4, Pringle 4-0-23-0, Gooch 4-0-281.
2nd inns: Lever 18-2-104-2, Foster 20-4-79-3, Childs 9.1-2-23-2, Pringle 12-1-45-2.

David East hooked Botham for two sixes and also hit seven fours to at least see the County into three figures. Only Richards and Botham were able to contend with a pitch that continued to favour bowlers when Somerset's turn came to bat. Richards drove a catch low to cover after making 53 from 52 balls (with 10 fours) while Botham hit six fours from the first seven balls he faced from Graham Gooch before a straight six against John Lever gave Somerset the lead. Resuming on 36 on day two, Botham, who was by now struggling against a throat infection, was never able to take command so necessary to build his team a large lead. John Lever and Neil Foster bowled unchanged to remove three of the last four wickets and the latter also had a hand in the dismissal of Marks – run out by Foster in his follow-through. By the time Essex came to bat in their second innings – trailing by 71 – the pitch was taking an increasing amount of spin as off-break duo Marks and Harman set about taking advantage. A six-hour century, made across the last two sessions of day two and the morning session of day three, by Brian Hardie underpinned Essex's bid to set their opposition a testing run-chase. In the end it was a target that would prove to be tantalisingly out of Somerset's reach.

Britannic Assurance County Championship

Essex v Kent

4-day match | **Venue:** County Ground, Chelmsford **Result:** Essex won by 8 wickets

Graham Gooch: Essex best

Essex began a journey into the unknown when the 1988 campaign brought the introduction of four-day Championship cricket – three such matches being played by each county at the start of the season and three more at the end sandwiching the traditional three-day fayre. The host county were no strong advocates of the innovation and their mindset would not have altered as Kent opening pair Mark Benson and Neil Taylor put on a first-wicket partnership of 208 in 83 overs. Kent pressed on to 400-7 on the second morning before prematurely declaring, a decision that Essex captain Graham Gooch believes was "a tactical mistake". The Essex opener made the visitors pay as he took full advantage of an easy-paced pitch to reach his century by the close of day two. Gooch was particularly severe on Chris Penn, pulling the seamer to the boundary to bring up his 50 from 86 balls and crashing a straight drive off the same bowler 67 balls later to register his 100.

The England batsman ploughed on remorselessly on day three to record his career-best Essex score of 275 – although, with his 333 for England still two years in the future, he remembers leaving the crease with a tinge of regret. "My abiding memory of that innings was that I was pretty upset for giving away my wicket (bowled by left-arm spinner Richard Davis)," Gooch laments. "I played a

Essex's left-arm spinner John Childs was rewarded for a fine career with a belated England call-up towards the end of this 1988 season – featuring twice in the series against West Indies. The slow bowler started his campaign well as he picked up a five-wicket haul in the opening Championship match against Kent. It was an unexpected bonus at that time of the year, as he remembers: "I was quite buoyant going into the season [with the advent of four-day games] as it was an opportunity for me to bowl a lot more overs – though the spinners didn't normally come into their own until around June and the Festival weeks. So I wasn't anticipating bowling an awful lot of overs in this match. You don't expect those [five-wicket hawls] coming along till later in the season. It was a typical belter of a Chelmsford wicket but if you can build up pressure you can get wickets."

Toss: Kent won the toss and decided to bat.
Umpires: R Julian, KJ Lyons.

KENT

Batsman	1st innings		2nd innings	
MR Benson	c East b Topley	110	c Gooch b Topley	13
NR Taylor	b Topley	94	c Miller b Childs	24
SG Hinks	c Prichard b Gooch	35	st East b Miller	10
CJ Tavaré	c East b Topley	13	c East b Childs	0
*CS Cowdrey	c Border b Pringle	48	(6) c Gooch b Childs	54
GR Cowdrey	c Gooch b Lever	35	(7) b Topley	145
†SA Marsh	lbw b Lever	7	(8) c Border b Lever	120
C Penn	not out	25	(9) c Prichard b Topley	1
RP Davis	not out	10	(5) c Border b Childs	1
AP Igglesden	did not bat		c Fletcher b Childs	3
HL Alleyne	did not bat		not out	0
Extras	(2 b, 15 lb, 5 nb, 1 w)	23	(3 b, 10 lb)	13
Total	(7 wickets, declared, 152 overs)	400	(all out, 117.2 overs)	384

Fall: 1st inns: 1-208, 2-209, 3-254, 4-295, 5-327, 6-352, 7-363. **2nd inns:** 1-27, 2-49, 3-49, 4-49, 5-89, 6-122, 7-344, 8-357, 9-372, 10-384.
Bowling: 1st inns: Lever 33-11-62-2, Topley 39-6-124-3, Pringle 37-7-77-1, Gooch 9-3-19-1, Childs 24-6-65-0, Miller 7-1-30-0, Border 3-1-6-0. **2nd inns:** Lever 19-4-85-1, Topley 21.2-5-57-3, Childs 45-16-113-5, Miller 28-6-95-1, Border 4-0-21-0.

ESSEX

Batsman	1st innings		2nd innings	
GA Gooch	b Davis	275	lbw b Davis	73
BR Hardie	c CS Cowdrey b Penn	20	c Taylor b CS Cowdrey	22
PJ Prichard	c Benson b Penn	0	(4) not out	15
AR Border	c Marsh b CS Cowdrey	31	(3) not out	55
DR Pringle	c Marsh b Alleyne	128	did not bat	
*KWR Fletcher	c sub b Davis	58	did not bat	
G Miller	b Davis	16	did not bat	
†DE East	c Tavaré b Davis	29	did not bat	
TD Topley	c Marsh b Penn	1	did not bat	
JK Lever	not out	13	did not bat	
JH Childs	b Davis	7	did not bat	
Extras	(6 b, 24 lb, 7 nb, 1 w)	38	(1 b, 4 lb)	5
Total	(all out, 161.5 overs)	616	(2 wickets, 21.2 overs)	170

Fall: 1st inns: 1-33, 2-33, 3-126, 4-385, 5-539, 6-543, 7-591, 8-594, 9-606, 10-616. **2nd inns:** 1-53, 2-150.
Bowling: 1st inns: Igglesden 13-2-57-0, Alleyne 20-2-80-1, Penn 41-7-160-3, CS Cowdrey 31-3-93-1, Davis 39.5-8-132-5, GR Cowdrey 17-1-64-0. **2nd inns:** Alleyne 6-0-40-0, CS Cowdrey 7-0-59-1, Davis 4.2-0-34-1, GR Cowdrey 4-0-32-0.

reckless shot and should have redoubled my efforts at that stage. I should have gone on to get 300 because up until then opportunities to score 300 were few and far between." Trailing by 216 on first innings, the game seemed up for Kent on the final morning when they lurched to 122-6. Maiden centuries from Graham Cowdrey and Steve Marsh then averted an innings defeat in a stand of 222 in 52 overs but then Allan Border took a fine, tumbling catch at midwicket with a record Kent seventh-wicket partnership – and safety – in sight. Needing 169 off 25 overs, Essex began their second innings against a side that took to the field with a limping Penn and without knee-injury victim Alan Igglesden. A new Test and County Cricket Board (TCCB) regulation meant players could not be substituted until five overs had elapsed.

Essex ran out winners with 22 balls to spare as Gooch continued his fine early-season form with 73 off 64 balls while Border hit 55 not out off 39 balls to see his side home. The total number of runs (1570) was the highest aggregate for a Championship match and the third highest in England (a sign of things to come in four-day cricket).

Britannic Assurance County Championship

Essex v Leicestershire

4-day match

Venue: County Ground, Chelmsford **Result:** Draw

Few matches encapsulated the 'Year of the Bat' in 1990 more than Essex's opening home game of the campaign against Leicestershire. The Test and County Cricket Board (TCCB) had decided before the season that pitches with a green tinge were a thing of the past and cricket balls with less pronounced seams would make life doubly hard for bowlers. It was no surprise, therefore, when Leicestershire captain Nigel Briers chose to bat on a sunny first morning at Chelmsford. Briers, himself, took advantage of what the 1991 *Essex Yearbook* termed a "straw-coloured pitch" as he and Boon put on 142 for the first wicket before lunch. However, off-spinner Peter Such was to make a favourable impression on his first appearance for the County, claiming three wickets in his opening spell of 20 overs. The slow bowler struck with his first ball after the resumption when Boon played back and was trapped leg before. Briers was then caught down the leg-side before Such took a low return

Runs on the board:
Paul Prichard *(left)*
and Graham Gooch

catch to dismiss James Whittaker. Leicester became so bogged down that they missed out on a fourth batting point by six runs as they could only advance to 294-4 off 100 overs. Laurie Potter's 62 in 45 overs typified the visitors' difficulties. Shoots of a recovery began to be planted by Chris Lewis who straight drove Such for six just before the close to bring up his half-century. The all-rounder – who was dropped late on day one on 38 – was given two more lives on the second day at 143 and 169 as he advanced his maiden century to within 11 of a double ton. Lewis batted six hours and 10 minutes, driving five sixes against the spinners as well as hitting 15 fours to dominate Leicestershire's highest score since 1947 of 520. Essex's reply began well as Graham Gooch and Paul Prichard's second-wicket partnership moved to 76 by the close and the Essex duo advanced their alliance to 403 on day three as 554 runs were struck by the County on Saturday. Their partnership – the highest ever compiled for any Essex wicket – came off 496 balls with Gooch's 215 spanning 309 deliveries, containing one six and 28 fours, while Paul Prichard's career-best 245 arrived in 318 balls with two sixes and 31 fours. Neil Foster carried on the momentum as he ended the day on 83 not out and was given time, when the game resumed on Monday, to complete a maiden first-class hundred off 79 balls (including five sixes

Essex batsman Paul Prichard recorded a career-best 245 against Leicestershire as batsmen took a firm grip on proceedings: "It was a case of just keeping on batting," Prichard explains. "At the time you are not aware of records because you have your mind set on doing your job out in the middle. Batting alongside Graham Gooch made life easier because he had that aura over bowlers that made them slightly daunted by him. I would say a career-best innings has to be near the top [in terms of their best] for any batsman – whatever the conditions. But I think the best and most satisfying innings was the 25 coming in at seven in the John Player League against Yorkshire in 1985 that helped us to win the title on the last day of the season – that was the best under pressure. After that comes my 92 against Leicestershire in the Benson & Hedges Cup Final [in 1998] and then this 245."

Toss: Leicestershire won the toss and decided to bat.
Umpires: KE Palmer, DR Shepherd.

LEICESTERSHIRE

TJ Boon	lbw b Such	90	c Waugh b Childs	89
*NE Briers	c Garnham b Such	65	c Garnham b Such	104
JJ Whitaker	c and b Such	31	b Stephenson	15
L Potter	c Prichard b Waugh	62	not out	16
JDR Benson	c Shahid b Foster	8	not out	10
CC Lewis	not out	189	did not bat	
†P Whitticase	lbw b Waugh	0	did not bat	
MI Gidley	c and b Shahid	9	did not bat	
JP Agnew	lbw b Shahid	37	did not bat	
GJF Ferris	c Waugh b Foster	11	did not bat	
AD Mullally	b Foster	3	did not bat	
Extras	(1 b, 9 lb, 1 nb, 4 w)	15	(5 b, 3 lb, 6 nb, 1 w)	15
Total	**(all out, 181 overs)**	**520**	**(3 wickets, 89 overs)**	**249**

Fall: 1st inns: 1-145, 2-178, 3-197, 4-214, 5-303, 6-309, 7-458, 8-460, 9-498, 10-520. **2nd inns:** 1-170, 2-205, 3-236.
Bowling: 1st inns: Foster 41-8-102-3, Andrew 20-3-72-0, Waugh 23-5-76-2, Childs 41-14-88-0, Such 43-7-118-3, Shahid 13-1-54-2. **2nd inns:** Foster 8-2-30-0, Andrew 9-1-31-0, Childs 33-10-93-1, Such 19-9-29-1, Shahid 11-3-42-0, Stephenson 9-5-16-1.

ESSEX

*GA Gooch	c Whitticase b Lewis	215
JP Stephenson	c Lewis b Mullally	35
PJ Prichard	c Briers b Mullally	245
ME Waugh	b Lewis	43
BR Hardie	not out	74
†MA Garnham	b Lewis	0
NA Foster	run out	101
N Shahid	did not bat	
JH Childs	did not bat	
SJW Andrew	did not bat	
PM Such	did not bat	
Extras	(9 b, 20 lb, 16 nb, 3 w)	48
Total	**(6 wickets, declared, 158.5 overs)**	**761**

Fall: 1st inns: 1-82, 2-485, 3-551, 4-587, 5-589, 6-761.
Bowling: 1st inns: Mullally 31-3-124-2, Agnew 35.5-4-170-0, Ferris 23-2-100-0, Lewis 28-3-115-3, Potter 14-0-91-0, Gidley 25-3-121-0, Benson 2-0-11-0.

and eight fours). Essex declared on 761-6 – their highest total in the Championship and the fifth largest for all counties until Lancashire eclipsed it later on the same day. There was still time for Briers and Boon to put on another century stand – the first time in 25 years an opening pair had added century stands in both innings for Leicester – before the toiling bowlers were finally put out of their misery with an early close to proceedings at 5.30pm. Gooch's innings was the sign of things to come for him in a prolific season that also included his 333 for England against India. Although a batsman for all conditions, the opener was happy to admit everything was stacked against the bowlers in this game and over the course of the season as a whole. "The previous year [1989] had seen a cricket ball used that had a more courser/durable seam and the bowlers took full advantage," Gooch explains. "As a result, such an adjustment was made in 1990 that meant the balls didn't do much at all – couple that with the wickets being flat and it was a good year to be a batsman! "Leicestershire got stuck in with the bat in this match and were cock-a-hoop with their score [520] – they thought they were in the pound seats. It didn't turn out that way and we decided our best option was to go past their total and try to bat just once."

Britannic Assurance County Championship

Essex v Middlesex

Venue: County Ground, Chelmsford **Result:** Essex won by an innings and 208 runs

Essex went into their final match of the 1991 season knowing victory over their great rivals Middlesex would see them win the Championship for the fifth time after finishing runners-up in the two previous campaigns. On first inspection of the scorecard, it appeared Essex's march to the title went unhindered almost from ball one right until Neil Foster completed a fine personal season by claiming the last wicket. One shadow hovered over the County Ground and its inhabitants on the first morning when Middlesex were being shot out for 51 in 103 minutes, however. Two years earlier, Essex had been deducted 25 points for what had been considered a 'sub-standard' pitch at Southend – a decision that would go a long way to denying them the title in 1989. After winning the toss, Essex Captain Graham Gooch, chose to bowl first in the hope that a well-grassed wicket would generate most assistance on the first day. However, even Gooch could not have anticipated

A job well done: Neil Foster (left) and Graham Gooch

that he would have been required to don the pads himself before lunch on the first day. Middlesex's first four wickets went down in the space of 12 balls, with the score stuck on five, as Foster and Derek Pringle took advantage of movement off the seam. The visitors' innings went from bad to worse and it was only because of Foster's removal from the attack that they were able to surpass 50 as Neil Williams chanced his arm. As Gooch revealed, Middlesex couled count themselves fortunate to have survived for even this long as the spectre of Southchurch Park 1989 remained at the back of his mind. "Coming to Chelmsford with the chance of clinching the Championship was the ideal scenario," Gooch proffered. "Our aim was to produce a wicket that gave a balance between bat and ball but as we had moved into September there was always the prospect of early movement. Having been docked points a couple of years previously, I was so concerned that I took Neil Foster off when we had them at 30-8 and brought on Steve Andrew. Any concerns about the pitch proved unfounded when we batted – there was nothing wrong with it!" Indeed, no batsman made a better fist of putting the pitch into perspective than Gooch, who reached a double-century in the last over of the first day when he swatted a Mike Gatting long-hop to the boundary. By that point Essex were already 23 ahead having lost John Stephenson and Paul Prichard cheaply. Pakistan overseas batsman Salim Malik – who proved a roaring success in his first season with the Club – then joined his skipper in making batting on an up-to-then apparent terror track look plain-sailing. The game changed when the silky right-hander hit three fours in his first five balls to begin a 182-run stand

Neil Foster called his 1991 campaign "the best season I ever had". Graham Gooch was grateful to have enjoyed the services of such a performer during his time as Captain. "Neil Foster was a class act," Gooch asserts. "He was always managing his knee and was in a lot of pain towards the end of his career. He was a classical English bowler who was always asking questions of the batsman. He had a lovely action, bowled at a lively pace and was very accurate in getting the ball to move away from the batsman. Barring injury he would have played a lot more for England. Neil also captained the side that year [1991] so he was a big reason why we were successful."

Toss: Essex won the toss and decided to field.
Umpires: SB Hassan, NT Plews.

MIDDLESEX

MA Roseberry	b Pringle	2		c Gooch b Pringle	99
M Keech	hit wkt b Foster	3		c Garnham b Foster	0
*MW Gatting	lbw b Pringle	0		c Gooch b Foster	35
MR Ramprakash	c Pringle b Foster	0		b Foster	19
KR Brown	c Gooch b Foster	4		c Hussain b Pringle	59
PN Weekes	run out	5		b Andrew	0
JE Emburey	lbw b Pringle	1		lbw b Topley	37
NF Williams	c Hussain b Andrew	23		c Topley b Foster	6
DW Headley	c Garnham b Foster	1	(10)	c Salim Malik b Foster	22
†P Farbrace	not out	12	(9)	c Topley b Foster	8
NG Cowans	c Hussain b Andrew	0		not out	8
Extras		0		(5 lb, 9 w)	14
Total	**(all out, 24.3 overs)**	**51**		**(all out, 94.4 overs)**	**307**

Fall: 1st inns: 1-5, 2-5, 3-5, 4-5, 5-12, 6-15, 7-15, 8-26, 9-51, 10-51. **2nd inns:** 1-5, 2-63, 3-91, 4-213, 5-222, 6-225, 7-262, 8-268, 9-278, 10-307.
Bowling: 1st inns: Foster 11-6-18-4, Pringle 12-3-25-3, Andrew 1.3-0-8-2. **2nd inns:** Foster 30.4-4-104-6, Pringle 20-9-38-2, Andrew 13-1-48-1, Topley 19-5-70-1, Stephenson 5-1-10-0, Salim Malik 7-0-32-0.

ESSEX

*GA Gooch	c Weekes b Williams	259
JP Stephenson	lbw b Headley	18
PJ Prichard	lbw b Williams	11
Salim Malik	c Brown b Headley	80
N Hussain	c Farbrace b Cowans	57
NV Knight	c Farbrace b Weekes	61
†MA Garnham	not out	24
DR Pringle	not out	14
NA Foster	did not bat	
TD Topley	did not bat	
SJW Andrew	did not bat	
Extras	(14 b, 11 lb, 15 nb, 2 w)	42
Total	**(6 wickets, declared, 123 overs)**	**566**

Fall: 1st inns: 1-37, 2-74, 3-256, 4-395, 5-494, 6-539.
Bowling: 1st inns: Williams 30-7-140-2, Cowans 26-7-70-1, Headley 30-3-153-2, Gatting 16-0-62-0, Emburey 14-0-87-0, Weekes 4-0-21-1, Roseberry 3-0-8-0.

in 31 overs that ended when he was caught in the gully. Gooch ploughed on remorselessly and became so comfortable that he advanced down the pitch to fast bowler Norman Cowans, straight driving him to the boundary three times in an over. Gooch's 245 went into day two, spanning 380 balls and he hit two sixes and 37 fours as he dominated a huge Essex first innings. Trailing by 515, with two days and 52 overs remaining, it seemed that there was no way back for the reigning champions. When opener Matthew Keech was then out to the first ball he faced from Foster, the end seemed nigh but rain and a stubborn fourth-wicket stand between Mike Roseberry and Keith Brown then ensured the home side needed to return for what they hoped would be the final day of their season. Roseberry and Brown carried their partnership to 112 before the latter fell to Pringle's second ball of the day but victory – and the title – was achieved 25 minutes after lunch when Malik caught Dean Headley in the gully off Foster to give the bowler his sixth wicket of the innings and 10th of the match. Having overseen two recent near-misses in the Championship, Gooch was relieved to have cause for celebration again when he took the microphone on the balcony after the match: "I am a bit emotional actually," Gooch said. "It doesn't often happen to me."

Essex v Lancashire

Venue: County Ground, Chelmsford **Result:** Essex won by 1 wicket

Arguably for the first, but certainly not the last, time a famous Essex victory was earned in a significant part to the batting exploits of John Childs. The veteran had proved himself a magnificent acquisition since joining from Gloucestershire in 1985 but it was for his slow bowling that he was synonymous. Childs was chosen as the spin option to replace the injured Peter Such against a formidable Lancashire team that dominated in one-day cricket during the late eighties and early nineties. The left-armer proved to be one of Essex's more economical bowlers on the day as the County conceded their highest total in the Gillette Cup and NatWest Trophy of 318-8. Lancashire captain Neil Fairbrother had little

hesitation in choosing to bat first on a typically flat Chelmsford wicket. Graeme Fowler and Nick Speak laid the platform for a sizeable total in a second-wicket partnership of 89 while Ian Austin and Dexter Fitton issued the coup de grace by smashing 40 from 20 balls at the end of the innings. Having proved expensive with the ball Stephenson atoned with the bat as he and Graham Gooch put on an unbroken opening stand of 116 from 25 overs by the tea interval. Both then fell within two overs after the break to halt the County's progress. Gooch was an unlikely victim of occasional leg-spinner Mike Atherton who was pressed into action due to a groin injury to Phil DeFreitas, who broke down in his first over. Childs recalls the outcome of a pre-match fitness test involving the England fast bowler being a pivotal factor in the final outcome. "What I first remember about the day is that DeFreitas had gone through a

Mike Garnham: nerveless performance

physical warm-up test before the game and said to his captain [Fairbrother] that he was fit to play," Childs explains. "He bowled three balls and went off injured. Lancashire had backed themselves with five genuine bowlers as the scorecard shows." Mark Waugh and Paul Prichard added 46 for the third-wicket before the former was bowled by Mike Watkinson just before bad light was offered. Play was held up for half-an-hour in late afternoon with Essex on 179-3 off 33 overs. Upon the resumption the batting side lost five wickets for 45 and, as the light deteriorated, the outcome of the match looke ominous for Essex with 91 required from little more than 10 overs with two wickets left. Mike Garnham and Don Topley then put on 54 in six overs before the latter was run out by a direct hit from the boundary. Last man Childs joined Garnham with 37 needed in a little

In only his fourth NatWest Trophy appearance for Essex in eight years, John Childs batted in a 60-overs match for the County for the first time. The left-hander's overdue march to the crease was rewarded by 13 valuable runs out of a last-wicket stand of 37 with Mike Garnham that saw his team home. Not everyone had total faith in the number 11 batsman's prospects, however, as the man himself explains:
"Lancashire were so much in charge and I heard a lot of people left the ground by the time I went in," Childs remembers. "But people got wind of what was happening and came back from the pubs to see the end of the game, indicating what they thought of my batting!"

Toss: Essex won the toss and decided to field.
Umpires: RA White, PB Wight.

LANCASHIRE

		Runs	Balls	Mins	4s	6s
G Fowler	c Prichard b Topley	66	95	109	8	-
MA Atherton	c Shahid b Pringle	8	20	31	-	-
NJ Speak	c Garnham b Pringle	60	102	125	4	-
*NH Fairbrother	run out	28	42	38	1	-
GD Lloyd	lbw b Stephenson	24	38	37	1	-
M Watkinson	c Stephenson b Topley	40	29	45	5	1
PAJ DeFreitas	b Stephenson	0	2	1	-	-
ID Austin	not out	33	26	42	4	1
†WK Hegg	st Garnham b Stephenson	7	9	10	1	-
JD Fitton	not out	17	9	15	3	-
DK Morrison	did not bat					
Extras	(19 lb, 10 nb, 6 w)	35				
Total	**(8 wickets, 60 overs)**	**318**				

Fall: 1-36, 2-127, 3-186, 4-192, 5-249, 6-249, 7-261, 8-278.
Bowling: Foster 12-1-47-0, Topley 8-0-51-2, Pringle 12-3-50-2, Stephenson 12-0-78-3, Gooch 4-0-22-0, Childs 12-1-51-0.

ESSEX

		Runs	Balls	Mins	4s	6s
*GA Gooch	c Hegg b Atherton	49	71	115	3	-
JP Stephenson	c DeFreitas b Morrison	75	94	120	10	-
ME Waugh	b Watkinson	25	36	42	1	1
PJ Prichard	c Hegg b Fitton	28	37	95	1	-
NV Knight	run out	1	7	16	-	-
N Shahid	b Atherton	12	21	25	-	-
DR Pringle	c Hegg b Morrison	16	18	26	-	1
NA Foster	b Watkinson	11	13	13	-	1
†MA Garnham	not out	53	37	36	5	-
TD Topley	run out	15	17	30	2	-
JH Childs	not out	13	11	14	2	-
Extras	(13 lb, 3 nb, 5 w)	21				
Total	**(9 wickets, 59.5 overs)**	**319**				

Fall: 1-123, 2-133, 3-179, 4-183, 5-194, 6-208, 7-228, 8-228, 9-282.
Bowling: DeFreitas 0.3-0-5-0, Atherton 11.2-0-83-2, Watkinson 12-2-39-2, Morrison 12-0-72-2, Austin 12-1-58-0, Fitton 12-0-49-1.

more than three overs. Wicket-keeper/batsman Garnham took the bulk of the strike as the equation was whittled down to 14 off the last over – a tall order but home side's chances were improved by the choice of bowler to finish off the innings. Childs takes up the story: "Fairbrother gambled on the game not going down to the last over. It didn't pay off and you don't often see a part-time leg-spinner [Atherton] bowl the last over. After Mike [Garnham] hit a single off the first ball, I recall him urging me to get a single [to get him back on strike] but Lancashire were wise to that and had a reasonably attacking in/out field to save the single. Atherton bowled two leg-spinners close to the left-hander's slot which I hit over mid-wicket for four. But I was still aware the batsman was at the wrong end. So I managed to squirt a single and gave the strike to Mike – who had played an exceptional innings – and he finished the game off with a straight boundary. As all good batsmen do, he didn't leave it to the last ball." Garnham's 53 not out earned him the man-of-the-match award in a match that thrilled a BBC television audience as well as a fervent Chelmsford attendance. In a remarkable batting effort, Essex had made the highest score recorded by a side batting second to win a match in the competition.

Britannic Assurance County Championship

Essex v Hampshire

4-day match   **Venue:** County Ground, Chelmsford **Result:** Essex won by 8 wickets

It was fitting that Essex clinched the 1992 Championship against Hampshire as the turning point in the County's season had come against the same opposition in June when they claimed an unlikely victory. Following on at Bournemouth, Essex found themselves just 14 ahead with three second-innings wickets in hand. A late-order rally was then followed by a stunning bowling display late on the final day to dismiss the home side for 80 and claim a 79-run victory. By the time both sides arrived at Chelmsford, Hampshire, who led the table at the time of the previous meeting, had slipped out of title contention. Essex, on the other hand, recovered from losing three of their opening seven matches to surge to the top of the table. Victory against the southern county would see the home team retain the title with two games to spare. What followed was a thrilling encounter with many twists and turns before Essex imposed themselves on the game at the last. A slow Chelmsford wicket proved difficult for batsmen to dominate and it was not until the 17th over that Kevan James glanced Don Topley for four to register the first boundary of the match. An intriguing sub-plot came when David Gower arrived at the crease, shortly after the release of his autobiography in which he had been critical of Essex and England captain Graham Gooch's time in charge of the national set-up. Gower took 14 off an over from Mark Ilott and had made 30 off 35 balls before holing out to Paul Prichard at cover in, of all people, Gooch's third over – at which point the swing bowler removed himself from the attack and did not bowl again for the rest of the innings. Shaun Udal made a career-best at the time of 44 but Hampshire were bowled out just

**Spin twins:
Peter Such** *(left)*
and John Childs

before the close for 233. That total began to look competitive when Essex trailed by 14 on day two as last pair Peter Such and John Childs came together at the crease. What followed was an entertaining and hugely-unlikely stand of 79 in 17 overs between two of the lesser-accomplished batsmen on the county circuit. Young Hampshire left-armer Ian Turner had bowled well up to that point as he achieved his maiden five-wicket haul. His fellow spinners seemed able to play him better than most, however, so Hampshire captain Mark Nicholas decided he would turn up the heat to finish the innings off. But, as the 1993 Essex Yearbook recorded, West Indian fast bowler Malcolm Marshall went the same way as his team-mates as the partnership escalated into match-changing proportions: "They (Such and Childs) treated the Hampshire attack with disdain and, in particular, were severe on Malcolm Marshall, Such attacking him cross-batted from outside the leg-stump repeatedly hitting him to the extra cover boundary. It was enormous fun for the

Peter Such offers his version of the crucial 79-run last-wicket partnership he shared with John Childs in Essex's first innings. "During my stay at the crease I felt a combination of nerves and fear as the finest fast bowler in the world was running in at me. It's not nice trying to bat against someone like Malcolm Marshall when you are number nine, 10 or 11 because you don't have the same reactions or degree of ability as the other batsmen. I decided to have a slog at him – backing away to leg and thrashing to the off-side. We were always going to play our shots but fortunately we had put on a crucial 70 or 80 before one of us got out."

Toss: Hampshire won the toss and decided to bat.
Umpires: G Sharp, AGT Whitehead.

HAMPSHIRE

KD James	b Topley	20	(2)	lbw b Pringle	15
TC Middleton	c Garnham b Ilott	17	(1)	c Stephenson b Pringle	2
DI Gower	c Prichard b Gooch	30		c Prichard b Ilott	4
RA Smith	c Ilott b Childs	23		b Such	23
*MCJ Nicholas	c Ilott b Childs	19		b Childs	0
MD Marshall	lbw b Such	39		c Prichard b Childs	12
JR Ayling	c Gooch b Such	5		c Ilott b Childs	31
†AN Aymes	b Such	13		c Childs b Pringle	65
SD Udal	c Such b Pringle	44		st Garnham b Stephenson	32
IJ Turner	c Topley b Such	8		c Garnham b Ilott	16
KJ Shine	not out	4		not out	5
Extras	(4 b, 4 lb, 3 w)	11		(8 b, 10 lb, 6 w)	24
Total	**(all out, 109.3 overs)**	**233**		**(all out, 105.3 overs)**	**229**

Fall: 1st inns: 1-35, 2-72, 3-72, 4-108, 5-117, 6-146, 7-168, 8-184, 9-209, 10-233. **2nd inns:** 1-15, 2-22, 3-35, 4-37, 5-55, 6-63, 7-119, 8-172, 9-217, 10-229.
Bowling: 1st inns: Pringle 18.3-7-32-1, Ilott 27-13-60-1, Topley 11-2-34-1, Gooch 3-1-5-1, Childs 30-11-71-2, Such 20-9-23-4. **2nd inns:** Pringle 20.3-8-42-3, Ilott 16-4-44-2, Topley 2-0-7-0, Childs 35-17-67-3, Such 29-13-46-1, Stephenson 3-2-5-1.

ESSEX

*GA Gooch	c Smith b Ayling	22	c Middleton b Turner	19
JP Stephenson	c Aymes b Marshall	6	not out	83
JJB Lewis	c Aymes b Ayling	43	b Turner	4
PJ Prichard	b Turner	82	not out	55
NV Knight	b Turner	5	did not bat	
†MA Garnham	b Turner	14	did not bat	
DR Pringle	lbw b Turner	14	did not bat	
TD Topley	b Turner	16	did not bat	
MC Ilott	c Middleton b Udal	2	did not bat	
PM Such	not out	35	did not bat	
JH Childs	b Ayling	43	did not bat	
Extras	(2 b, 5 lb, 8 nb, 1 w)	16	(3 lb, 1 nb)	4
Total	**(all out, 110.2 overs)**	**298**	**(2 wickets, 44.2 overs)**	**165**

Fall: 1st inns: 1-12, 2-50, 3-142, 4-159, 5-185, 6-188, 7-216, 8-219, 9-219, 10-298. **2nd inns:** 1-24, 2-32.
Bowling: 1st inns: Marshall 24-7-40-1, Shine 5-0-25-0, Ayling 15.2-0-44-3, Turner 38-12-81-5, Udal 24-2-91-1, Nicholas 1-0-3-0, James 3-0-7-0. **2nd inns:** Marshall 11-3-33-0, Ayling 9-3-34-0, Turner 14-5-54-2, Udal 10-0-40-0, Smith 0.2-0-1-0.

crowd and the stand was invaluable to Essex because it gave them a 65-run lead on first innings." When Hampshire went into lunch on day three at 37-4 it appeared the game was firmly in Essex's grasp and, at 63-6, a three-day finish was on the cards. Hampshire wicketkeeper Adrian Aymes was then given solid support by Jon Ayling and Udal – the latter in a stand of 53 that spanned 26 overs – to breathe some life back into the game. It was an hour before the first wicket of the day – Hampshire's ninth – fell on the final morning and it took the new ball to achieve the breakthrough (Turner caught behind off Ilott). Aymes, partnered for the 10th wicket by a hobbling Kevin Shine (who was unable to bowl later in the day) was the last batsman to fall when he was caught at long-on after four hours of resistance. With the County set 165 to win off 80 there was plenty of time to achieve the required victory (although rain had been expected to play a part as the day went on). Turner continued to trouble the Essex batsmen on a pitch still helpful for the spinners and his removal of Graham Gooch and Jon Lewis either side of lunch made life somewhat tougher for a period. John Stephenson and Paul Prichard then added 133 in 31 overs (the highest partnership of the match) as victory – and the title – was secured with more than two hours to spare at 3.35pm.

Britannic Assurance County Championship
Northamptonshire v Essex

4-day match   **Venue:** Wardown Park, Luton **Result:** Northamptonshire won by 2 wickets

Despite the valiant efforts of Mark Ilott, Essex were unable to prevent Championship leaders Northants maintaining their place at the head of the table in a thrilling match that was completed by the middle session of day two. Left-arm quicks held sway as both Ilott and fellow England bowler Paul Taylor claimed 23 victims between them as they took advantage of late swing under cloud cover – with conditions especially favourable on day one. Ilott entered

the match having just returned from a groin injury that had kept him out of the previous two Championship matches. However, after seeing Taylor and David Capel dismiss Essex for just 127 (a recovery in itself thanks to a hard-hitting 52 not out from Robert Rollins) there was no time for the pace bowler to ease himself back in gently. Ilott notes, "When you see a fellow swing bowler taking wickets you do tend to think 'if he can do that so can I'. But it can put pressure on you when you are expected to take wickets, in the same way as it does for a spinner on a turning pitch. I could see from the way our batters coped that it was swinging and if bowlers were doing well then so could I too. I always backed myself to bowl well."

The pace man proceeded to rip through the Northants line-up, taking 9-19 as the hosts were dismissed for 46 – their lowest score since the Second World War. Ilott's haul included a hat-trick of lbw's although it was not, as reported at the time, the second occasion he had achieved such a feat (his three successive wickets for Watford Under-15s were not all leg before victims but it was true

Mark Ilott:
heroic in defeat

that he turned to his father, John, was who the umpire and shouted "howzat, dad' on the third delivery). Ilott's career-best bowling featured a spell of five wickets for no runs after tea during which time he became the first bowler to achieve a hat-trick of leg-before decisions in the Championship since Mike Proctor in 1979 for Gloucestershire against Yorkshire at Cheltenham. Graham Gooch thus began the Essex second innings at 5pm in bright sunlight but that

Fifteen years later, Mark Ilott can look back philosophically on a match that Essex had been expected to win after the extraordinary events of day one: "After three innings were completed in one day the wicket had undergone three lots of rolling – so that would have taken some of the bite out. I don't recall it swinging less but they got the highest total of the match on the second day which suggested something must have changed. It certainly didn't go as flat as a pancake but it was not as bowler-friendly. At the end of the match I ended up thinking 'how can you take 14 wickets and lose?!' Had we won I would have been a major contributor. Looking back, the pain of losing has lessened whereas my career-best is still there. But at the time I was hugely annoyed to have taken 14 wickets and been on the losing side."

Toss: Northamptonshire won the toss and decided to field.
Umpires: DJ Constant, RA White.

ESSEX

GA Gooch	b Taylor	4	lbw b Mallender		20
DDJ Robinson	b Mallender	8	lbw b Mallender		3
ME Waugh	lbw b Taylor	12	lbw b Taylor		9
N Hussain	b Kumble	27	c Capel b Taylor		0
*PJ Prichard	c Montgomerie b Capel	11	lbw b Taylor		0
RC Irani	lbw b Capel	0	c Montgomerie b Taylor		26
†RJ Rollins	not out	52	c Warren b Taylor		4
MC Ilott	lbw b Capel	1	c Bailey b Taylor		0
DM Cousins	b Capel	0	b Taylor		17
PM Such	b Kumble	2	run out		19
JH Childs	c Warren b Capel	4	not out		3
Extras	(4 lb, 2 nb)	6	(6 lb)		6
Total	**(all out, 48.1 overs)**	**127**	**(all out, 28.1 overs)**		**107**

Fall: 1st inns: 1-6, 2-22, 3-24, 4-44, 5-44, 6-78, 7-79, 8-79, 9-88, 10-127. **2nd inns:** 1-16, 2-33, 3-35, 4-35, 5-35, 6-63, 7-63, 8-68, 9-103, 10-107.
Bowling: 1st inns: Taylor 10-1-18-2, Mallender 8-0-22-1, Curran 6-1-15-0, Capel 14.1-3-29-5, Kumble 10-2-39-2. **2nd inns:** Taylor 14.1-2-50-7, Mallender 8-3-22-2, Curran 4-0-22-0, Kumble 2-0-7-0.

NORTHAMPTONSHIRE

RR Montgomerie	b Ilott	18	(2)	c Hussain b Ilott	18
MB Loye	lbw b Ilott	3	(3)	lbw b Irani	14
RJ Bailey	lbw b Ilott	0	(4)	lbw b Ilott	1
*AJ Lamb	c Rollins b Ilott	19	(5)	not out	50
†RJ Warren	b Ilott	0	(6)	c Hussain b Waugh	25
KM Curran	lbw b Ilott	6	(7)	c Prichard b Waugh	24
DJ Capel	c Rollins b Irani	0	(8)	c Robinson b Ilott	6
JN Snape	lbw b Ilott	0	(9)	lbw b Ilott	14
A Kumble	lbw b Ilott	0	(10)	not out	17
NA Mallender	lbw b Ilott	0	(1)	lbw b Ilott	8
JP Taylor	not out	0		did not bat	
Extras		0		(4 b, 2 lb, 8 nb, 1 w)	15
Total	**(all out, 20.1 overs)**	**46**		**(8 wickets, 56 overs)**	**192**

Fall: 1st inns: 1-17, 2-17, 3-39, 4-39, 5-45, 6-46, 7-46, 8-46, 9-46, 10-46. **2nd inns:** 1-24, 2-49, 3-53, 4-56, 5-94, 6-131, 7-142, 8-161.
Bowling: 1st inns: Ilott 10.1-2-19-9, Cousins 4-0-9-0, Irani 6-2-18-1. **2nd inns:** Ilott 22-0-86-5, Irani 17-7-53-1, Waugh 17-4-47-2.

wasn't to be the end of the drama for the day. Taylor, who had made a relatively understated impact in the first innings with 2-18, returned figures of 7-50 as Essex made 20 less than in their first innings. Incredibly there was still time on day one for Northants to begin their pursuit of 189 for victory – a total that would constitute by far the highest score of the match.

The home side took an 'all or nothing' approach to their batting on the second day and their method paid dividends as captain Allan Lamb saw them home with a 71-ball half-century (an innings that included six fours, a rare commodity in this match). Ilott kept his side in the match with another five wickets – also having Lamb dropped by Nasser Hussain – and the game was still in the balance when he trapped Jeremy Snape lbw to leave Northants 28 runs short with two wickets remaining. Lamb was then joined by Indian spinner Anil Kumble who blazed away for 17 not out to see his team home. The Northants skipper noted at the time, "He (Kumble) said, 'leave it to me, captain', so I did. After that I never doubted we would win."

National Westminster Bank Trophy, Final
Essex v Warwickshire

60-overs match   **Venue:** Lord's Cricket Ground, St John's Wood **Result:** Essex won by 9 wickets

Much importance was always placed on winning the toss during the NatWest Trophy finals of the late '80s and '90s, with 10 of the previous 11 finals being won by the team batting second. Despite taking full advantage of the early movement precipitated by a 10.30am start, however, Essex had very recent precedence as to why they should have taken nothing for granted at the mid-way stage. For it was Essex who were the sole team over those earlier 11 Lord's showpieces to have floundered in the second innings – to such an extent that they were bowled out for 57 by Lancashire in the most recent final. Nonetheless, the County will have been proud of their work in the field as they restricted the favourites to 170-8 from their 60 overs. Preparations for the match were complicated by the death of Diana, Princess of Wales, the previous weekend, with her funeral taking place on the original day of the scheduled fixture. Not only did that mean the match was put

back by a day but Essex's pre-match work-out took place at Regent's Park as Lord's was shut on the Saturday. Warwickshire had comfortably beaten Essex in both four-day and one-day league matches at the end of August and were bidding for their third NatWest Trophy victory in five years. Ashley Cowan and Mark Ilott had both performed well in the previous year's final in defeat and again set the tone for a good display in the field. With the pitch offering sideways movement, Cowan swung the third legitimate ball of the day prodigiously into Nick Knight's pads and the former Essex left-hander realised his mistake in shouldering arms long before a simple leg-before appeal was upheld. Cowan struck again in his

**Ashley Cowan:
in the swing of things**

fourth over – Neil Smith, attempting a pinch-hitting role in difficult circumstances, driving at an out-swinger to be caught at second slip by Stuart Law. David Hemp – who had made hundreds in the quarter-final and semi-final – was run out by Paul Grayson's underarm throw and then Trevor Penney was the victim of another Cowan out-swinger. All this time Warwickshire were barely able to get their scoring rate above two runs per over as the entire Essex attack showed admirable discipline. Dominic Ostler – who had been dropped at slip by Cowan on five – gave Irani due reward for bowling through the pain barrier when he top-edged a pull to Danny Law on the grandstand boundary. That description was to do the catch a disservice, however, as the fielder made a routine catch into a work of art as he needed four grabs before completing the dismissal. Off-spinner Peter Such then encapsulated

Fast bowler Ashley Cowan's outstanding bowling effort came near the end of a fine campaign that earned him a place in England's touring squad over the winter to the West Indies. Looking back, the right-armer believes his performance against Warwickshire pushed his claims but an England call was not at the top of his thoughts leading up to the game: "I'd had a reasonably successful year – in what was only my second full season – and I didn't think about that [being called up by England]," Cowan stresses. "It was a Lord's final, the first one had been a shambles so I just wanted to get on with it and enjoy the occasion. As it turned out it was a nice day with a full house and a lot of people behind us. I'm sure the performance in the final helped and we had featured on television in the run-up to the final so that would have helped too. But I would like to think they took into consideration my whole season."

Toss: Essex won the toss and decided to field.
Umpires: MJ Kitchen, P Willey, JH Hampshire (TV).

WARWICKSHIRE

		Runs	Balls	4s	6s	S-Rate
NV Knight	lbw b Cowan	0	3	-	-	0.00
*NMK Smith	c SG Law b Cowan	5	19	1	-	26.32
DL Hemp	run out (Hussain)	21	67	3	-	31.34
DP Ostler	c DR Law b Irani	34	106	3	-	32.08
TL Penney	c Rollins b Cowan	5	36	-	-	13.89
DR Brown	c DR Law b Ilott	37	62	1	-	59.68
G Welch	c and b Such	2	11	-	-	18.18
AF Giles	run out (Grayson)	21	33	2	-	63.64
†KJ Piper	not out	15	19	1	-	78.95
AA Donald	not out	3	5	-	-	60.00
GC Small	did not bat					
Extras	(5 b, 15 lb, 2 nb, 5 w)	27				
Total	**(8 wickets, 60 overs)**	**170**				

Fall: 1-1, 2-12, 3-45, 4-74, 5-90, 6-95, 7-147, 8-156.
Bowling: Cowan 12-3-29-3, Ilott 12-3-29-1, Irani 12-4-22-1, SG Law 12-4-38-0, Such 11-1-32-1.

ESSEX

		Runs	Balls	4s	6s	S-Rate
*PJ Prichard	lbw b Donald	57	45	7	1	126.67
SG Law	not out	80	71	10	1	112.68
N Hussain	not out	25	43	4	1	58.14
RC Irani	did not bat					
DDJ Robinson	did not bat					
AP Grayson	did not bat					
DR Law	did not bat					
†RJ Rollins	did not bat					
AP Cowan	did not bat					
MC Ilott	did not bat					
PM Such	did not bat					
Extras	(5 lb, 4 w)	9				
Total	**(1 wicket, 26.3 overs)**	**171**				

Fall: 1-109.
Bowling: Welch 5-0-34-0, Brown 4-0-29-0-3, Small 7-0-43-0, Donald 6-0-36-1, Giles 4-1-20-0, Penney 0.3-0-4-0.

the Essex display with a diving one-handed catch off his own bowling to remove Graeme Welch. Warwickshire's later batsmen ensured their side lasted their full allocation but early wickets were vital in the reply if they were to have any chance of pulling off an unlikely victory. As it transpired, Essex's openers, Paul Prichard and Stuart Law, made hay while the sun shone and they had already reached their all-out total of the previous final by the end of the sixth over. Warwickshire's trump card, South African pace bowler Allan Donald, was introduced into the attack in that sixth over and he was promptly dispatched for 12. Essex found the boundary 11 times in the first seven overs – as many as Warwickshire had managed in 60 overs – and Prichard swept Giles for six before going back to Donald and being trapped lbw. The batting side had already made 109 off just 14 overs by that stage and victory was well in sight. Tea was taken with 19 runs needed and Law needed just nine balls after the break to achieve them. Essex's triumph was completed by 5.19pm with the entire match spanning just 86.3 overs – five balls fewer than the previous year. There had been one earlier nine-wicket finish in the final, also against Warwickshire by Surrey in 1982, but this victory was achieved with fewer overs bowled – an emphatic way to banish the memories of 1996.

Benson & Hedges Cup, Final

Essex v Leicestershire

50-overs match | **Venue:** Lord's Cricket Ground, St John's Wood **Result:** Essex won by 192 runs

A tale of two bowling performances went a long way to deciding what was – at the time – scheduled to be the last Benson & Hedges Cup Final. Although the 50-overs format returned briefly a few years later – with Essex again reaching the final only to lose to Warwickshire in 2002 – this was to be the last time the County got their hands on the trophy. Leicestershire captain Chris Lewis – standing in for James Whittaker, absent with a leg injury – gleefully elected to field after winning the toss in anticipation of claiming the new ball himself. The England all-rounder spectacularly wasted the opportunity, however, as his first spell ended with figures of 4-0-24-0. Fellow opening bowler Alan Mullally fared a little better as he removed Stuart Law cheaply but was nonetheless responsible for seven of the 18 wides bowled by the Midlands county. Essex skipper Paul Prichard, playing his first game of the season in the competition due to a bout of shin splints, looked in fine touch from the off and his partnership of 134 with Nasser Hussain was even more commendable in light of the favourable bowling conditions. The opener twice carved sixes over extra cover with Hussain effecting a similar stroke for good measure. Essex's final total of 268-7 looked a daunting proposition for the opposition as all-rounder Ronnie Irani agreed: "When we all got back into the dressing room after our innings, we thought we would win the game easily because we had scored 100 runs above par on that wicket." Any visions of a victory lap had to be put on hold, however, as the predicted rain arrived during the interval to wash out the remainder of the day. Back came the teams on the Sunday – the same day as the France '98 World Cup Final – with the possibility of a bowl-out looming because of the weather. Essex pace man Mark Ilott recalls, "We went into the nets and practiced indoors just in case but the forecast was not too bad. We were always hopeful of getting out there. I would have been one of those chosen along with Peter Such, Paul Grayson, Ronnie Irani and Stuart Law. Those five were thought to be the most accurate." Play did eventually resume at 3.25pm and this time conditions were put into perspective by the opening bowlers. "We bowled better," Ilott asserts. "Just like Warwickshire the previous year [in the

Joyful and triumphant: Essex celebrate another one-day title

Essex all-rounder Ronnie Irani gave particular praise to Mark Ilott for his bowling effort in this and the side's two other finals over the space of three seasons in the '90s. Irani remarked: "Mark Ilott was unplayable in our two NatWest Trophy Finals [against Lancashire in 1996 and Warwickshire in 1997] and this Benson & Hedges Cup Final. We decided the Pavilion End should have been renamed the 'Mark Ilott End'!" When this quote was put to the man himself, Ilott admits his satisfaction at his returns on the big occasion: "I'd not really thought about it that way before," the left-armer stated, "but I do recall Ian Botham coming up to me before the Benson and Hedges Cup Final in 2002 asking why I wasn't playing because my record at Lord's was very good. On that occasion Andy Clarke had done very well in the semi-final so I understood that he couldn't be left out but I'm proud of my career at Lord's."

Toss: Leicestershire won the toss and decided to field.
Umpires: R Julian, MJ Kitchen, JC Balderstone (TV).

ESSEX

		Runs	Balls	4s	6s	S-Rate
*PJ Prichard	c Simmons b Williamson	92	113	11	2	81.42
SG Law	c Mullally b Wells	6	24	-	-	25.00
N Hussain	c Smith b Lewis	88	102	8	1	86.27
RC Irani	c Maddy b Mullally	32	37	2	1	86.49
DR Law	c Lewis b Williamson	1	5	-	-	20.00
AP Grayson	not out	9	7	2	-	128.57
†RJ Rollins	c Brimson b Mullally	0	2	-	-	0.00
SD Peters	b Mullally	9	8	1	-	112.50
AP Cowan	not out	3	2	-	-	150.00
MC Ilott	did not bat					
PM Such	did not bat					
Extras	(2 b, 8 lb, 18 w)	28				
Total	**(7 wickets, 50 overs)**	**268**				

Fall: 1-40, 2-174, 3-234, 4-244, 5-245, 6-250, 7-265.
Bowling: Mullally 10-1-36-3, Lewis 9-0-59-1, Wells 10-0-34-1, Simmons 9-1-67-0, Brimson 2-0-13-0, Williamson 10-0-49-2.

LEICESTERSHIRE

		Runs	Balls	4s	6s	S-Rate
DL Maddy	c SG Law b Cowan	5	41	-	-	12.20
IJ Sutcliffe	c SG Law b Cowan	1	12	-	-	8.33
BF Smith	c SG Law b Cowan	0	1	-	-	0.00
PV Simmons	b Ilott	2	4	-	-	50.00
VJ Wells	lbw b Ilott	1	10	-	-	10.00
A Habib	lbw b Ilott	5	15	1	-	33.33
†PA Nixon	not out	21	36	3	-	58.33
*CC Lewis	c Peters b Irani	0	14	-	-	0.00
D Williamson	c Hussain b SG Law	11	18	2	-	61.11
AD Mullally	lbw b Irani	1	12	-	-	8.33
MT Brimson	b SG Law	0	5	-	-	0.00
Extras	(8 lb, 4 nb, 17 w)	29				
Total	**(all out, 27.4 overs)**	**76**				

Fall: 1-6, 2-6, 3-10, 4-17, 5-31, 6-31, 7-36, 8-67, 9-73, 10-76.
Bowling: Ilott 8-2-10-3, Cowan 10-2-24-3, Irani 6-2-21-2, SG Law 3.4-0-13-2.

NatWest Trophy Final], Leicestershire thought they had it in the bag. Alan Mullally had said that he would be confident chasing anything under 300. Overhead conditions didn't change too much so the ball swung on both days. The rain meant there was a bit of moisture so it moved a lot for me and Ashley Cowan. Ashley also bowled at a good pace and we were too much for Leicestershire on the day. Overall we bowled and batted better than them and it meant more because they were so confident and cocky about it – for me that made it sweeter than the Warwickshire game." After Cowan removed the openers, Ilott then claimed the prize wicket of West Indian Phil Simmons to leave the batting side in tatters. Essex's left-armer conceded just four runs off the bat in eight overs as the match turned into a procession of hapless batsmen returning to the pavilion. Darren Maddy (the winner of five Gold awards in seven matches leading up to the game) managed five singles in 14 overs before providing Law with his third slip catch. Indeed it was Law who finished the job off with two wickets as Leicestershire recorded the lowest score in a B & H Final. During a year in which Essex finished bottom of the County Championship, resulting in Prichard's resignation as captain, this victory was undoubtedly a memory to savour.

Essex v Surrey

45-overs match **Venue:** Castle Park Cricket Ground, Colchester **Result:** Essex won by 23 runs

Essex's first foray into staging floodlit cricket proved to be a resounding success both on and off the field at Castle Park in 2000. Tickets sold out well in advance as many of an eventual 6,000 crowd were in place in time to see Essex begin their innings – the shape of things to come for floodlit cricket in Essex. It was an attraction that took on a new dimension once permanent lights were erected at Chelmsford in 2003. Surrey went into the match unbeaten in Norwich Union National League Division Two and with the knowledge that victory would secure them the title with games to spare. The Lions fielded a full-strength team with a host of household names including Alec Stewart, Graham Thorpe, Alex Tudor and Saqlain Mushtaq. Essex, by contrast, had endured an inconsistent campaign and were out of contention for promotion with four games remaining. Parachutists, cheerleaders and Essex batsmen striding to the crease with their own signature tune was the order of the day as the match began under bright

Lighting up Colchester: Essex President Doug Insole, Essex Chairman David Acfield and former Prime Minister John Major at Castle Park

sunshine. Essex's opening duo, Nasser Hussain and Stuart Law, kept the smiles on the faces of the home support as they put on 161 in 32 overs for the first wicket. England captain Hussain made a timely return to form after a poor Test campaign against West Indies, a series that was just about to climax at The Oval. The right-hander hooked and on-drove Tudor for three successive fours in the sixth over as the home team reached 100 by the 19th over. Law was the more explosive of the pair as he made his 50 from 45 balls – including a pull for six off Tudor. Ian Salisbury – despite conceding 11 in his first over – and Adam Hollioake then turned the game back on an even footing by the end of the innings as they instigated an astonishing collapse. Eight wickets were shared by the pair in the last 13 overs for the cost of just 49 runs as the hosts were only able to sneak above 200 despite their flying start. With Surrey's top six containing five players with England experience – former Essex batsman Nadeem Shahid being the odd man out – all

---

Essex wicketkeeper James Foster was making just his third National League appearance in this fixture with Surrey. The youngster made 11 not out and took a fine catch low to his right to dismiss Nadeem Shahid as he tasted victory for the first time. Foster recalls: "They had a star-studded line-up and I can remember Graham Thorpe sledging me when I was coming into bat, accusing me of strutting to the crease because you could choose your own music and I picked 'Fly Away' by Lenny Kravitz. Alec Stewart was one of my heroes so I was awe-struck playing against him. Surrey were the form team and they had brought champagne with them because they thought they were just going to rock up and win. We got a decent score – but not what it could have been – and with their line-up they thought they were going to walk it. Stewart walked in to 'Let Me Entertain You' and we thought 'here we go, he might well do that', but we beat a team littered with internationals and it was a great feeling. Playing under lights in front of a crowd that was so pro-Essex was brilliant to be involved in."

Toss: Essex won the toss and decided to bat.
Umpires: JH Hampshire, DR Shepherd.

ESSEX

		Runs	Balls	4s	6s	S-Rate
N Hussain	c Stewart b Hollioake	57	102	4	-	55.88
SG Law	c Hollioake b Salisbury	92	94	11	1	97.87
GR Napier	c Bicknell b Salisbury	2	8	-	-	25.00
*RC Irani	c Bicknell b Hollioake	8	18	-	-	44.44
SD Peters	c Brown b Salisbury	7	10	1	-	70.00
AP Grayson	c Stewart b Salisbury	0	2	-	-	0.00
†JS Foster	not out	11	15	-	-	73.33
DR Law	c Thorpe b Hollioake	2	11	-	-	18.18
AP Cowan	c Shahid b Hollioake	3	5	-	-	60.00
TJ Mason	not out	8	7	1	-	114.29
AC McGarry	did not bat					
Extras	(5 b, 4 lb, 4 nb, 3 w)	16				
Total	**(8 wickets, 45 overs)**	**206**				

Fall: 1-161, 2-164, 3-168, 4-180, 5-180, 6-180, 7-187, 8-197.
Bowling: Bicknell 7-0-27-0, Tudor 6-0-44-0, Saqlain Mushtaq 9-1-34-0, Ratcliffe 5-0-22-0, Salisbury 9-2-32-4, Hollioake 9-0-38-4.

SURREY

		Runs	Balls	4s	6s	S-Rate
AD Brown	b McGarry	27	38	3	-	71.05
†AJ Stewart	c DR Law b Cowan	13	19	2	-	68.42
N Shahid	c Foster b Irani	14	23	2	-	60.87
GP Thorpe	c Mason b Grayson	19	37	-	-	51.35
IJ Ward	b DR Law	25	64	-	-	39.06
*AJ Hollioake	c Napier b DR Law	36	41	4	-	87.80
JD Ratcliffe	c Cowan b McGarry	9	8	1	-	112.50
AJ Tudor	c Irani b DR Law	3	6	-	-	50.00
MP Bicknell	not out	15	9	2	-	166.67
IDK Salisbury	run out	0	4	-	-	0.00
Saqlain Mushtaq	c DR Law b Cowan	4	13	-	-	30.77
Extras	(9 lb, 2 nb, 7 w)	18				
Total	**(all out, 43.3 overs)**	**183**				

Fall: 1-28, 2-58, 3-58, 4-95, 5-149, 6-154, 7-161, 8-164, 9-164, 10-183.
Bowling: Cowan 8.3-0-38-2, DR Law 8-1-45-3, Irani 8-1-23-1, McGarry 8-2-20-2, Mason 6-0-29-0, Grayson 5-0-19-1.

looked set fair for the visitors to clinch the title. Essex fast bowler Ashley Cowan explains why their exalted opponents were such a tough proposition at the time. "Surrey were considered as the Man. Utd of cricket because money was starting to change the way that cricket was moving," Cowan explains. "They were the first county that paid cricketers according to who they were and how they performed rather than on a structured capping system. There was a lot of money flying around and they had lots of internationals as well as good overseas players and they weren't shy to pay them well. You always knew you were up against it when you played them as they were a team of Superstars but sometimes they played as individuals." Cowan made a crucial early breakthrough when he removed Stewart to lift home spirits and the match was in the balance when Surrey stumbled to 95-4. A partnership of 54 between Ian Ward and Hollioake then saw the visitors need 63 off the last 10 overs with six wickets left but Danny Law dismissed both in quick succession to trigger a dramatic collapse that saw the Lions lose their last six batsmen for 39 runs inside nine overs. Cowan finished the match off at 10.30pm by removing Saqlain to put the seal on a hugely successful experiment for the County.

PPP Healthcare County Championship, Division Two

Essex v Warwickshire

4-day match **Venue:** County Ground, Chelmsford **Result:** Essex won by 6 wickets

Having failed to make the cut for Division One when the Championship was split at the end of the 1999 season, the County found themselves chasing a return to the top-flight in the following campaign. That pursuit came down to the last match of the season when Essex hosted Warwickshire in a 'winner takes all' clash for one of the three promotion spots. Essex Captain Ronnie Irani chose to bowl first despite apparently favourable batting conditions – a decision that meant the County needed to take their chances when they came along. As it transpired the bowling was awry and catches went down as Warwickshire opening pair Mike Powell and Mark Wagh batted for 59 overs in a partnership of 230. A run out appeared the likeliest mode of dismissal, with Essex's attack labouring, and so it proved as Powell was thrown out by Irani when backing too

far up at the non-striker's end. Dominic Ostler then helped Wagh take the score up to 306 before Peter Such triggered a collapse with three quick wickets. Wagh was the second of his three victims before the close after the opener had struck 137. The right-hander – missed by Stuart Law at slip on 18 and 48 – had been drafted into the side in recent weeks in the absence of the injured Nick Knight and his century at Chelmsford – on the back of several other solid

TV star: Stephen Peters (*left*) talks to SKY's Bob Willis after his match-winning innings

displays – saw him awarded his county cap, a day after asking for release from his contract. An eventful match for Wagh continued on day two when umpires John Hampshire and Barry Dudleston advised Warwickshire captain Neil Smith to remove him from the attack as they were not satisfied with the legality of the off-spinner's action. Smith had earlier declared at 400-8 to deny Essex a third bowling point with such fine margins still needing to be considered at that stage. Law fell to a brilliant right-handed catch by Trevor Penney at cover to leave the home side in trouble at 63-3. A combination of Darren Robinson's excellent strokeplay – particularly off his legs – and Irani's fighting spirit then

Peter Such was the pick of the Essex bowlers as they struggled for wickets in Warwickshire's first innings although rain meant the off-spinner played little part over the remainder of the match as he watched Ronnie Irani and Stephen Peters complete a successful run-chase. Such is full of praise for the role 21-year-old Peters played on that final day.

"Stephen Peters was the difference in that game," Such claims. "He played very well and was a very fine young player at the time. Credit to him for starting to turn that potential into genuine runs over the latter part of his career [with third county Northamptonshire]. He also played an excellent knock in the 1998 Benson & Hedges quarter-final at Lord's in a very tight game so we knew he had the ability to play important innings – it was his consistency that was an issue."

Toss: Essex won the toss and decided to field. .
Umpires: B Dudleston, JH Hampshire, JW Lloyds (TV).

WARWICKSHIRE

MJ Powell	run out	106	(2)	not out	0
MA Wagh	c Prichard b Such	137	(1)	not out	8
DP Ostler	b Such	32		did not bat	
DL Hemp	c Foster b Anderson	11		did not bat	
A Singh	c and b Such	7		did not bat	
TL Penney	not out	28		did not bat	
DR Brown	b Ilott	15		did not bat	
*NMK Smith	b Ilott	13		did not bat	
†KJ Piper	c Prichard b Cowan	0		did not bat	
CE Dagnall	not out	6		did not bat	
A Richardson	did not bat			did not bat	
Extras	(4 b, 9 lb, 30 nb, 2 w)	45			0
Total	(8 wickets, declared, 125.2 overs)	400		(no wicket, declared, 0.3 overs)	8

Fall: 1st inns: 1-230, 2-306, 3-315, 4-321, 5-329, 6-348, 7-370, 8-379.
Bowling: Cowan 29-6-115-1, Ilott 25-10-64-2, Irani 13-5-18-0, Anderson 30.2-6-107-1, Such 28-7-83-3.
2nd inns: Robinson 0.3-0-8-0.

ESSEX

PJ Prichard	lbw b Dagnall	0	c Singh b Brown	19
AP Grayson	lbw b Brown	17	c Piper b Dagnall	7
DDJ Robinson	c Ostler b Smith	92	c Hemp b Dagnall	5
SG Law	c Penney b Richardson	10	lbw b Richardson	8
*RC Irani	not out	72	not out	64
SD Peters	c Brown b Smith	1	not out	77
†JS Foster	not out	7	did not bat	
AP Cowan	did not bat		did not bat	
RSG Anderson	did not bat		did not bat	
MC Ilott	did not bat		did not bat	
PM Such	did not bat		did not bat	
Extras	(1 lb, 8 nb)	9	(8 b, 4 lb, 2 nb, 8 w)	22
Total	(5 wickets, declared, 77 overs)	208	(4 wickets, 38.4 overs)	202

Fall: 1st inns: 1-0, 2-38, 3-63, 4-179, 5-183. **2nd inns:** 1-36, 2-46, 3-51, 4-64 .
Bowling: 1st inns: Dagnall 19-8-48-1, Richardson 20-4-57-1, Brown 17-3-49-1, Smith 20-3-49-2,
Wagh 1-0-4-0. **2nd inns:** Richardson 10-1-57-1, Dagnall 11.4-2-57-2, Brown 11-1-51-1, Smith 5-0-21-0,
Hemp 1-0-4-0.

pulled Essex round in a partnership of 116 for the fourth-wicket. Essex were well on their way to avoiding the follow-on at the close of play although a significant first-innings deficit seemed likely. As it turned out, day three's wash-out favoured the hosts as Warwickshire by now had no option but to risk defeat to claim the victory that was a necessity to gain promotion. Essex could have batted on to 350 and collected enough bonus points to send them into Division One with a draw – but at 208-5 that target was still a long way off. Irani's negotiating skills worked a treat as Essex were left to score 201 from a minimum of 56 overs. Time was never likely to be a problem for the batting side but wickets did seem an issue when Law was the fourth batsman to fall at 64. Irani was then joined by youngster Stephen Peters and the fifth-wicket pair added 138 in 25 overs to win the match and gain promotion with plenty of time and 17.2 overs in hand. Peters' 77 not out came off just 84 balls with 13 boundaries while Irani played a Captain's innings with an unbeaten 64 off 77 balls. Irani's first full season at the helm ended in champagne-popping balcony celebrations – due reward for leading from the front after a successful personal Championship season of 1175 runs @ 55.95 and 42 wickets @ 24.

Frizzell County Championship, Division Two

Essex v Nottinghamshire

4-day match **Venue:** County Ground, Chelmsford **Result:** Essex won by 7 wickets

Having clinched promotion to Division One during the final game of the 2000 season, a similar prospect awaited Essex in the last match of 2002 following an ignominious top-flight campaign in between. An instant return to the First Division always seemed likely as just one bonus point was required in the home fixture with Nottinghamshire – a feat achieved just after lunch on day one when Graham Napier trapped Darren Bicknell leg before. A minimum of 10 points were needed to claim the Division Two title while their opponents would take

Will Jefferson:
standing tall

top spot with a victory. Notts' batsman Usman Afzaal looked to be taking the match away from the hosts when he compiled a fluent century. The left-hander took full toll of anything loose outside off-stump and straight drove one six just short of the press box on his way to 134 off 167 balls but his dismissal triggered a collapse as James Middlebrook picked up three wickets in four balls. When Greg Smith edged Napier to first slip the visitors had slipped from 238-4 to 265-9. Wicket-keeper/batsman Chris Read then swung lustily in a last-wicket stand of 76 with A J Harris before the former was eventually caught at mid-on after striking 10 fours and one six in his 82-ball 73. Notts ended the first day slightly the happier of the two sides and their mood was boosted further still on day two by securing their own promotion when leg-spinner Stuart MacGill removed Aftab Habib to claim Essex's sixth wicket. Habib batted fluently for an even half-century but his removal came in the middle of a collapse that saw Essex's last seven wickets go down for 69 runs. Essex were in the process of negating Nottinghamshire's 59-run first-innings lead on day three reducing their rivals to 149-7 before Bilal Shafayat – who was dropped on 33 and 58 – and Paul Franks then added 87 in 21 overs as Notts were finally bowled out for 280. That left Essex needing 340 to win in 31 overs plus the last day but their task appeared a tall one as the pitch was taking an increasing amount of turn and Australian Test bowler MacGill was in the opposition's ranks. Despite the loss of Darren Robinson and John Stephenson, Essex finished the evening in optimistic mood as Will Jefferson and Mark Waugh added an unbeaten 59 in the last 12

Essex opener Will Jefferson considers his match-winning century against Nottinghamshire as the best innings he ever played for the County. The right-hander also pays tribute to the part a legendary Australian played in the run-chase: "I remember vividly having Mark Waugh at the other end [during a 135-run third-wicket stand] and what an influence he had been on the whole squad during the last month of the season [filling in for Andy Flower as overseas player]. Myself and Mark traded boundaries early on the final morning, which gave us an enormous boost and eased the pressure. I don't think I have ever timed the ball any better than some of the shots I played in that innings – particularly on the off-side. To score such a big and influential hundred, and get capped, was an amazing couple of days. It remains one of the highlights of my career."

Toss: Essex won the toss and decided to field.
Umpires: B Leadbeater, JF Steele. **Referee:** R Subba Row.

NOTTINGHAMSHIRE

Batsman	Dismissal (1st inns)	Runs	Dismissal (2nd inns)	Runs
*JER Gallian	lbw b Stephenson	23	(2) c Jefferson b Dakin	12
GE Welton	c Jefferson b Dakin	1	(1) b Middlebrook	23
DJ Bicknell	lbw b Napier	53	(4) lbw b Stephenson	31
U Afzaal	c Jefferson b Middlebrook	134	(5) c Foster b Grant	0
BM Shafayat	lbw b Stephenson	4	(6) b Dakin	70
P Johnson	c Foster b Dakin	16	(7) c Foster b Napier	13
†CMW Read	c Middlebrook b Dakin	73	(8) b Dakin	18
PJ Franks	c Habib b Middlebrook	0	(9) c Grayson b Stephenson	33
SCG MacGill	c Grayson b Middlebrook	0	(11) not out	9
GJ Smith	c Stephenson b Napier	4	(10) c Habib b Middlebrook	16
AJ Harris	not out	16	(3) lbw b Stephenson	17
Extras	(8 b, 1 lb, 8 nb)	17	(5 b, 9 lb, 18 nb, 6 w)	38
Total	**(all out, 86.5 overs)**	**341**	**(all out, 76.3 overs)**	**280**

Fall: 1st inns: 1-7, 2-50, 3-160, 4-195, 5-238, 6-250, 7-250, 8-250, 9-265, 10-341. **2nd inns:** 1-34, 2-43, 3-90, 4-93, 5-99, 6-123, 7-149, 8-236, 9-262, 10-280.
Bowling: 1st inns: Dakin 18.5-2-87-3, Napier 15-3-65-2, Stephenson 11-2-42-2, Grant 15-2-62-0, Middlebrook 25-8-69-3, Grayson 2-0-7-0. **2nd inns:** Dakin 19-3-49-3, Napier 14-2-50-1, Middlebrook 11.3-3-37-2, Grant 14-0-66-1, Stephenson 13-4-45-3, Grayson 5-1-19-0.

ESSEX

Batsman	Dismissal (1st inns)	Runs	Dismissal (2nd inns)	Runs
DDJ Robinson	c MacGill b Smith	41	b Franks	22
WI Jefferson	lbw b Harris	0	not out	165
JP Stephenson	c Read b Harris	65	b MacGill	4
ME Waugh	b Franks	49	not out	57
A Habib	c Harris b MacGill	50	did not bat	
*AP Grayson	c Read b MacGill	2	did not bat	
†JS Foster	c Shafayat b Franks	29	did not bat	
JM Dakin	c Read b Harris	1	did not bat	
JD Middlebrook	not out	25	did not bat	
GR Napier	lbw b Franks	0	did not bat	
JB Grant	lbw b MacGill	0	did not bat	
Extras	(1 b, 5 lb, 14 nb)	20	(9 lb, 10 nb)	19
Total	**(all out, 88.4 overs)**	**282**	**(3 wickets, 68.2 overs)**	**343**

Fall: 1st inns: 1-2, 2-87, 3-144, 4-213, 5-222, 6-233, 7-244, 8-281, 9-281, 10-282. **2nd inns:** 1-57, 2-70, 3-205.
Bowling: 1st inns: Smith 17-3-60-1, Harris 20-10-42-3, Franks 21-7-50-3, MacGill 28.4-4-116-3, Shafayat 2-0-8-0. **2nd inns:** Smith 11-1-63-0, Harris 11-2-65-0, MacGill 25-1-121-1, Franks 14-5-54-2, Shafayat 6-0-19-0, Johnson 1.2-0-12-0.

overs of the day and capitalising on anything loose from MacGill. The towering 6' 10½" opener Jefferson used his great reach to good effect as he struck 11 fours in his half-century – a portent of what was to follow on day four. Notts would still have been confident of victory – and the title – going into the final day but Jefferson and Waugh added 57 in the first eight overs to lift the home crowd. Australian maestro Waugh, who had been a hugely popular overseas player for the County between 1988 and 1995, signed off in his last first-class innings for the Club with a typically stylish 76. The right-hander hit 47 in 45 minutes at the start before Habib carried on the momentum with some fluent strokeplay of his own as the three Essex batsmen put on 198 runs in 34 overs in the first session to leave just 16 needed after lunch. Jefferson fittingly struck the 29th boundary of his innings 20 balls into the resumption to complete a masterful run-chase as he reached an unbeaten 165 off 214 deliveries to cap a fine first full season for the opener that culminated in the award of his County cap. It was also a highly satisfactory season for new Head Coach Graham Gooch in his first year at the helm with promotion having also been achieved in the National Cricket League.

totesport League, Division One

Essex v Hampshire

45-overs match **Venue:** Castle Park Cricket Ground, Colchester **Result:** Essex won by 12 runs

There have been many outstanding one-day sides in Essex's history but few have been as dominant as the team that carried all before them in the 2005 totesport League. Having just survived the drop from Division One the previous season, hopes were understandably muted going into the following campaign. Yet, in retrospect, a squad containing batsmen such as Andy Flower and Ronnie Irani, bowlers of the quality of Danish Kaneria and Darren Gough along with a surfeit of all-rounders including Ravi Bopara, Grant Flower, Ryan ten Doeschate and Andre Adams had every right to feel confident about their prospects.

photo: GalvinEyes

Such was Essex's superiority that the title was secured with three matches to spare, thanks to a dramatic victory over Hampshire at Colchester. It was to prove a day of high-drama all-round at Castle Park as spectators were kept up-to-date over the tannoy with news of England's own nail-biting win over Australia in the penultimate Ashes Test at Trent Bridge. At that stage it seemed unlikely that fans of England and Essex would be toasting a double success that evening as the visitors made a good fist of their pursuit of 223 from 45 overs. The home side's innings was a stop-start affair with two stands of note mixed with

Nearly there: Andre Nel *(far left)* is congratulated by James Foster, Ronnie Irani and Ravi Bopara after bowling Dimitri Mascarenhas in the final over

collapses either side. Will Jefferson featured in both sizeable partnerships as he joined Ronnie Irani in a 70-run alliance for the first-wicket before adding 68 with James Middlebrook for the fifth-wicket. Jefferson was the pick of the batsmen with 88 before picking out mid-wicket off Andy Bichel, soon to become an Essex player himself. The rangy opener told the Essex Eagles official programme for the subsequent home match with Worcestershire that a final total of 222-9 was short of their target. "At one stage Ronnie [Irani] and I were going well and I think we scored 270-280 the previous year [at Colchester] so we were a little under-par from that. We got off to a tremendous start but they

Leg-spinner Danish Kaneria enjoyed an outstanding totesport League campaign, taking 16 wickets @ 17.37. The Pakistani worked in tandem with off-spinner James Middlebrook to frequently put the squeeze on the opposition during the middle overs. True to form, the spin twins claimed five wickets in the title-winning match against Hampshire with Kaneria taking 3-26 from his nine overs. Although there were still three matches remaining, Kaneria believes victory at Colchester was crucial following a defeat and 'No Result' in their previous two one-day league fixtures: "The Hampshire game was really special because we knew if we won this one, we won the totesport League. That was a game where we had lost our momentum and we would have been under immense pressure [had we lost] – then we would have lost two games and anything could have happened after that. We just went out with a positive frame of mind and no matter how many runs we made we would just go out and win that game."

Toss: Essex won the toss and decided to bat.
Umpires: MJ Harris, VA Holder.

ESSEX

		Runs	Balls	Mins	4s	6s	S-Rate
WI Jefferson	c McLean b Bichel	88	106	131	10	1	83.02
*RC Irani	b Watson	29	41	53	3	-	70.73
GW Flower	c Watson b Mascarenhas	6	11	9	1	-	54.55
A Flower	run out	7	10	11	-	-	70.00
RS Bopara	c Bichel b Mascarenhas	4	11	10	-	-	36.36
JD Middlebrook	b Tremlett	33	39	43	3	-	84.62
RN ten Doeschate	c McLean b Tremlett	12	16	27	1	-	75.00
†JS Foster	c Watson b Bichel	1	6	4	-	-	16.67
GR Napier	b Tremlett	17	18	27	2	-	94.44
Danish Kaneria	not out	12	10	11	2	-	120.00
A Nel	not out	5	3	2	1	-	166.67
Extras	(4 lb, 2 nb, 2 w)	8					
Total	**(9 wickets, 45 overs)**	**222**					

Fall: 1-70, 2-81), 3-92, 4-101, 5-169, 6-171, 7-172, 8-196, 9-214.
Bowling: Bichel 9-3-45-2, Tremlett 9-1-48-3, Watson 7-1-30-1, Mascarenhas 9-0-32-2, Udal 8-0-37-0, Ervine 1-0-11-0, Lamb 2-0-15-0.

HAMPSHIRE

		Runs	Balls	Mins	4s	6s	S-Rate
JP Crawley	c Nel b Middlebrook	84	106	127	10	-	79.25
†N Pothas	c A Flower b Danish Kaneria	49	62	69	7	1	79.03
SM Ervine	b Danish Kaneria	6	14	12	-	-	42.86
SR Watson	c Bopara b Middlebrook	3	9	7	-	-	33.33
GA Lamb	run out	27	34	48	-	1	79.41
AJ Bichel	c Nel b Danish Kaneria	1	9	4	-	-	11.11
AD Mascarenhas	b Nel	15	17	25	1	-	88.24
KJ Latouf	b Bopara	8	12	12	-	-	66.67
JJ McLean	not out	4	5	6	-	-	80.00
*SD Udal	not out	2	2	1	-	-	100.00
CT Tremlett	did not bat						
Extras	(2 lb, 9 w)	11					
Total	**(8 wickets, 45 overs)**	**210**					

Fall: 1-95, 2-105, 3-114, 4-173, 5-175, 6-182, 7-198, 8-206.
Bowling: Napier 6-0-44-0, Nel 9-1-33-1, Bopara 7-0-40-1, Danish Kaneria 9-2-26-3, Middlebrook 9-0-37-2, GW Flower 5-0-28-0.

[Hampshire] showed that even if you get off to a good start, if you take them down in the middle of the innings then you could cause problems and put the pressure on."

Hampshire began their run-chase well and it took a good catch by Andy Flower off Kaneria to end the opening stand at 95 with Nic Pothas the batsman to go. Fellow opener John Crawley lasted until the 37th over but when he chipped James Middlebrook to Andre Nel at long-on, the nerves set in for the visitors. From 173-3, needing less than six-runs-per-over, Hampshire fell away to the extent that 25 were needed off the last two overs. By the time Nel came to bowl the final six balls 18 runs were still required and when the South African bowled Dimitri Mascarenhas off the second delivery, it was game over.

Essex's vocal and enthusiastic balcony celebrations were hugely merited in the midst of a campaign that saw them win 13 and lose just one of 16 matches to ultimately win the title by a comprehensive 14-point margin.

Tour Match

Essex v Australians

2-day match **Venue:** The Ford County Ground, Chelmsford **Result:** Draw

Few cricket fans in the United Kingdom will forget the summer of 2005 as England and Australia fought out one of, if not the, greatest Ashes series of all time. Essex played their part in capturing the mood when they hosted the tourists on a gloriously sunny weekend in early September. Essex aficionados had long been championing the burgeoning talents of young batsmen Alastair Cook and Ravi Bopara but this was the match when they burst on to the national consciousness. Left-hander Cook had been in particularly impressive form over the course of the season with plenty of wise pundits pushing his claims for a place in the full England squad. The opener settled his nerves, after Essex won the toss and elected

photo: Kieran Galvin

**Alastair Cook:
Aussie basher**

to bat, when he struck three boundaries in Brett Lee's second over. As Cook recalls, however, it wasn't all plain sailing early on: "I scored a lot of runs that summer and remember at the time thinking about what it would be like to face Australia after watching the Ashes. When I went out to bat I was just interested in getting off the mark and there was a very close lbw appeal against Brett Lee second or third ball." Opening partner Will Jefferson played his part in the run-fest with 64 in a stand of 140 for the first-wicket. But this was just the hors d'oeuvres for a sumptuous main course provided by Cook and Bopara that lasted past tea as the young duo added 270 for the second wicket. Cook needed just 49 balls to register his half-century and shortly after lunch, having faced another 58 dekiveries, he moved into three figures. By contrast, Bopara's century was relatively sedate at 184 balls as the Australian bowlers toiled. Leg-spinner Stuart MacGill, who had been touted for a call-up for the fifth Test, did himself no favours as he was milked to all parts of the Chelmsford ground for 128 runs in 24 overs. Cook was dominant off both front and back foot as he completed his double-century off just 232 balls with 30 fours and one six. The 20-year-old added three more boundaries before he was finally dismissed while Bopara also stepped up a gear after reaching his century – finishing with 17 fours and two sixes. Both fell in quick succession but James Foster and James Middlebrook carried on in the same vein to bring up the 500 just before the close – the perfect end to an incredible day of run-gathering by the home side.

Media hype was the order of the day throughout the 2005 season as the Ashes reached a thrilling crescendo. As a result, Essex's match against Australia was afforded more column inches and subjected to more speculation than might otherwise have been the case. Essex's double centurion Alastair Cook was not immune to the circus going on around the game in the build-up. "I do remember hearing as the fixture approached that Australia would probably put out a weakened team – possibly even club cricketers – rather than risk their big guns just ahead of the last Test," Cook notes. "But Ricky Ponting, Shane Warne and Glenn McGrath were the only three [major players] who didn't play. They still put out Brett Lee, Mike Kasprowicz, Jason Gillespie and Stuart MacGill so it was a quality bowling attack."

Toss: Essex won the toss and decided to bat.
Umpires: RJ Bailey, P Willey.

ESSEX

WI Jefferson	b Kasprowicz	64
AN Cook	c Gillespie b Kasprowicz	214
RS Bopara	b Tait	135
ML Pettini	c Hayden b Tait	8
†JS Foster	not out	38
JD Middlebrook	not out	26
*RC Irani	did not bat	
TJ Phillips	did not bat	
GR Napier	did not bat	
AP Palladino	did not bat	
A Nel	did not bat	
JS Ahmed	did not bat	
Extras	(4 b, 5 lb, 8 nb)	17
Total	**(4 wickets, declared, 105 overs)**	**502**

Fall: 1st inns: 1-140, 2-410, 3-434, 4-441.
Bowling: 1st inns: Lee 13-0-69-0, Gillespie 22-3-80-0, Tait 15-1-72-2, MacGill 24-0-128-0, Kasprowicz 19-2-85-2, Hodge 12-1-59-0.

AUSTRALIANS

JL Langer	c Cook b Middlebrook	87
ML Hayden	retired out	150
SM Katich	c Pettini b Napier	72
BJ Hodge	c Foster b Phillips	166
*†AC Gilchrist	c Palladino b Middlebrook	8
BJ Haddin	st †Pettini b Phillips	59
B Lee	not out	7
JN Gillespie	not out	4
SW Tait	did not bat	
SCG MacGill	did not bat	
MS Kasprowicz	did not bat	
RT Ponting	did not bat	
Extras	(1 lb, 5 nb, 2 w)	8
Total	**(6 wickets, 95 overs)**	**561**

Fall: 1st inns: 1-213, 2-244, 3-378, 4-389 , 5-550, 6-550.
Bowling: 1st inns: Nel 10-1-41-0, Palladino 12-1-81-0, Napier 12-1-77-1, Ahmed 15-0-95-0, Middlebrook 23-3-110-2, Phillips 20-0-137-2, Cook 3-0-19-0.

Bopara had to wait a little longer for an international call-up but Cook was playing Test cricket just a matter of months after this performance. As a result, the now firmly-established England player readily acknowledges this innings was a defining moment in his career. "Looking back I would have to," Cook affirms. "In terms of helping Essex to win, obviously it wasn't significant. But personally that innings was one that just put me ahead of the contenders [for an England place]. At the time I was in the pack of the next 10 batsmen but that 200 pushed me forward, made me jump out of the pack and got people to notice me." Australia put the pitch into perspective when they plundered 561-6 from just 95 overs on the second day of a fixture that was not recorded as a first-class match. Matthew Hayden – who had been struggling for form in the Test series – hammered 150 while his opening partner Justin Langer just missed out on his century as the experienced duo added 213 for the first wicket. Brad Hodge – who was not selected for a Test all summer – carried on the theme once Hayden retired out as he struck 166 at just under a run-a-ball. England went on to draw the final Test at the Oval to win back the Ashes but there will always be a little part of that summer that will be forever Essex.

Friends Provident Trophy, Quarter-Final

Leicestershire v Essex

50-overs match   **Venue:** Grace Road, Leicester **Result:** Essex won by 118 runs

Ravi Bopara took his first tentative steps on the international stage in 2007 when he steadily forced his way into the One-Day International team. Later that year the youngster played in all three Tests of the tour to Sri Lanka but such was the limit of his success in those matches that the 2008 domestic season became one of redemption.Bopara proved he would not wilt at this first major setback as he was outstanding with bat and ball as Essex dominated the one-day game that year. The right-hander's crowning glory was his innings against Leicestershire in the quarter-final of the Friends Provident Trophy.

photo: GalvinEyes

Ravi Bopara:
innings of a lifetime

Essex Captain Mark Pettini may have been regretting his decision to bat first when the visitors found themselves on 37-3 with Garnett Kruger and Dillon du Preez taking advantage of any early morning assistance on offer. Ryan ten Doeschate then joined Bopara to steady the innings with a stand of 67 but it was not until James Foster joined Bopara at the crease that the innings really got going. The duo batted splendidly to set a new record fifth-wicket partnership in the competition for the County of 190 in 28 overs.

Leicester had no answer to the might of Bopara's bat as the Forest Gate-born batsman struck his century in 85 balls and then moved onto 150 off another 36. A mammoth 111 runs came in the last 10 overs including 70 in the last five as the penultimate over from Du Preez yeilded 24 runs. Needing eight from the last over to reach his 200, Bopara carved the penultimate ball over cover for his 10th six to reach the landmark and bring up his fourth 50 off just 16 balls and in so doing, he became the seventh batsman to score a double-century in one-day cricket (Surrey's Ali Brown having achieved the feat twice). In addition, he broke the record for the highest individual score by an Essex batsman in one-day cricket of 198 not out by Graham Gooch against Sussex in the Benson & Hedges Cup in 1982. Quoted

Graham Gooch had become the County's batting coach by the time of Bopara's innings. The legendary opening batsman was quoted in the Essex Eagles matchday programme shortly after the innings about Bopara's effort and losing his place in the record books:
"It's a fantastic achievement," Gooch said. "I'm absolutely delighted for him. I had a fantastic day at Sussex in 1982 [when he struck 198 not out] but this couldn't have happened to a more gifted player. That innings was what you call a 'Daddy Hundred'. A century in a one-day game will usually win your team the game but to score 200 out of 350 is an unbelievable performance. What he did is testament to the talent of this boy. Ravi is nowhere near his peak and will get better as the years go on."

Toss: Essex won the toss and decided to bat.
Umpires: RJ Bailey, IJ Gould.

ESSEX

		Runs	Balls	Mins	4s	6s	S-Rate
*ML Pettini	c Dippenaar b Kruger	18	15	20	2	-	120.00
JER Gallian	c Ackerman b Kruger	9	18	28	2	-	50.00
V Chopra	b du Preez	6	13	12	1	-	46.15
RS Bopara	not out	201	138	165	18	10	145.65
RN ten Doeschate	b Allenby	27	31	41	4	-	87.10
†JS Foster	c Dippenaar b du Preez	61	76	99	3	-	80.26
JD Middlebrook	not out	13	9	14	1	1	144.44
GR Napier	did not bat						
DD Masters	did not bat						
Danish Kaneria	did not bat						
AJ Tudor	did not bat						
Extras	(9 lb, 6 w)	15					
Total	**(5 wickets, 50 overs)**	**350**					

Fall: 1-28, 2-34, 3-37, 4-104, 5-294.
Bowling: du Preez 10-0-60-2, Kruger 10-0-70-2, Malik 8-0-68-0, Allenby 10-0-61-1, Henderson 10-0-59-0, Snape 2-0-23-0.

LEICESTERSHIRE

		Runs	Balls	Mins	4s	6s	S-Rate
HD Ackerman	c Foster b Tudor	4	2	1	1	-	200.00
MAG Boyce	c Foster b Masters	57	69	106	5	-	82.61
HH Dippenaar	c Foster b Tudor	18	25	21	3	-	72.00
J Allenby	c Gallian b Napier	6	10	11	-	-	60.00
*†PA Nixon	b Middlebrook	62	64	78	5	-	96.88
J du Toit	c Pettini b ten Doeschate	35	26	35	4	1	134.62
JN Snape	b Napier	21	24	32	2	-	87.50
D du Preez	not out	9	14	22	-	-	64.29
CW Henderson	b Bopara	2	5	6	-	-	40.00
MN Malik	b Bopara	0	1	1	-	-	0.00
GJP Kruger	c Chopra b ten Doeschate	2	6	5	-	-	33.33
Extras	(2 lb, 14 w)	16					
Total	**(all out, 41 overs)**	**232**					

Fall: 1-4, 2-32, 3-53, 4-157, 5-162, 6-217, 7-220, 8-228, 9-228, 10-232.
Bowling: Tudor 6-0-38-2, Napier 8-0-48-2, Masters 8-0-35-1, Bopara 6-0-34-2, Danish Kaneria 3-0-25-0, ten Doeschate 7-0-32-2, Middlebrook 3-0-18-1.

in the 2009 *Essex Yearbook*, Bopara explained how an individual score of 200 was far from his mind in the early overs of the day. "I wasn't sure that I could score a double hundred in a one-day game – it's just not something you think of," he said. "You think of hundreds and even 150 but I never thought of 200. I certainly wasn't thinking about it after the first 10 overs of that match at Leicester because we were 30-odd for 3 and the ball was nipping about a bit. I thought to myself 'we'll do well to get to 200 here' and if we do that then at least we've got a chance as we'll have some runs on the board."

In fact, Leicestershire only managed 31 more than Bopara as a team when their turn came to bat. The only moments of concern for the visitors came during a stand of 104 between Matt Boyce and Paul Nixon for the fourth-wicket before Boyce became Foster's third victim and Middlebrook removed Nixon with his fifth delivery to end the match as a contest. There was still time for Bopara to pick up two wickets in two balls although by then he had already done more than enough to claim the Man-of-the-Match award!

Essex v Sussex

20-overs match | **Venue:** The Ford County Ground, Chelmsford **Result:** Essex won by 128 runs

Few domestic innings can have seized the moment more perfectly than Graham Napier's effort in the Twenty20 Cup against Sussex in 2008. Crowds were increasing year-on-year in the Twenty20 format in England while India had just cottoned on to the phenomenal by holding the inaugural Indian Premier League (IPL) earlier that year. Credibility begat money for 20-overs cricket and the Essex cricketer became an overnight star. Contract offers from India poured in and while the all-rounder was unable to fully capitalise on his world-breaking exploits it did change his life to some extent. Earlier on in the season the all-rounder had even been considering a career outside of cricket as injuries hampered his progress after being

photo: Warren Page, CalvinEyes

Graham Napier:
new sensation

an England one-day prospect at one stage. But Napier fought his way back into the Essex side and was beginning to find his form again in all facets of the game by the time Sussex visited for a Twenty20 Cup game. As luck would have it, SKY's television cameras were on hand to capture an innings the like of which viewers can rarely, if ever, have seen. A packed house at Chelmsford were the chosen few to watch the carnage for themselves but vigilance was the order of the day as the ball flew to all parts of the ground. Essex had just started to experiment with Napier at number three in the order – with mixed results up to then – as they looked to hit upon a winning formula. The right-hander came to the crease early on to join Jason Gallian in a stand of 77 in nine overs but it was the home side's third-wicket partnership that really got things moving with James Foster an unlikely junior partner in a stand of 119 in seven overs despite hitting 48 from 23 balls. Shortly, after reaching a 29-ball fifty, he drove two sixes over long-off and picked up another over deep backward square-leg off consecutive Dwayne Smith deliveries. Only another 15 balls were needed to reach his century and he made his intentions clear that 150 was in his sights when Chris Liddle was hit for three successive on-side sixes. Such punishment was nothing to that incurred by James Kirtley in the final over of the innings, however, as Napier struck 29 – including four sixes – to register his third 50 off 13 balls to ensure that Essex's very own master blaster equalled the record for the most sixes in an innings in any form of the game. He broke various records in the T20-format and his 152 not out remained the highest score in the Twenty20 Cup by the end of the 2010 season. Speaking in the

Essex wicketkeeper-batsman James Foster hit seven boundaries and one six of his own as he shared in an Essex competition-record third-wicket stand of 119. Looking back on the match two years later, the former England gloveman considers the significance of Graham Napier's innings that evening.

"It put Napes [Napier] on the map," Foster recalls. "The IPL had just started and he was in prime position to take advantage of it all, especially with that game being on telly. It showed everyone the potential for players to make a lot of money out of being successful at the Twenty20 format. Napes had quite a lot of huge knocks on telly that year and that raised his profile and he ended up playing for the Mumbai Indians. That was an indication of a change of the face of cricket right there."

Toss: Essex won the toss and decided to bat.
Umpires: B Dudleston, NJ Llong, RT Robinson (TV).

ESSEX

		Runs	Balls	Mins	4s	6s	S-Rate
*ML Pettini	c Liddle b Martin-Jenkins	4	9	8	1	-	44.44
JER Gallian	c Liddle b Yardy	26	29	41	3	-	89.66
GR Napier	not out	152	58	66	10	16	262.07
†JS Foster	b Hamilton-Brown	48	23	27	7	1	208.70
RN ten Doeschate	not out	4	2	5	1	-	200.00
GW Flower	did not bat						
NJ Dexter	did not bat						
JD Middlebrook	did not bat						
DD Masters	did not bat						
Danish Kaneria	did not bat						
MA Chambers	did not bat						
Extras	(3 lb, 2 nb, 3 w)	8					
Total	**(3 wickets, 20 overs)**	**242**					

Fall: 1-13, 2-90, 3-209.
Bowling: Martin-Jenkins 4-1-17-1, Kirtley 4-0-67-0, Liddle 4-0-49-0, Smith 2-0-33-0, Yardy 4-0-52-1, Hamilton-Brown 2-0-21-1.

SUSSEX

		Runs	Balls	Mins	4s	6s	S-Rate
CD Nash	c Pettini b Masters	8	11	12	1	-	72.73
MW Goodwin	b Chambers	23	17	30	4	-	135.29
DR Smith	lbw b Chambers	21	11	10	2	2	190.91
MJ Prior	c Pettini b Chambers	8	6	5	-	1	133.33
*CJ Adams	c Dexter b Middlebrook	5	12	19	-	-	41.67
MH Yardy	b Middlebrook	15	14	16	1	1	107.14
RJ Hamilton-Brown	c Pettini b ten Doeschate	7	10	12	-	-	70.00
RSC Martin-Jenkins	c Napier b Middlebrook	10	12	12	-	-	83.33
†AJ Hodd	b Danish Kaneria	2	4	4	-	-	50.00
CJ Liddle	lbw b Danish Kaneria	0	3	3	-	-	0.00
RJ Kirtley	not out	1	1	1	-	-	100.00
Extras	(4 b, 3 lb, 2 nb, 5 w)	14					
Total	**(all out, 16.4 overs)**	**114**					

Fall: 1-24, 2-56, 3-66, 4-66, 5-92, 6-94, 7-109, 8-112, 9-113, 10-114.
Bowling: Masters 3-0-20-1, Napier 2-0-20-0, Chambers 3-0-31-3, Danish Kaneria 2.4-0-8-2, ten Doeschate 3-0-15-1, Middlebrook 3-0-13-3.

aftermath of his performance, Napier was still coming to terms with an innings that he will remain synonymous with. "I had one of those days where everything clicked together and seemed to work," Napier said. "Whatever I tried came off. Even my mis-hits went for six when some days you'd get caught on the boundary. I can't explain how or why it happened but it just came off. The pleasing bit was that virtually every six cleared the boundary by a long way." Essex's 242-3 was the fourth-highest total in Twenty20 cricket at the time so the chances of Sussex returning home as victors was slim at the midway point. So it proved as young fast bowler Maurice Chambers served notice of his rich potential by dismissing Sussex's three most destructive batsmen – Dwayne Smith, Matt Prior and Murray Goodwin – as the visitors were bowled out for 114. Napier continued his form over the remainder of the season and eventually plumped for Mumbai Indians in the IPL. A lack of opportunities – he was granted just one appearance by Mumbai in two seasons and has never been selected to play for the full England team – as well as a serious back injury meant Napier struggled to build on his successes of 2008 over the following two years. But whatever happens over the remainder of his career he will always have this match to savour.

Friends Provident Trophy, Final

Essex v Kent

50-overs match | **Venue:** Lord's Cricket Ground, St John's Wood **Result:** Essex won by 5 wickets

Every Cup Final needs a hero but the chances of this particular showpiece being dominated by Grant Flower had appeared slim midway through the 2008 season. The Zimbabwean's form was sketchy and he found himself in and out of the side. Departure at the end of the campaign seemed the likeliest course of action and Sussex had already been in discussions with the player. As Indian

photo: Kieran Galvin

Grant Flower:
calming influence

Summer's go, however, this one was right up there as the right-hander finished his season with a flourish. Add in useful slow left-arm bowling together with his outstanding fielding ability and people were starting to wonder how the award of a new contract could ever have been in doubt. Kent were left cursing his resurgence not once but twice as Flower denied them at the last in both the NatWest Pro40 Division Two title race and here at Lord's. Essex had earlier lost to the Spitfires in the Twenty20 Cup semi-final, meaning revenge was in the air at the home of cricket. David Masters and Graham Napier had formed an outstanding double act as Essex's opening attack in one-day cricket that year and they took full advantage of being given first use of the ball. James Foster's ability to stand up to the seamers was a major factor in their ability to strangle the opposition batsmen and he was in the action early on when he caught Kent skipper Rob Key. Wickets then fell at regular intervals as the Kent middle order played extravagantly in their attempts to break the shackles. Martin van Jaarsveld held the innings together but he was just as culpable as his team-mates when, on 58, he pulled Chris Wright to Alastair Cook at mid-wicket. Ryan McLaren and Yasir Arafat then ensured they

gave themselves something to bowl at by playing sensibly to lift their side to 214 all out off the final ball of the innings. Kent's score was slightly below par but on a slow pitch there was still plenty of work to do for the Essex batsmen. Everything was going to plan at 88-2 in the 22nd over but then Ravi Bopara and Alastair Cook – the latter inexplicably cutting a long-hop to extra-cover – fell in successive Robbie Joseph overs. Foster then helped Flower add 68 in 96 balls with the electric running between the wickets turning ones into twos on several occasions. Essex's fleetness of foot was not disturbed by the emergence of Ryan ten Doeschate at the fall of Foster – Joseph's third wicket as the pace bowler

Essex captain Mark Pettini was in his first full season in charge in 2008 and was able to enjoy phenomenal success that year. Not only did he lift the Friends Provident Trophy but he also carried off the NatWest Pro40 Division Two title and steered his troops to Twenty20 Cup Finals Day. Victory at Lord's stood out among the crowd of moments to savour in 2008.
Pettini told the *2009 Essex Yearbook*: "It was my first Lord's final so to win it as Captain was something special and still makes me smile when I think about it now. It will always be one of the fondest memories of my career."

Toss: Kent won the toss and decided to bat.
Umpires: NJ Llong, G Sharp, RA Kettleborough (TV).

KENT

		Runs	Balls	Mins	4s	6s	S-Rate
JL Denly	b Napier	11	19	22	2	-	57.89
*RWT Key	c Foster b Masters	7	13	18	1	-	53.85
M van Jaarsveld	c Cook b Wright	58	75	125	4	-	77.33
JM Kemp	b Masters	16	31	39	2	-	51.61
DI Stevens	c Foster b Wright	0	6	4	-	-	0.00→
†GO Jones	lbw b Danish Kaneria	19	39	32	3	-	48.72
Azhar Mahmood	c Flower b Danish Kaneria	2	8	7	-	-	25.00
R McLaren	b Bopara	63	71	79	4	-	88.73
Yasir Arafat	b Bopara	27	34	38	2	-	79.41
JC Tredwell	run out (Cook→ten Doeschate)	0	0	1	-	-	0.00
RH Joseph	not out	2	5	6	-	-	40.00
Extras	(7 lb, 2 nb)	9					
Total	**(all out, 50 overs)**	**214**					

Fall: 1-15, 2-19, 3-58, 4-59, 5-94, 6-100, 7-138, 8-204, 9-209, 10-214.
Bowling: Masters 10-2-34-2, Napier 8-1-23-1, Wright 8-0-36-2, Bopara 8-0-46-2, Danish Kaneria 10-0-42-2, ten Doeschate 6-0-26-0.

ESSEX

		Runs	Balls	Mins	4s	6s	S-Rate
*ML Pettini	lbw b Azhar Mahmood	10	18	30	1	-	55.56
JER Gallian	b Azhar Mahmood	28	45	62	3	-	62.22
AN Cook	c Stevens b Joseph	33	51	73	4	-	64.71
RS Bopara	lbw b Joseph	7	20	33	-	-	35.00
GW Flower	not out	70	97	105	6	-	72.16
†JS Foster	c Jones b Joseph	18	35	56	1	-	51.43
RN ten Doeschate	not out	30	29	38	2	-	103.45
GR Napier	did not bat						
CJC Wright	did not bat						
DD Masters	did not bat						
Danish Kaneria	did not bat						
Extras	(7 lb, 4 nb, 11 w)	22					
Total	**(5 wickets, 48.5 overs)**	**218**					

Fall: 1-32, 2-60, 3-88, 4-93, 5-161.
Bowling: Azhar Mahmood 9.5-0-53-2, Yasir Arafat 9-1-40-0, Joseph 10-1-40-3, McLaren 10-0-34-0, Stevens 8-0-35-0, Tredwell 2-0-9-0.

worked up a fine head of steam. Ten Doeschate offered one chance – when he pulled to the boundary – but his boundless energy galvanised his senior partner in the race towards their target. The Eagles reached the final two overs needing just three runs for victory – although even a tie would have been enough having scored more runs than their opponents after 15 overs – and Flower duly finished the game with a long-on boundary. Flower's 97-ball 70 not out was perfectly timed on a wicket that he acknowledged after the match was difficult to bat on throughout. "The way the ball was moving around it was probably in Kent's favour [at 93-4] – these games are a lot about momentum," Flower stated. "But we weren't chasing a massive total so we just needed a couple of partnerships – which I got with James Foster and Ryan ten Doeschate – and then the game would swing back our way." As a veteran of 67 Test matches and over 200 ODIs, plenty of golden days had been garnered over Flower's career. Nonetheless, that one fine day at Lord's will remain one of his most treasured memories. "It [my innings] ranks up there," Flower opined. "As you get older you know you haven't got many more moments like this and to play with such a great bunch of guys at Lord's…you can't put a price on that."

Kent v Essex

40-overs match **Venue:** St Lawrence Ground, Canterbury **Result:** Essex won by 4 wickets

Essex's 2008 season was punctuated by a succession of magnificent individual one-day innings – evidenced by four entries from that season in this book. While Graham Napier and Ravi Bopara hit the headlines for their spectacular big-hitting, Grant Flower took a more measured approach in carving his name into Essex folklore. The Zimbabwean had already broken Kent hearts a month earlier in the Friends Provident Trophy Final at Lord's when the two sides met again in another 'winner takes all' encounter at Canterbury. On this occasion, the NatWest Pro40 Division Two title was at stake with defeat likely to result in a play-off spot for promotion at best. Essex went into the match unbeaten in

photo: Galvineyes

their first seven 40-overs games of the season while Kent had suffered just one defeat thus far. Spitfires captain Rob Key was determined he would do all he could to avoid another defeat to their fierce rivals by recording a career-best one-day score. The England batsman reached his 104-ball century with three successive boundaries down to fine-leg off Ryan ten Doeschate on his way to 120 not out.

Canterbury tales: Essex claim another victory over Kent

Essex's pursuit of 247 was always likely to be an arduous one but Yasir Arafat made it harder still when he bowled Eagles skipper Mark Pettini with the first ball of the innings. Jason Gallian – who had been in prolific 40-overs form all season – and Ravi Bopara then added 113 in 24 overs before the former edged behind in Darren Stevens' first over. The Kent all-rounder struck again to remove Bopara soon after but while Flower was still at the crease, there remained high hopes of an Essex victory. Wickets fell around him but Flower marched on to a half-century as the target hovered into view. Thirty-nine were

Essex all-rounder Graham Napier's Annus Mirabilis ended on an unfortunate note at Canterbury when he was stretchered off the field (a sight regularly seen in football but not so common in cricket). The pace bowler recalled the incident for his website (www.grahamnapier.com): "The ball was hit back to me off the last delivery of my spell [by Rob Key] and I managed to stop it. But in trying to avoid standing on the ball in my follow-through I landed on the side of my right foot. I felt immediate pain and heard a crunch – which was obviously a worry. I wasn't concerned there was a break but the ligaments connected to the ankle can play havoc further down the line if the injury is not immediately treated properly. Umpire Ian Gould insisted I was carried off on a stretcher as a precaution to make sure there was no further damage – that wasn't my choice but it was the sensible one!

"Our Physio [Pete Gettings] taped up my ankle so that, together with painkillers, I was not in too much discomfort. As the game got tighter I padded up and was ready to contribute to the cause if needed – although I wasn't very mobile so James Foster was ready to act as my runner."

Toss: Essex won the toss and decided to field.
Umpires: IJ Gould, P Willey, NL Bainton (TV).

KENT

KENT		Runs	Balls	Mins	4s	6s	S-Rate
JL Denly	c Foster b Masters	11	19	21	1	-	57.89
*RWT Key	not out	120	117	155	15	1	102.56
M van Jaarsveld	run out	61	55	66	4	3	110.91
MJ Walker	b ten Doeschate	19	26	22	1	-	73.08
DI Stevens	run out	18	15	19	3	-	120.00
Azhar Mahmood	c Wright b ten Doeschate	1	3	3	-	-	33.33
R McLaren	not out	5	6	14	-	-	83.33
†GO Jones	did not bat						
Yasir Arafat	did not bat						
JC Tredwell	did not bat						
RH Joseph	did not bat						
Extras	(5 lb, 2 nb, 4 w)	11					
Total	**(5 wickets, 40 overs)**	**246**					

Fall: 1-18, 2-131, 3-164, 4-218, 5-220.
Bowling: Napier 8-0-44-0, Masters 8-1-21-1, Bopara 7-0-53-0, Wright 4-0-23-0, Middlebrook 6-0-33-0, Flower 2-0-13-0, ten Doeschate 5-0-54-2.

ESSEX

ESSEX		Runs	Balls	Mins	4s	6s	S-Rate
*ML Pettini	b Yasir Arafat	0	1	1	-	-	0.00
JER Gallian	c Jones b Stevens	51	71	86	4	-	71.83
RS Bopara	c Azhar Mahmood b Stevens	59	83	99	5	-	71.08
GW Flower	not out	68	42	61	7	-	161.90
†JS Foster	run out	19	15	13	2	-	126.67
RN ten Doeschate	c Denly b McLaren	1	3	4	-	-	33.33
JK Maunders	b Yasir Arafat	11	11	12	1	-	100.00
JD Middlebrook	not out	13	11	12	-	1	118.18
GR Napier	did not bat						
CJC Wright	did not bat						
DD Masters	did not bat						
Extras	(9 lb, 6 nb, 10 w)	25					
Total	**(6 wickets, 39 overs)**	**247**					

Fall: 1-0, 2-113, 3-144, 4-176, 5-188, 6-217.
Bowling: Yasir Arafat 8-2-32-2, Joseph 5-0-31-0, McLaren 7-0-45-1, Azhar Mahmood 7-0-45-0, Tredwell 8-0-58-0, Stevens 4-0-27-2.

needed from the last five overs and the target was down to 30 when James Middlebrook joined Flower at the crease. Middlebrook hit the only six of the innings in the 38th over to relieve the pressure as Kent's fielding and bowling became increasingly ragged.

With the equation down to 10 runs from two overs, just six of those balls were needed as Middlebrook hit the winning run to shatter Kent once more. Results elsewhere meant Kent even missed out on a play-off as Key and his men were left to reflect on a season of what-might-have-been's. For Essex, it put a fine seal on a marvellous one-day season when Flower proved himself a man for the big occasion. The right-hander's 42-ball 68 not out was another fine example of how to time a run-chase to perfection.

Flower told the 2009 *Essex Yearbook* that both of his season-defining innings against Kent had their merits: "I probably had to play more shots [at Canterbury] as there was more pressure to score. But it was a flatter wicket than Lord's and I got some bad balls which I put away."

LV= County Championship, Division Two

Derbyshire v Essex

4-day match **Venue:** The County Ground, Derby **Result:** Essex won by 5 wickets.

Promotion back to the top-flight of the County Championship had eluded Essex since they were relegated in 2003. A run of three wins and two draws in their previous five games left Essex's fate in their own hands as they went to Derby for their final Second Division match of the 2009 season. The visitors needed a minimum of 19 points to be certain while Derby – 10 points behind – also harboured ambitions of joining champions Kent in Division One in 2010. Northamptonshire were the biggest threat to the County, however, and their early victory over Leicestershire in their last fixture meant victory for Essex became essential. Derby were hampered by the absence of swine-flu victims

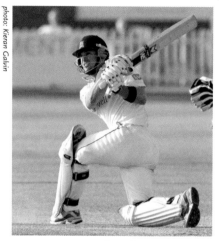

photo: Kieran Galvin

Ryan ten Doeschate:
in control

Tim Groenewald and Tom Lungley while they will have been grateful for Essex captain Mark Pettini's decision to field as Graeme Wagg, Greg Smith and Jamie Pipe also felt unwell on day one. Despite help from a green pitch and early morning moisture, Essex failed to take advantage of conditions as Derbyshire captain Chris Rogers made an opening day double-hundred. The Australian enjoyed a huge slice of luck on 134, when he played on to David Masters without dislodging the bail, but otherwise the left-hander looked imperious during an innings that spanned almost seven hours in total. Essex came back into the match on day two after Graham Napier eventually dismissed Rogers at the end of a 329-ball vigil that included 31 fours and one six. Leg-spinner Danish Kaneria then picked up his maiden first-class hat-trick – Smith bowled around his legs, Wagg lbw sweeping and Jonathan Clare playing round a top-spinner – to cap a fine season for the Pakistani. The Essex reply got off to a disasterous start when Wagg removed openers John Maunders and Alastair Cook in a six-over spell that afforded the medium-pacer figures of 2-5. Tom Westley and Matt Walker steadied the Essex ship and took their third-wicket partnership to 224 on the third day. Westley's maiden first-class century was the main factor in the visitors avoiding the follow-on and picking up the batting bonus points needed to keep Essex in the promotion hunt. Essex were ultimately set 359 from a minimum of 65 overs on

Essex First-Team Coach Paul Grayson rubbished suggestions after the match that the County's target – 359 in 65 overs – had been favourable. "Our victory target was labelled in some quarters as being generous but a big chase, at six an over on a fourth-day pitch, was never going to be easy – even if we made it look that way thanks to a terrific effort under pressure. In our position we would have attempted to chase down any target but credit to [Derbyshire coach] John Morris and [captain] Chris Rogers for at least making it a realistic one. John told me that had it not been for the way Essex had played in previous years then we might not have had a game at all on that final day. As it was, we had set them a target of 266 in 65 overs at Derby the previous year – which they got – so John said he felt he should be fair to us in return by offering us a game this time."

Toss: Essex won the toss and decided to field.
Umpires: SA Garratt, RA Kettleborough, RJ Bailey (TV).

DERBYSHIRE

*CJL Rogers	c Masters b Napier	222	c Cook b Danish Kaneria		42
WL Madsen	lbw b Wright	16	c Walker b Wright		0
GT Park	c Walker b Wright	57	not out		103
DJ Redfern	c Maunders b Wright	48	did not bat		
WW Hinds	b Masters	37	b Danish Kaneria		36
JL Sadler	c Walker b Masters	8	not out		27
GM Smith	b Danish Kaneria	6	(4) c and b Danish Kaneria		16
†DJ Pipe	c Walker b Wright	21	did not bat		
GG Wagg	lbw b Danish Kaneria	0	did not bat		
JL Clare	lbw b Danish Kaneria	0	did not bat		
PS Jones	not out	19	did not bat		
Extras	(5 b, 24 lb, 10 nb, 1 w)	40	(8 lb, 8 nb)		16
Total	**(all out, 128.4 overs)**	**474**	**(4 wickets, declared, 64 overs)**		**240**

Fall: 1st inns: 1-61, 2-182, 3-312, 4-400, 5-420, 6-429, 7-439, 8-439, 9-439, 10-474. **2nd inns:** 1-20, 2-63, 3-85, 4-143.
Bowling: 1st inns: Masters 33-10-72-2, Wright 27.4-5-97-4, Napier 34-6-111-1, Danish Kaneria 22-1-114-3, ten Doeschate 7-1-34-0, Westley 5-1-17-0. **2nd inns:** Napier 10-2-30-0, Wright 16-2-59-1, ten Doeschate 5-0-26-0, Danish Kaneria 17-1-36-3, Westley 3-0-3-0, Cook 7-0-40-1, Pettini 6-0-38-0.

ESSEX

JK Maunders	c Rogers b Wagg	5	c Wagg b Smith		55
AN Cook	c Pipe b Wagg	8	c Sadler b Clare		25
T Westley	c Pipe b Jones	132	c Jones b Wagg		40
MJ Walker	c Hinds b Clare	75	c Sadler b Smith		18
*ML Pettini	c Madsen b Jones	14	not out		85
†JS Foster	c Redfern b Clare	15	c Park b Smith		13
RN ten Doeschate	run out	41	not out		108
GR Napier	c Pipe b Clare	0	did not bat		
CJC Wright	not out	24	did not bat		
Danish Kaneria	c Madsen b Wagg	10	did not bat		
DD Masters	did not bat		did not bat		
Extras	(11 b, 6 lb, 14 nb, 1 w)	32	(5 b, 4 lb, 4 nb, 2 w)		15
Total	**(9 wickets, declared, 107.5 overs)**	**356**	**(5 wickets, 60 overs)**		**359**

Fall: 1st inns: 1-9, 2-14, 3-238, 4-244, 5-271, 6-299, 7-299, 8-346, 9-356. **2nd inns:** 1-45, 2-114, 3-139, 4-160, 5-203.
Bowling: 1st inns: Jones 28-3-87-2, Wagg 31.5-10-79-3, Smith 10-0-41-0, Clare 23-4-64-3, Park 9-0-43-0, Hinds 6-0-25-0. **2nd inns:** Jones 11-0-68-0, Wagg 19-0-102-1, Clare 6-0-35-1, Smith 18-0-96-3, Park 1-0-12-0, Madsen 4-0-29-0, Redfern 1-0-8-0.

the final day to claim victory in a match during which they had been second-best for much of the time. Wickets fell at regular intervals and at 203-5 the game was firmly in Derbyshire's favour. At that point Ryan ten Doeschate joined skipper Pettini and the sixth-wicket pair added an astonishing 156 unbeaten runs in 17.3 overs to see Essex over the line with overs to spare. Ten Doeschate's 108 not out from 59 balls – with nine fours and eight sixes – earned most of the plaudits but Pettini's 94-ball 85 was equally pivotal. All-rounder ten Doeschate had been an increasing force within the Essex ranks since joining the County in 2003. This hundred proved his status as a 'man for the moment' when nerves of steel were the order of the day. Ten Doeschate recalled, "When I walked out to bat, I said to myself that if I could score a quick 50 and Mark (Pettini) was still there, then we could win the game. I didn't really feel any pressure because, to be honest, I love that sort of situation. Mark and I maintained the run-rate that was required and we had a few big overs from time to time that kept us where we wanted to be. Although I've scored a few centuries, in terms of what this one means to the team, this is by far the most important. Every hundred is enjoyable but this one is very treasured."

Friends Provident t20, South Division

Essex v Surrey

20-overs match | **Venue:** The Ford County Ground, Chelmsford **Result:** Essex won by 6 wickets.

Essex's bid to reach Twenty20 Cup Finals Day for the third time in five years could scarcely have begun less favourably. Three defeats in their opening four group fixtures meant there was little room to manoeuvere for the Eagles when they visited the formidable Somerset team in their next match. Just as things seemed to be taking a turn for the better, however, in-form Ryan ten Doeschate sustained a hamstring injury when going well on 48 not out. The Netherlands international would miss the remainder of the group stage and join Graham Napier (stress fracture of the back) as key long-term absentees. Enter New Zealander Scott

photo: Nick Wood

**Scott Styris:
perfect timing**

Styris, who picked up the mantle with bat and ball to not only help turn likely defeat into victory at Taunton but also inspire the team's march to the knockout stage. The all-rounder's crowning glory came in the home tie with Surrey in front of the television cameras. Surrey were in the ascendancy for the vast majority of the game but found themselves denied at the last by an incredible batting performance from the Kiwi. Steven Davies had earlier dominated the first innings of the match as he fired 89 off 50 balls to see the Lions to a formidable 187-6. The wicket-keeper/batsman hammered three sixes and 11 boundaries in sharing stands of 64 in 38 balls with Jason Roy and 82 in eight overs with Mark Ramprakash. Davies was eventually caught at deep mid-wicket by Grant Flower to become one of three victims for leg-spinner Danish Kaneria. In the final equation, Chris Wright's final over – which cost just five runs and accounted for Andrew Symonds and Gareth Batty – proved crucial to the outcome. Essex's response began poorly as Alastair Cook and Matt Walker fell cheaply but Ravi Bopara and Styris began to make progress in a stand of 47 in seven overs. Bopara struggled to find his timing on this occasion, however, and it was no surprise when he holed out on the midwicket boundary for 27 off 33 balls. A daunting 113 were needed in 10.5 overs at that point but Tim Phillips provided Styris with invaluable support as the overseas star went into overdrive. The right-hander reached a 32-ball 50 with his third six but 79 were still required from the last five overs. The fourth-wicket pair hit 54 between overs sixteen and eighteen but Chris Tremlett appeared to have swung the game decisively back in Surrey's favour when the penultimate over cost just three runs and accounted for the wicket of Phillips – caught off a hook on the deep

> Essex wicketkeeper – and interim captain of the time – James Foster was new to the crease for the final over, after Tim Phillips had fallen.
> "We needed 22 from the last over and I was thinking 'Oh God, if we get a single now then it's all down to me'" Foster recalls. "But I didn't have to do it because Scott [Styris] just went 'bang, bang, bang' and finished it with one ball to spare. We had no right to win that game because we were so far behind the eight ball but Scott played like only Scott could do which he did throughout his stint for us."

Toss: Essex won the toss and decided to field.

Umpires: NGB Cook, JH Evans, B Dudleston (TV).

SURREY

		Runs	Balls	Mins	4s	6s	S-Rate
*RJ Hamilton-Brown	run out	7	5	6	1	-	140.00
†SM Davies	c Flower b Danish Kaneria	89	50	59	11	3	178.00
JJ Roy	st Foster b Danish Kaneria	29	17	23	3	1	170.59
MR Ramprakash	st Foster b Danish Kaneria	35	29	34	5	-	120.69
A Symonds	b Wright	17	10	12	1	1	170.00
SJ Walters	not out	7	6	12	-	-	116.67
GJ Batty	b Wright	0	2	1	-	-	0.00
CP Schofield	not out	1	1	2	-	-	100.00
TE Linley	did not bat						
A Nel	did not bat						
CT Tremlett	did not bat						
Extras	(2 w)	2					
Total	**(6 wickets, 20 overs)**	**187**					

Fall: 1-9, 2-73, 3-155, 4-167, 5-182, 6-182.

Bowling: Wright 4-0-31-2, Styris 3-0-27-0, Masters 4-0-42-0, Bopara 3-0-35-0, Danish Kaneria 4-0-32-3, Phillips 2-0-20-0.

ESSEX

		Runs	Balls	Mins	4s	6s	S-Rate
RS Bopara	c Walters b Schofield	27	33	42	2	-	81.82
AN Cook	c Batty b Tremlett	11	9	13	2	-	122.22
MJ Walker	c Ramprakash b Linley	1	4	6	-	-	25.00
SB Styris	not out	106	50	59	6	8	212.00
TJ Phillips	c Walters b Tremlett	30	25	33	2	1	120.00
*†JS Foster	not out	0	0	2	-	-	0.00
GW Flower	did not bat						
JC Mickleburgh	did not bat						
DD Masters	did not bat						
Danish Kaneria	did not bat						
CJC Wright	did not bat						
Extras	(4 b, 3 lb, 4 nb, 2 w)	13					
Total	**(4 wickets, 19.5 overs)**	**188**					

Fall: 1-18, 2-28, 3-75, 4-166.

Bowling: Nel 4-0-36-0, Tremlett 4-1-31-2, Linley 4-0-28-1, Symonds 2.5-0-45-0, Batty 2-0-16-0, Schofield 3-0-25-1.

backward square-leg boundary. All of Essex's flickering hopes rested with Styris as he prepared to face Australian all-rounder Symonds with 22 needed off the last six balls. A boundary from the first ball jangled Surrey nerves and then when Styris mowed the second ball over mid-wicket for six, the game began to swing inexorably towards the home side. Another two runs were taken off the third ball and then Styris found the mid-wicket boundary once more to bring up his 100 after 49 balls – the second 50 coming off 17 deliveries. Needing six off the last two deliveries, Essex's newest hero backed away to leg and drove the ball over extra-cover for his eighth maximum of the innings to claim a remarkable victory with one ball to spare. Styris was rightfully proud of his effort when speaking to the SKY cameras shortly after his maiden T20 century. "That was probably my best innings in Twenty20 cricket," he acknowledged. "It was a great batting wicket and both sides scored pretty easily. With that short boundary you never felt you were out of the game so I was really pleased that I could help the boys cross the line. We are here to entertain the crowd and hopefully we did that and hopefully I did that as well." Few in the sell-out Ford County Ground crowd would have disagreed.

Friends Provident t20, Quarter-Final
Essex v Lancashire

20-overs match   **Venue:** The Ford County Ground, Chelmsford **Result:** Essex won by 8 wickets

photos: Nick Wood

Essex supporters have never been short of entertainment and memorable finishes since the Twenty20 Cup began its life in 2003. Few have matched the quarter-final against Lancashire in 2010 for drama as the County pulled off a thrilling run-chase with five balls to spare. The hosts went into the match without five of their leading T20 players but showed the squad's strength-in-depth as a couple of the team's relatively unsung heroes saved the day with the bat. Essex had earlier begun the match in fine style when David Masters pinned Stephen Moore in front of his stumps with the first delivery. The visitors recovered from this disastrous opening to reach 33-1 before rain delayed proceedings for 35 minutes. Chris Wright struck in his first over upon the resumption when Steven Croft was caught at mid-wicket but Tom Smith

Dynamic duo:
Mark Pettini *(top)*
and Matt Walker

and Paul Horton then added 51 in less than six overs before the former was magnificently caught by a diving Grant Flower at deep mid-wicket. Sajid Mahmood was unexpectedly promoted up the order but repaid the faith shown in his batting with 34 off 17 balls. He and Horton put on 49 before Wright removed both in the 17th over on his way to a fine analysis of 4-25. However, Glen Chapple ensured the momentum was with Lancashire at the end of the innings by scoring all but one of the 28 runs made in the last two overs. Essex's challenging run-chase made an unfavourable beginning when form-man Ravi Bopara was dismissed in the third over. Fellow opener Mark Pettini was then joined by Matt Walker and the second-wicket pair reached their half-century stand in less than six overs before doubling their stand at the same rate. Pettini, who had just returned to the side after taking a break

Having recently taken on the Essex captaincy, James Foster had a night to remember as he saw his team close to the finishing line with 16 not out off five balls in the penultimate over. "When Mark [Pettini] got out I remember feeling very nervous because we still had a lot of runs to get. When you have a new batsman coming to the crease it can potentially slow things up and would have put even more pressure on Walks [Matt Walker]. I remember not being able to see the ball very well from [Glen] Chapple but if it was in my slot I was going to hit it over extra-cover. I got a couple of boundaries away early and that settled the nerves. Then I started playing around in the crease which Chapple wasn't very happy with, which I knew was a good sign. If I was standing outside off-stump he was asking me if I was going to stay there because he was going to come round the wicket. I hit a few boundaries to settle the nerves and then Walks finished it off. I remember him being the sweatiest man in the world and that wasn't helped by him also diving around on what was the wet grass by that point. I regretted doing that [hugging him] afterwards because I got drenched by his sweat! It was a serious knock from him."

Toss: Essex won the toss and decided to field.
Umpires: JH Evans, NJ Llong, NGB Cook (TV).

LANCASHIRE

		Runs	Balls	Mins	4s	6s	S-Rate
SC Moore	lbw b Masters	0	1	1	-	-	0.00
TC Smith	c Flower b Phillips	35	32	46	4	-	109.38
SJ Croft	c Phillips b Wright	27	18	22	3	1	150.00
PJ Horton	lbw b Wright	44	30	44	3	1	146.67
SI Mahmood	b Wright	34	17	24	3	2	200.00
†GD Cross	c Walker b Wright	9	8	10	1	-	112.50
*G Chapple	not out	28	14	13	2	1	200.00
MJ Chilton	not out	1	1	5	-	-	100.00
G Keedy	did not bat						
SD Parry	did not bat						
SC Kerrigan	did not bat						
Extras	(1 b, 2 nb, 2 w)	5					
Total	**(6 wickets, 20 overs)**	**183**					

Fall: 1-0, 2-42, 3-93, 4-142, 5-143, 6-164.
Bowling: Masters 4-0-26-1, Carter 4-0-44-0, Chambers 4-0-51-0, Wright 4-0-25-4, Phillips 3-0-25-1, Flower 1-0-11-0.

ESSEX

		Runs	Balls	Mins	4s	6s	S-Rate
ML Pettini	b Mahmood	81	56	79	7	1	144.64
RS Bopara	c Cross b Chapple	4	6	9	-	-	66.67
MJ Walker	not out	74	49	76	4	4	151.02
*†JS Foster	not out	16	5	8	3	-	320.00
GW Flower	did not bat						
T Westley	did not bat						
TJ Phillips	did not bat						
A Carter	did not bat						
DD Masters	did not bat						
CJC Wright	did not bat						
MA Chambers	did not bat						
Extras	(6 lb, 2 nb, 1 w)	9					
Total	**(2 wickets, 19.1 overs)**	**184**					

Fall: 1-17, 2-164.
Bowling: Chapple 4-0-30-1, Smith 3-0-41-0, Mahmood 4-0-29-1, Parry 2-0-24-0, Kerrigan 4-0-38-0, Keedy 2.1-0-16-0.

following his relinquishing of the captaincy, batted superbly with the pressure of leadership off his shoulders. The right-hander was given one life – when he was dropped on 70 by Tom Smith off Gary Keedy – before Mahmood bowled him with the last ball of the 18th over. New captain James Foster entered the fray with 20 needed off the last two overs but a testing prospect was made to look simple as he struck Chapple for three successive boundaries. Walker fittingly ended the match off the first ball of the last over to send Essex to Twenty20 Cup Finals Day for the third time in five years. Batting hero Walker paid tribute to the spirit within the Essex camp after triumphing with a depleted team. "We were probably a bit light on batting with Cooky [Alastair Cook] not being around so when you lose your best player [Ravi Bopara] there is always a bit of pressure," Walker explained to Essex TV. "But we showed just how much of a team we are in this campaign – we lost Ryan [ten Doeschate] pretty early on, Napes [Graham Napier] hasn't played any part of it, Cooky's been in and out, Ravi's been in and out, and we just got on with it. Sometimes when you lose your best players, it spurs you on and gives the other lads a chance to impress and inspires you to step up and do your job."

Bibliography

We have consulted several newspapers, local and national and quoted from The Times, Western Daily Press and Daily Herald. We have used as invaluable reference sources the CricketArchive website and have occasionally quoted from the following books:

Wisden Book of Cricketers' Lives
Wisden Cricketers' Almanacks
The Fast Men by David Frith
Famous Cricketers of Essex by Dean Hayes
The Cricketer
Essex County Cricket Club – The Official History by David Lemmon and Mike Marshall
They Made Cricket by G.D.Martineau
Ken Farnes, Diary of an Essex Master written by David Thurlow
Essex CCC Yearbooks and Handbooks
Wickets, Catches and the Odd Run by Trevor Bailey
Great One-Day Cricket Matches by David Lemmon
Gooch – My Autobiography by Graham Gooch and Frank Keating
Essex Cricket Matchday Programmes
Essex Cricket Members' Magazines

FRONT AND BACK COVER PICTURES

Front cover pictures *(from top clockwise)*: Essex with the Friends Provident Trophy in 2008, Essex in the 1890s, Graham Napier, Trevor Bailey and Doug Insole, Frederick Fane, Keith Fletcher with the John Player League trophy in 1985, Graham Gooch, Essex with the Benson & Hedges Cup in 1998

Back cover pictures *(from top to bottom)*: Essex v the Australians at Southend in 1948, Matt Walker takes the plaudits after completing victory over Lancashire in the 2010 FPt20 match at Chelmsford